Herong's Tutorial Examples

Android
Tutorials

Herong Yang
HerongYang.com/Android

Android Tutorials -

Herong's Tutorial Examples

v3.05, 2023

Herong Yang

This book is a collection of notes and sample codes written by the author while he was learning Android system. Topics include Installing of Android SDK on Windows, Creating and running Android emulators, Developing First Android Application - HelloAndroid, Creating Android Project with 'android' Command, Building, Installing and Running the Debug Binary Package, Inspecting Android Application Package (APK) Files, Using Android Debug Bridge (adb) Tool, Copying files from and to Android device, Understanding Android File Systems, Using Android Java class libraries, Using 'adb logcat' Command for Debugging. Updated in 2023 (Version v3.05) with ADB tutorials.

Table of Contents

Keywords: Android, SDK, Application, Development

About This Book

This section provides some detailed information about this book - Android Tutorials - Herong's Tutorial Examples.

Title: Android Tutorials - Herong's Tutorial Examples

Author: Herong Yang - Contact by email via herong_yang@yahoo.com.

Category: Computers / Operating Systems / Android

Version/Edition: v3.05, 2023

Number of pages in PDF format: 346

Description: This book is a collection of notes and sample codes written by the author while he was learning Android system. Topics include Installing of Android SDK on Windows, Creating and running Android emulators, Developing First Android Application - HelloAndroid, Creating Android Project with 'android' Command, Building, Installing and Running the Debug Binary Package, Inspecting Android Application Package (APK) Files, Using Android Debug Bridge (adb) Tool, Copying files from and to Android device, Understanding Android File Systems, Using Android Java class libraries, Using 'adb logcat' Command for Debugging. Updated in 2023 (Version v3.05) with ADB tutorials.

Keywords: AAPT, Android, ADB, API, Dalvik, emulator, Java, layout, logcat, shell, SDK, USB, view.

Copyright:

Revision history:

* Version 3.05, 2023. Updated ADB tutorials.

- Version 3.00, 2015. Added Android SDK R24 tutorials.

- Version 2.00, 2012. Added Android file system tutorials.

- Version 1.00, 2011. First edition.

Web version: https://www.herongyang.com/Android - Provides free sample chapters, latest updates and readers' comments. The Web version of this book has been viewed a total of:

- 1,587,674 times as of December 2022.

- 1,519,503 times as of December 2021.

- 1,427,094 times as of December 2020.

- 1,332,564 times as of December 2019.

- 1,234,855 times as of December 2018.

- 1,145,846 times as of December 2017.

- 1,041,100 times as of December 2016.

- 890,202 times as of December 2015.

- 602,466 times as of December 2014.

- 293,074 times as of December 2013.

- 106,324 times as of December 2012.

PDF/EPUB version: https://www.herongyang.com/Android/PDF-Full-Version.html - Provides information on how to obtain the full version of this book in PDF, EPUB, or other format.

Installing JDK 1.8 on Windows System

This chapter provides tutorial notes on installing JDK (Java Development Kit) on Windows systems. Topics include downloading and installing Java SE Development Kit 8u45; compiling and executing Java programs; setting up JAVA_HOME environment variable.

Takeaways:

- The latest version of JDK is Java SE Development Kit 8u45.

- "javac class_name.java" is the command to compile a Java source code into a Java class code.

- "java -cp . class_name" is the command to launch the JVM to run a Java class code.

- "JAVA_HOME" is the environment variable required to run some development tools to build and test Android apps.

Downloading and Installing JDK 1.8

This section describes how to download and install Java SE Development Kit (JDK) 8u45 on a Windows system.

Since Android apps are developed in Java language, you need to have a copy of JDK (Java Development Kit) installed on your computer first. The latest version of JDK is Java SE Development Kit 8u45. Here is what I did to download and install Java SE Development Kit 8u45 on my Windows 7 system.

1. Open the Java SE Download page with this URL: http://www.oracle.com/technetwork/java/javase/downloads/.

2. Click the download button below "JDK" in the "Java SE 8u45" section. You will see a new page with a list of different download files of "Java SE Development Kit 8u45".

3. Click the "Accept License Agreement" option.

4. Locate the line "Windows x86 175.98 MB" and click on "jdk-8u45-windows-i586.exe" to start download.

5. Save the download file to C:\download\jdk-8u45-windows-i586.exe and wait for the download to finish.

6. Double-click on C:\download\jdk-8u45-windows-i586.exe to start the installation wizard. The installation wizard will guide you to finish the installation.

Java SE Development Kit (JDK) 8 Setup

To verify the installation, open a command window to try the java command. If you are getting the following output, your installation was ok:

```
C:\herong>"\Program Files\Java\jdk1.8.0_45\bin\java.exe" -version

java version "1.8.0_45"
Java(TM) SE Runtime Environment (build 1.8.0_45-b15)
Java HotSpot(TM) Client VM (build 25.45-b02, mixed mode)
```

Writing My First Java Program

This section provides a tutorial example on how to write, compile, and execute the first Java program with JDK 1.8.

When JDK is installed on your machine, it provides two commands for you to compile and run Java programs.

- "javac class_name.java" - Compiles a Java program stored a file named with the program class name.

- "java -cp . class_name" - Runs a compiled Java program. "-cp ." specifies the current directory as the class path.

Let's try these commands with a very simple Java program.

First use NotePad to enter the following Java program into a file called Hello.java:

```
class Hello {
    public static void main(String[] a) {
        System.out.println("Hello world!");
    }
}
```

Then compile this program in a command window with the "javac" command:

```
C:\herong>"\Program Files\Java\jdk1.8.0_45\bin\javac.exe" Hello.java
```

To execute the program, use the java command:

```
C:\herong>"\Program Files\Java\jdk1.8.0_45\bin\java.exe" Hello
Hello world!
```

Congratulations, you have successfully entered, compiled and executed your first Java program.

Setting JAVA_HOME Environment Variable

This section provides a tutorial example on how to set up JAVA_HOME environment variable to run development tools to build and test Android apps.

After installing JDK, you need to make sure the JAVA_HOME environment variable is set to the new JDK folder. This is needed to run development tools to build and test Android apps. Here is how you set and verify the JAVA_HOME environment variable.

1. Go to "Control Panel\System and Security\System" and click "Advanced system settings" on the left. You see the System Properties dialog box displayed with the "Advanced" tab opened.

2. Click the "Environment Variables" button. You see the Environment Variables dialog box displayed.

3. Enter or modify the JAVA_HOME entry to be "\Program Files\Java\jdk1.8.0_45\". Then click OK to close dialog boxes.

4. Start command line window and try the following commands:

```
C:\herong>set JAVA_HOME

C:\herong>"%JAVA_HOME%\bin\java" -version
java version "1.8.0_45"
Java(TM) SE Runtime Environment (build 1.8.0_45-b15)
Java HotSpot(TM) Client VM (build 25.45-b02, mixed mode)
```

If you get similar output, you know your JAVA_HOME environment variable is correct.

Installation of Android SDK R24 and Emulator

This chapter provides tutorials and notes on installation of Android SDK R24 and emulator. Topics include downloading and installing Android SDK R24; installing Android latest platform; creating Android virtual device; running Android emulator; running emulator's built-in Web browser.

Takeaways:

- The Android SDK starter package does not contain library packages for any specific Android platforms.

- The SDK Manager allows you to view and install Android platform packages that are available from the Android developer center.

- The AVD (Android Virtual Device) Manager allows you to create and launch Android emulators for specific Android platforms and devices.

- The AVD Manager R24 can emulate different type of devices, like tablet, smart phone, smart TV, and smart watch.

- The Android emulator provides a number of built-in applications that are ready to run.

- The Android emulator R24 uses cable LAN for Internet connection by default. You need to disable the cable LAN driver, if you are using Wi-Fi.

- The Android emulator R24 performance is very poor on Windows 7 systems. You need to wait for about 10 minutes for the emulator to be fully loaded and show the starting screen.

- The Android emulator R24 resolution is very poor too.

Downloading and Installing Android SDK R24

This section provides a tutorial example on how to download and install Android SDK (Software Development Kit) Revision 24 on Windows systems.

If you want to develop applications for Android systems, you need to start with the following two steps to create an Android development environment on your Windows system:

- Download and install Android SDK starter package.

- Download and install libraries and tools to help you build applications for specific Android platforms.

Here is what I did to download and install the Android SDK Revision R24 starter package:

1. Go to the Android SDK download page at http://developer.android.com/sdk/.

2. Click "android-sdk_r24.3.2-windows.zip" in the Other Download Options - SDK Tools Only section near the bottom of the page. Follow instructions given on the page to finish the download

3. Save the downloaded file to C:\download\android-sdk_r24.3.2-windows.zip. The file size should be 187,488,291 bytes.

4. Unzip the downloaded file to C:\local\android-sdk-windows.

5. Double-click on "C:\local\android-sdk-windows\SDK Manager.exe". The "Android SDK Manager" windows will show up:

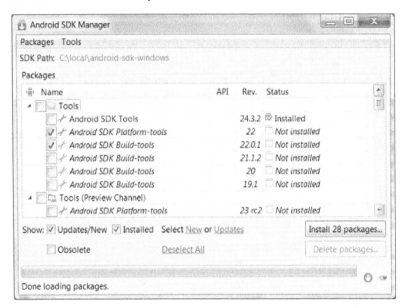

Android SDK Manager R24

Cool. Android SDK Revision 24 starter package is installed now. Read next tutorials to learn how to install Android platform emulator.

By the way, SDK Manager is a Java application and requires JDK to be installed in the "C:\Program Files" folder, like "C:\Program Files\Java\jdk1.8.0_45\". It does not use the JAVA_HOME environment variable.

Running Android SDK Manager R24

This section provides a tutorial example on how to run Android SDK Manager R24 to see what additional tools and libraries that are available from the Android developer center.

After installing the Android SDK starter package, you can use the Android SDK Manager to see what additional tools and libraries that are available from the Android developer center.

Double-click on "C:\local\android-sdk-windows\SDK Manager.exe". The "Android SDK Manager" windows will show up with a list of libraries and tools for different versions of Android platforms that are currently available for download:

- Tools/Android SDK Tools - Basic tools installed already as part of the starter package.

- Tools/Android SDK Platform-tools - Common tools for Android platforms.

- Tools/Android SDK Build-tools - Common tools to build applications.

- Android M (API22, MNC preview) (To be released in 2015 Q3) - Libraries and tools for Android M platforms.

- Android 5.1.1 (API22) (Released on Apr. 21, 2015) - Libraries and tools for Android 5.1.1 platforms.

- Android 5.0.1 (API21) (Released on Dec. 2, 2014) - Libraries and tools for Android 5.0.1 platforms.

- Android 4.4W.2 (API20) (Released on Oct. 21, 2014) - Libraries and tools for Android 4.4W.2 platforms.

- Android 4.4.2 (API19) (Released on Dec. 9, 2014) - Libraries and tools for Android 4.4.2 platforms.

- Android 4.3.1 (API17) (Released on Oct. 3, 2013) - Libraries and tools for Android 4.3.1 platforms.

- Android 4.1.2 (API16) (Released on October 9, 2012) - Libraries and tools for Android 4.1.2 platforms.

- Android 4.0.3 (API15) (Released on Dec. 16, 2011) - Libraries and tools for Android 4.03 platforms.

- Android 2.3.3 (API10) (Released on Feb. 9, 2011) - Libraries and tools for Android 2.3.3 platforms.

- Android 2.2 (API8) (Released on May 20, 2010) - Libraries and tools for Android 2.2 platforms.

- Extra - Additional libraries for USB driver and other interfaces.

Read the next tutorial on how to download and install libraries and tools for Android 5.1 platforms.

Installing Android Platform 4.0.3 and Libraries

This section provides a tutorial example on how to install Android platform libraries and tools using Android SDK Manager.

If you want to develop applications for mobile devices that are running the Android systems, you need to download and install libraries and tools for the latest Android platform using the Android SDK Manager:

1. Double-click on "C:\local\android-sdk-windows\SDK Manager.exe" to run the Android SDK Manager.

2. Review those libraries and tools that are preselected for you:

```
[ ] Tools
    [x] Android SDK Platform-tools
    [x] Android SDK Build-tools
        ...
[x] Android M (API 22, MNC preview)
    [x] Documentation for Android "MNC" Preview
    [x] SDK Platform Android M Preview
    [x] Sample for SDK API MNC Preview
    [x] Android TV Intel x86 Atom System Image
    [x] ARM 64 v8a System Image
    [x] ARM EABI v7a System Image
    [x] Intel x86 Atom_64 System Image
    [x] Intel x86 Atom System Image
    [x] MIPS System Image
    [x] Sources for Android 'MNC' Preview SDK
 [x] Android 5.1.1 (API 22)
    [x] SDK Platform
    [x] Sample for SDK
    [x] Android TV ARM EABI v7a System Image
```

```
    [x] Android TV Intel x86 Atom System Image

    [x] Android Wear ARM EABI v7a System Image

    [x] Android Wear Intel x86 Atom System Image

    [x] ARM EABI v7a System Image

    [x] Intel x86 Atom_64 System Image

    [x] Intel x86 Atom System Image

    [x] Google APIs

    [x] Google APIs ARM EABI v7a System Image

    [x] Google APIs Intel x86 Atom_64 System Image

    [x] Google APIs Intel x86 Atom System Image

    [x] Sources for Android SDK

...

[ ] Extras

    ...

    [x] Android Support Library

    [x] Google USB Driver

    ...
```

4. Click the "Install 28 packages..." button. The "Choose Packages to Install" window will show up:

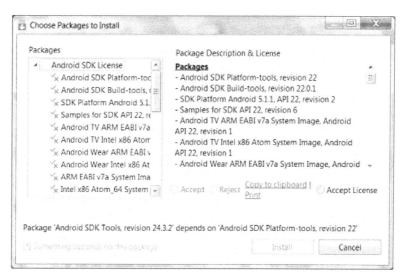

Android SDK Manager R24 - Installing Platform

5. Click the "Accept License" option, then "Install" button. Android SDK Manager will start to download those selected packages.

6. Wait for the download process to finish

Verifying Android Platform Installation

This section provides a tutorial example on how to verify Android platform installation using the 'android' tool provided in the Android SDK starter package.

After installing the latest Android platform packages using the Android SDK Manager, you need to run the "android" tool provided in the Android SDK starter package to verify the installation.

Go to a Windows command line window and run this command:

```
C:\herong\>\local\android-sdk-windows\tools\android list target
Available Android targets:
----------
id: 1 or "android-22"
     Name: Android 5.1.1
     Type: Platform
     API level: 22
     Revision: 2
     Skins: HVGA, QVGA, WQVGA400, WQVGA432, WSVGA, WVGA800 (default),
        WVGA854, WXGA720, WXGA800, WXGA800-7in
  Tag/ABIs : no ABIs.
```

The output confirms that:

- 1 Android platform is installed. The version number is 5.1.1, which was released on Apr. 21, 2015. The API (Application Programming Interface) level is 22. This platform should allow me to build and test my applications for any mobile devices that running Android 5.1.1 system.

Read the next tutorials on how to create and run an Android emulator on your Windows system.

Creating Android Virtual Device (AVD)

*This section provides a tutorial example on how to create an Android Virtual Device (AVD),
which is an emulator configuration that lets you to model an actual Android device.*

In order to run the Android emulator on your Windows system, you need to create an
Android Virtual Device (AVD), which is an emulator configuration that lets you to model
an actual device by defining hardware and software options to be emulated by the
Android Emulator.

Here is what I did to create an AVD:

1. Double-click on "C:\local\android-sdk-windows\AVD Manager.exe". The "Android
Virtual Device Manager" window shows up.

2. Click "Create" button. The "Create new Android Virtual Device (AVD)" window shows
up:

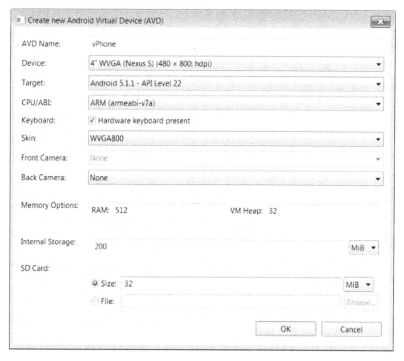

Create Android Virtual Device (AVD) - R24

3. Review and change settings to create virtual 4 inch phone:

```
Name: vPhone
Device: 4" WVGA (Nexus S)(480 x 800:hdpi)
Target: Android 5.1.1 - API Level 22
CPU/ABI: ARM (armeabi-v7a)
    [x] Hardware keyboard present
```

```
Skin: WVGA800
Front Camera: None
Back Camera: None
Memory Options:
   RAM: 512, VM Heap: 32
Internal Storage: 200 MiB
SD Card/Size: 32 MiB
```

4. Click "OK" button. A new virtual device simulating a phone will be created and listed on the AVD Manager screen.

Viewing Android Virtual Device (AVD) Details

This section provides a tutorial example on how to view details of a Android Virtual Device (AVD) created in the AVD Manager.

In the last tutorial, we have created a new AVD, called vPhone, to simulate a 4 inch phone. Now let's look at some details of this virtual device.

1. Double-click on "C:\local\android-sdk-windows\AVD Manager.exe". "vPhone" shows up in the AVD list.

2. Select "vPhone" and click the "Details..." button on the right side. The "AVD Details" box shows up.

3. Read the detail settings of the virtual device:

```
   Name: vPhone
CPU/ABI: ARM (armeabi-v7a)
   Path: C:\users\yang\.android\avd\vPhone.avd
 Target: Android 5.1.1 (API level 22)
   Skin: WVGA800
SD Card: 32M

-------------------------------------------------------

         hw.dPad: no
   hw.accelerometer: yes
     hw.device.name: 4in WVGA (Nexus S)
         vm.heapSize: 32
```

```
        skin.dynamic: no
 hw.device.manufacture: Generic
              hw.gps: yes
       hw.audioInput: yes
              tag.id: default
       hw.cpu.model: cortex-a8
     hw.camera.back: none
         hw.mainKeys: yes
      hw.lcd.density: 240
```

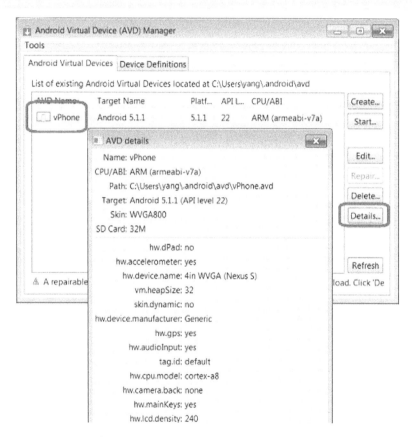

Android Virtual Device (AVD) Details - R24

Read next tutorial on how to run an Android emulator with the AVD.

Launching Android Emulator in AVD Manager

This section provides a tutorial example on how to launch an Android emulator with the Android Virtual Device (AVD) created in the AVD Manager.

Now I am ready to run a Android emulator with the AVD created in previous tutorials.

1. Double-click on "C:\local\android-sdk-windows\AVD Manager.exe". "vPhone" shows up in the AVD list.

2. Select "vPhone" and click the "Start" button on the right side. The "Launch Options" box shows up.

3. Review and change options:

```
Skin: WVGA800 (480x800)
Density: 240
[x] Scale display to real size

    Screen Size (in): 4.0
    Monitor dpi: 120
    Scale 0.51


[ ] Wipe user data
[ ] Launch from snapshot
[ ] Save to snapshot
```

3. Click the "Launch" button. The Android emulator window will show up with the word "android" displayed.

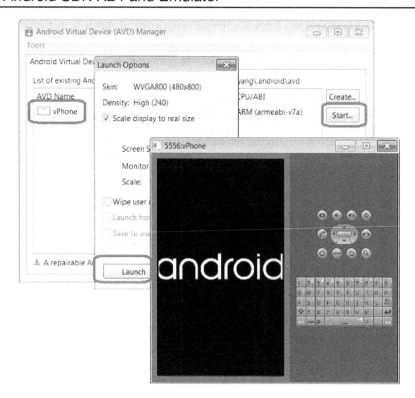

Android Virtual Device (AVD) Details - R24

Cool, I have an Android emulator started on my Windows system!

But where is the home screen to run apps on the emulator? I guess I need to wait for the emulator to get fully load. See the next tutorial on how to run apps on the emulator.

Android Emulator Starting Screens

This section provides a tutorial example on how to unlock the starting screen of an Android emulator by 'Swipe' up the lock icon.

After launching the Android emulator from the AVD Manager, the emulator displays the word "android" on the screen while loading all required code and data.

On my Windows computer, the loading process takes a long time. I have to wait for about 10 minutes before the starting screen shows up. May be my computer (with a 2.5 GHz processor and 4 GB of RAM) is not powerful enough to run Android SDK R24. Or it could be a code issue with Android SDK R24.

When the emulator is fully loaded, the starting screen shows up with the following information:

```
Battery status is 50% and charging
Clock shows the local time and date
A lock icon and a camera icon are located at the bottom
```

Click on the lock icon, it will say: "swipe up to unlock". How to swipe the lock on my Windows which is not a touch screen?

The answer is to select the lock icon and drag it up using the mouse to simulate the swipe gesture.

After unlocking the starting screen, the home screen shows up with the following information:

```
Make yourself at home
You can put your favorite apps here.


To see all apps, touch the circle.
```

Click the "Apps" icon in the circle. The application list screen shows up.

Congratulations, I have successfully created and started an Android emulator on my Windows system! But it's performance is very slow.

The Android emulator screen resolution is very poor too, see the screenshot below:

Android Emulator Starting and Home Screens - R24

Android Emulator Built-in Apps and Widgets

This section describes the built-in apps and widgets provided in an Android emulator generated from Android SDK R24.

After unlock the starting screen of the Android emulator, we look around on the emulator to try some built-in apps.

1. Click the "Apps" icon on the home screen. A list of all built-in apps shows up:

- API Demos - A collection of apps to demo Android API.

- Browser - A Web browser for you to browse Web pages on the Internet.

- Calculator - A simple calculator.

- Camera - An app to operate the built-in camera.

- Clock - A simple clock

- Contacts - A contact manager for you to record contact names and phone numbers.

- Custom Locale - An app to add other locales to support non-English languages.

- Dev Settings - An app to access development settings.

- Dev Tools - A collection of development tools.

- Downloads - An app to access the download folder.

- Email - A client app for you to connect to your email services.

- Gallery - An app to manage photos.

- Gestures Builder - A tool to build gestures.

- Messaging - A client app for you to send and receive messages.

- Music - An app to manage and listen music.

- Phone - A client app for you to make phone calls.

- Search - A Web app for you to use the Google search engine.

- Settings - An app for you to manage settings

- Speech Recorder - An app for you to record speeches.

2. Click the "Widgets" tab. A list of all built-in widgets shows up:

- Analog clock.

- API Demos

- Bookmark

- Calendar

Android Emulator R24 - Apps and Widgets

By the way, you can lock the screen with a password like "herong" to lock the screen by going to "Settings > Security".

Android Emulator Built-in Web Browser

This section provides a tutorial example on how to use the Android emulator's built-in Web browser to visit a web page. You need disable the cable LAN driver, if you are using Wi-Fi.

To the test emulator, let's use its browser to visit my home page.

1. Launch the Android emulator and unlock the screen.

2. Click the Browser icon and enter "herongyang.com" using the key pad on the screen.

3. Click the enter key. After some time, the browser returns an error message: "Webpage not available - The webpage at http://herongyang.com/ could not be loaded because: net::ERR_NAME_NOT_RESOLVED"

What's wrong with the emulator? Searching the Internet, I found a post on stackoverflow by Vaughn (http://stackoverflow.com/questions/2039964/how-to-connect -android-emulator-to-the-internet), which suggests to disable the network cable port, if you are using a Wi-Fi connection. Because the emulator is trying to obtain DNS service from the cable port.

4. On Windows 7 system, go to "Control Panel\Network and Internet\Network Connections"

5. Right-click on "Local Area Network", and then click "Disable".

6. Restart the emulator, try the browser again with http://herongyang.com/. Cool, the browser works!

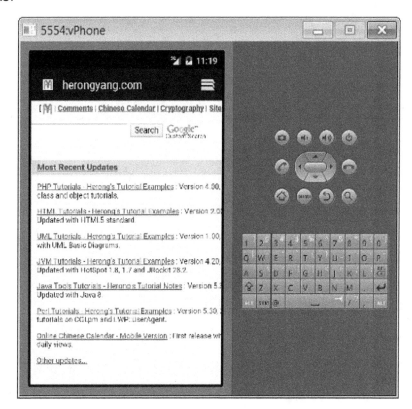

Android Emulator R24 - herongyang.com Page

As you can see, my home page is not responsive enough to fit in the 4 inch screen of the emulator. I still need to improve it.

Android Emulator for 7 Inch Tablet

This section provides a tutorial example on how to create and run an Android Emulator for 7 inch tablets.

While I was creating my "vPhone" AVD, I saw that the AVD Manager supports a number of device types:

- Nexus 7 (2012)(8.0",800 x 1280:tvdpi)

- Nexus 5 (4.95",1080 x 1920:xxhpi)

- ...

- Android Wear Round Chin (320 x 290:tvdpi)

- ...

- Android TV (720p) (1280 x 720:tvdpi)

- ...

- 10.1" WXVGA(Tablet)(1280 x 800:mdpi)

- 7" WSVGA(Tablet)(1024 x 600:mdpi)

- ...

So I decided to create another AVD to simulate a 7 inch tablet. Here are the parameters I used on the Create new AVD screen:

```
Name: vTablet
Device: 7" WSVGA(Tablet)(1024 x 600:mdpi)
Target: Android 5.1.1 - API Level 22
CPU/ABI: ARM (armeabi-v7a)
   [x] Hardware keyboard present
Skin: WSVGA
Front Camera: None
Back Camera: None
Memory Options:
   RAM: 512, VM Heap: 16
Internal Storage: 200 MiB
SD Card/Size: 32 MiB
```

Then I launched the vTablet AVD with "Scale display to real size" turned on. After about 10 minutes, my 7 inch tablet simulator was running on my Windows system.

After unlocking the screen and clicking the Apps icon, I saw the apps list screen.

Notice that there is no emulation of keyboard. But I can use the Windows keyboard for input.

Android Emulator R24 - 7 Inch Tablet

Android Emulator for Google Watch

This section provides a tutorial example on how to create and run an Android Emulator for Google watches.

I also create an Android Emulator for a smart watch with the following parameters on the Create new AVD screen:

```
Name: vWatch
```

```
Device: Android Wear Round (320 x 320:hdpi)

Target: Android 5.1.1 - API Level 22

CPU/ABI: Android Wear ARM (armeabi-v7a)

    [x] Hardware keyboard present

Skin: AndroidWearRound

Front Camera: None

Back Camera: None

Memory Options:

    RAM: 512, VM Heap: 32

Internal Storage: 200 MiB

SD Card/Size: 32 MiB
```

Then I launched the vWatch AVD with "Scale display to real size" turned on. After about 10 minutes, my smart watch simulator was running on my Windows system.

After clicking the power icon and waiting for another 5 minutes, my vWatch is fully working.

To see the list of apps, I had to press and hold down the power icon.

Android Emulator R24 - Google Watch

Missing Emulator Engine Program for 'arm' CPUS

This section provides a tutorial example showing the error of 'Missing emulator engine program for arm CPUS' when starting an Android emulator. This is caused missing emulator-arm.exe file in tools folder caused by anti-virus auto delete virus infected files.

A few days after I created my Android emulators, I started to get an error when starting any emulator in "AVD manager". The error says: "PANIC: Missing emulator engine program for 'arm' CPUS.", see the screenshot below.

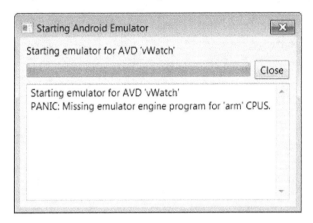

Android AVD Start Error - Missing 'arm' CPUS

Based on reports on the Internet, this error is caused by missing the emulator-arm.exe file in the "tools" folder. One possible root cause is the anti-virus program, which identifies the file as virus infected and deletes it automatically.

I am not sure what to the emulator-arm.exe file in my case. But I can run "SDK Manager", uninstall "Android SDK Tools 24.3.3" and install it again.

After reinstalling "Android SDK Tools 24.3.3", I see the file emulator-arm.exe is back in the tools folder. I have can start my Android emulator in AVD with no problem.

x86 Emulation Requires Hardware Acceleration

This section provides a tutorial example showing the error of 'x86 emulation currently requires hardware acceleration!' when starting an Android emulator, if the AVD is created to simulate Intel x86 CPU.

When running my Android emulators created to simulate ARM CPUs are very slow. It took about 10 minutes to get them fully started. So I decided to try emulating Intel CPUs.

1. Run AVD Manager and create a new Android emulator with the following parameters on the Create new AVD screen:

```
Name: ePhone
Device: 4" WVGA (Nexus S)(480 x 800:hdpi)
Target: Google APIs (Google Inc.) - API Level 22
CPU/ABI: Google APIs Intel Atom (x86)
    [x] Hardware keyboard present
Skin: WVGA800
Front Camera: None
Back Camera: None
Memory Options:
    RAM: 512, VM Heap: 32
Internal Storage: 200 MiB
SD Card/Size: 32 MiB
```

2. Click the "Start" to run "ePhone". I got a the following error:

```
ERROR: x86 emulation currently requires hardware acceleration!
Please ensure Intel HAXM is properly installed and usable.
CPU acceleration status: HAX kernel module is not installed!
```

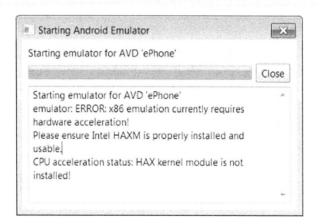

Android AVD Start Error - Intel HAXM Required

See the next tutorial on what is HAXM and how to install it.

HAXM - Hardware Accelerated Execution Manager

This section describes what is HAXM (Hardware Accelerated Execution Manager) and how to install it. HAXM requires Virtualization Technology (VT) to be enabled in the BIOS setup.

What Is HAXM (Hardware Accelerated Execution Manager)? HAXM is an Intel technology that reserves a portion of RAM to be used exclusively for specific programs like Android emulators. This, of course, will slow down the Windows system, because it runs on the remaining smaller RAM.

One way to install HAXM is to download the installer with Android SDK Manager:

1. Run Android SDK Manager and install "Intel x86 Emulator Accelerator (HAXM installer) 5.3" under the Extra section.

2. Run the installer, intelhaxm-android.exe, in the ".\extras\intel \Hardware_Accelerated_Execution_Manager\" Android SDK folder in a command line window.

3. Follow instructions given by the installer and use the suggested size, 1024 MB, for the reserved RAM.

4. Click "Next". I got the following error:

```
This computer meets the requirements for HAXM, but Intel
Virtualization Technology (VT-x) is not turned on. HAXM cannot be
installed until VT-x is enabled. Please refer to the Intel HAXM
documentation for more information.
```

Intel Accelerate HAXM Error - Virtualization Technology (VT) Required

To enable Virtualization Technology, I have to go to the BIOS setup. This requires some extra effort, so I am going to delay it to a later time.

Installing Apache Ant 1.9 on Windows System

This chapter provides tutorial notes on installing Apache Ant on Windows systems. Topics include downloading and installing Apache Ant 1.9.5; Ant build process preparation; creating an example Ant build file.

Takeaways:

- Apache Ant is a popular Java application build tool that allows you to automate the Java application build process.

- Apache Ant requires a build file in XML format that defines the build process in smaller steps.

- Apache Ant supports a set of commands that allows you to implement each build steps.

- If you are running JDK 1.8, you need to download and install Apache Ant 1.9. JDK 1.8 is not compatible with Ant 1.8.

Downloading and Installing Apache Ant 1.9

This section describes how to download and install Apache Ant 1.9.5 on a Windows system. Apache Ant is a popular Java application build tool that allows you to automate the Java application build process.

To develop Android applications in Java language, you also need to install Apache Ant, which is a popular Java application build tool that allows you to automate the Java application build process.

Here is what I did to download and install Apache Ant 1.9.5 on my Windows system.

1. Go to Apache Ant home page: http://ant.apache.org/ and click "Download / Binary Distributions" in the menu.

2. Click the link "apache-ant-1.9.5-bin.zip" next to ".zip archive:" in the "Current Release of Ant" section to start download.

3. Save the download file to C:\download\apache-ant-1.9.5-bin.zip and wait for the download to finish.

4. Unzip C:\download\apache-ant-1.9.5-bin.zip to folder C:\local\apache-ant-1.9.3.

5. Set JAVA_HOME as a system environment variable to point to the JDK 1.8 home folder:

```
set "JAVA_HOME=C:\Program Files\Java\jdk1.8.0_45"
```

To verify the installation, open a command window to try the "ant" command. If you are getting the following output, your installation is done correctly:

```
C:\herong>\local\apache-ant-1.9.5\bin\ant -version
Apache Ant(TM) version 1.9.5 compiled on May 31 2015
```

Preparations on Using Apache Ant Tool

This section describes how to prepare yourself to use the Apache Ant tool: create proper folder structure; define smaller build steps; put build steps into an Ant build file; implement each build step with Ant commands.

In order to use Apache Ant to help you to build a Java application, you need to prepare the following items:

1. Organize your application files in a nice folder structure. Here is an example:

```
.\                - Home folder to store all files of the application
.\src             - Source folder to store Java source files
```

```
.\build          - Build output folder
.\build\classes  - Class folder to store resulting class files
.\build\jar      - JAR folder to store resulting JAR files
```

2. Divide the build process into smaller steps. Here are some examples of build steps:

```
clean    - To clean up the build output folder
compile  - To compile all Java source files into class files
jar      - To build the JAR file from class files
run      - To execute the main class from the JAR file
```

3. Define all build steps in an Ant build file called .\build.xml. The build file is an XML file with the following structure:

```
<project>
    <target name="build_step_1">
        build_command_1
        build_command_1
        . . .
    </target>
    <target name="build_step_2">
        . . .
    </target>
    . . .
</project>
```

4. Implement each build step with Ant commands. Here is an example of implementing the "compile" build step with 3 Ant commands:

```
    <target name="compile">
        <delete dir="build/classes"/>
        <mkdir dir="build/classes"/>
        <javac srcdir="src" destdir="build/classes"/>
    </target>
```

After finishing implementing all build steps in the build file, you are ready to run the Ant tool to build your application. See next tutorial for a simple build file example.

First Apache Ant Build File Example

This section provides a tutorial example on how to write an Apache Ant build file to compile and run a simple Java application, Hello.java.

Now let's try to create Apache Ant build file to build and run the Hello Java application.

1. Create the application home folder and sub solders:

```
C:\>mkdir \herong\Hello
C:\>mkdir \herong\Hello\src
C:\>mkdir \herong\Hello\build
```

2. Copy the application source file, Hello.java, into the source folder:

```
C:\>copy Hello.java \herong\Hello\src
```

3. Create the build file, .\build.xml, using a text editor:

```xml
<project>
<!-- build.xml
 - Copyright (c) 2015, HerongYang.com, All Rights Reserved.
-->
    <target name="compile">
        <delete dir="build"/>

        <mkdir dir="build/classes"/>
        <javac srcdir="src" destdir="build/classes"/>

        <mkdir dir="build/jar"/>
        <jar destfile="build/jar/Hello.jar" basedir="build/classes">
            <manifest>
                <attribute name="Main-Class" value="Hello"/>
            </manifest>
        </jar>
    </target>

    <target name="run">
```

```
            <java jar="build/jar/Hello.jar" fork="true"/>
    </target>
</project>
```

4. Test the build process with the "ant" command:

```
C:\>cd \herong\Hello
C:\herong\Hello>\local\apache-ant-1.9.5\bin\ant compile
Buildfile: C:\herong\Hello\build.xml

compile:
    [delete] Deleting directory C:\herong\Hello\build
    [mkdir] Created dir: C:\herong\Hello\build\classes
    [javac] C:\herong\Hello\build.xml:9:
    warning: 'includeantruntime' was not set, defaulting
    to build.sysclasspath=last; set to false forepeatable builds
    [javac] Compiling 1 source file to C:\herong\Hello\build\classes
    [mkdir] Created dir: C:\herong\Hello\build\jar
      [jar] Building jar: C:\herong\Hello\build\jar\Hello.jar

BUILD SUCCESSFUL
Total time: 0 seconds

C:\herong\Hello>\local\apache-ant-1.9.5\bin\ant run
Buildfile: C:\herong\Hello\build.xml

run:
      [java] Hello world!

BUILD SUCCESSFUL
Total time: 0 seconds
```

Congratulations, you have successfully created a working Apache Ant build file!

Note that if you are using Ant 1.8 with JDK 1.8, you will get the following error:

```
BUILD FAILED
C:\herong\Hello\build.xml:9: Class not found: javac1.8
```

You need replace Ant 1.8 with Ant 1.9.

Developing First Android Application - HelloAndroid

This chapter provides tutorial notes on developing the first Android application. Topics include creating Android projects using the 'android' command; modifying Java source code; building and installing binary packages of Android projects.

Takeaways:

- Eclipse with Android plugin can help you to create, build and run Android application projects automatically.

- Without Eclipse, you can use command line tools from Android SDK and Apache Ant to create, build and run Android application projects manually.

- The "android" command line tool can be used to create new application projects with default configurations, Java source code and resource files.

- The "android" command line tool also generates build XML files to help you build and install Android applications using the Apache Ant tool.

- Testing of Android applications can be done on Android emulators on Windows systems.

Creating Android Project with "android" Command

This section describes how to create an Android application project without using the Eclipse IDE. The 'android' command can be used to create a project with all the source code and directory stubs for your project, as well as an Apache Ant build file.

After installed Android SDK (Software Development Kit), JDK (Java Development Kit), and Apache Ant, I think I am ready to develop my first Android application by following the tutorials given in the Android SDK package.

Based on the "Hello, World" tutorial provided in the Android tutorials, There are 2 ways to create an Android application development project:

* Using the Eclipse IDE with the Android Eclipse plugin installed.

* Using the "android" command provided in the Android SDK package.

Since I don't have Eclipse installed on my system at this moment, I will try to follow the "android" command example given in the Android SDK manual:

```
android create project \
    --package com.example.helloandroid \
    --activity HelloAndroid \
    --target <id> \
    --path <path-to-your-project>/HelloAndroid
```

If I understand correctly, the above command will:

* Create an application folder called HelloAndroid under the current folder.

* Create all sub folders and configuration files that are required by the build process.

* Create all Java stub source code for the application.

* Create an Ant build file that can be used to build the application.

Note that "--target <id>" allows us to specify which target Android platform this application is for. See the next tutorial on how to identify a target platform.

Listing Target Android Platforms

This section provides a tutorial example on how to list all available target Android target platforms with the 'android list targets' command.

In order to run the "android create project" command, we need to specify "--target <id>" to identify a target Android platform.

The Android SDK manual suggests us to run the "android list targets" command to see what's available in your installation. Here is what I got on my Android SDK R24 installation:

```
C:\herong>\local\android-sdk-windows\tools\android list targets


Available Android targets:
----------
id: 1 or "android-19"
     Name: Android 4.4.2
     Type: Platform
     API level: 19
     Revision: 4
     Skins: HVGA, QVGA, WQVGA400, WQVGA432, WSVGA, WVGA800 (default),
         WVGA854, WXGA720, WXGA800, WXGA800-7in
  Tag/ABIs : default/armeabi-v7a, default/x86


----------
id: 2 or "android-22"
     Name: Android 5.1.1
     Type: Platform
     API level: 22
     Revision: 2
     Skins: HVGA, QVGA, WQVGA400, WQVGA432, WSVGA, WVGA800 (default),
         WVGA854, WXGA720, WXGA800, WXGA800-7in, AndroidWearRound, ...
  Tag/ABIs : android-tv/armeabi-v7a, android-tv/x86, ...


----------
id: 3 or "Google Inc.:Google APIs:19"
```

```
    Name: Google APIs

    Type: Add-On

    Vendor: Google Inc.

    Revision: 14

    Description: Android + Google APIs

    Based on Android 4.4.2 (API level 19)

    Libraries:
     * com.android.future.usb.accessory (usb.jar)
         API for USB Accessories
     * com.google.android.media.effects (effects.jar)
         Collection of video effects
     * com.google.android.maps (maps.jar)
         API for Google Maps
    Skins: HVGA, QVGA, WQVGA400, WQVGA432, WSVGA, WVGA800 (default),
        WVGA854, WXGA720, WXGA800, WXGA800-7in
 Tag/ABIs : default/armeabi-v7a


 ----------
id: 4 or "Google Inc.:Google APIs (x86 System Image):19"
    Name: Google APIs (x86 System Image)

    Type: Add-On

    Vendor: Google Inc.

    Revision: 14

    Description: Android x86 + Google APIs

    Based on Android 4.4.2 (API level 19)

    Libraries:
     * com.android.future.usb.accessory (usb.jar)
         API for USB Accessories
     * com.google.android.media.effects (effects.jar)
         Collection of video effects
     * com.google.android.maps (maps.jar)
         API for Google Maps
    Skins: HVGA, QVGA, WQVGA400, WQVGA432, WSVGA, WVGA800 (default),
        WVGA854, WXGA720, WXGA800, WXGA800-7in
 Tag/ABIs : default/x86


 ----------
```

```
id: 5 or "Google Inc.:Google APIs:22"
     Name: Google APIs
     Type: Add-On
     Vendor: Google Inc.
     Revision: 1
     Description: Android + Google APIs
     Based on Android 5.1.1 (API level 22)
     Libraries:
      * com.android.future.usb.accessory (usb.jar)
          API for USB Accessories
      * com.google.android.media.effects (effects.jar)
          Collection of video effects
      * com.google.android.maps (maps.jar)
          API for Google Maps
     Skins: HVGA, QVGA, WQVGA400, WQVGA432, WSVGA, WVGA800 (default),
          WVGA854, WXGA720, WXGA800, WXGA800-7in, AndroidWearRound, ...
  Tag/ABIs : google_apis/armeabi-v7a, google_apis/x86,
     google_apis/x86_64
```

Ok. It looks we can try "id: 2 or android-22", which is an "Android 5.1.1 Platform", for our first Android application.

See the next tutorial for an example on how to create an application project for target id 2 with the "android create project" command.

"HelloAndroid" - First Android Project

This section provides a tutorial example on how to create the first Android project, HelloAndroid, using the 'android' command. Java source file and resource files are automatically created.

Now let's try to create a new Android application project called: HelloAndroid. I want the project home folder to be \herong\HelloAndroid and source code package to be com.herongyang.

Go to a command window and run the following commands to create the project, HelloAndroid:

```
C:\>cd \herong
C:\herong>\local\android-sdk-windows\tools\android create project \
   --package com.herongyang --activity HelloAndroid \
   --target android-22 --path .\HelloAndroid

Created project directory: C:\herong\HelloAndroid
Created directory C:\herong\HelloAndroid\src\com\herongyang

Added file C:\herong\HelloAndroid\src\com\herongyang\HelloAndroid.java
Created directory C:\herong\HelloAndroid\res
Created directory C:\herong\HelloAndroid\bin
Created directory C:\herong\HelloAndroid\libs
Created directory C:\herong\HelloAndroid\res\values
Added file C:\herong\HelloAndroid\res\values\strings.xml
Created directory C:\herong\HelloAndroid\res\layout
Added file C:\herong\HelloAndroid\res\layout\main.xml
Created directory C:\herong\HelloAndroid\res\drawable-xhdpi

Created directory C:\herong\HelloAndroid\res\drawable-hdpi
Created directory C:\herong\HelloAndroid\res\drawable-mdpi
Created directory C:\herong\HelloAndroid\res\drawable-ldpi
Added file C:\herong\HelloAndroid\AndroidManifest.xml
Added file C:\herong\HelloAndroid\build.xml
Added file C:\herong\HelloAndroid\proguard-project.txt
```

The output from the command tells me that:

- A Java source code file, com\herongyang\HelloAndroid.java, is created in the .\src folder.

- 2 resource files, values\strings.xml and layout\main.xml, are created in the .\res folder.

- 3 project-level files, AndroidMainifest.xml, build.xml, and proguard-project.txt, are created in the .\ folder.

Remember that the "--target 2" identifies the "Android 5.1.1 Platform" in my Android SDK environment

See next tutorial on how to modify the Java source code generated by the "android" tool.

"HelloAndroid.java" - First Android Java Code

This section provides a tutorial example on how to review and modify the first Android Java code, HelloAndroid.java. The modification is to print out the 'Hello Android' text on mobile devices.

Before generating the project binary file, I reviewed and modified the Java source code in .\src\com\herongyang\HelloAndroid.java to print out the "Hello Android" text on the mobile device:

```
/* HelloAndroid.java
 * Copyright (c) 2015, HerongYang.com, All Rights Reserved.
 */
package com.herongyang;

import android.app.Activity;
import android.os.Bundle;
import android.widget.TextView;
public class HelloAndroid extends Activity {
    /** Called when the activity is first created. */
    @Override
    public void onCreate(Bundle savedInstanceState) {
        super.onCreate(savedInstanceState);
        TextView tv = new TextView(this);
        tv.setText("Hello, Android");
        setContentView(tv);
    }
}
```

The modification is based on the example code provided in the "Hello, World" tutorial in the Android documentation. The following explanations are copied from the documentation:

An Android user interface is composed of hierarchies of objects called Views. A View is a drawable object used as an element in your UI layout, such as a button, image, or (in this case) a text label. Each of these objects is a subclass of the View class and the subclass that handles text is TextView.

In this change, you create a TextView with the class constructor, which accepts an Android Context instance as its parameter. A Context is a handle to the system; it provides services like resolving resources, obtaining access to databases and preferences, and so on. The Activity class inherits from Context, and because your HelloAndroid class is a subclass of Activity, it is also a Context. So, you can pass this as your Context reference to the TextView.

Next, you define the text content with setText().

Finally, you pass the TextView to setContentView() in order to display it as the content for the Activity UI. If your Activity doesn't call this method, then no UI is present and the system will display a blank screen.

See next tutorial on how to generate the project binary file.

"ant debug" Command and Build Error

This section provides a tutorial example on the 'ant' build command. An error occurred when running 'ant debug'. The error message says '...${aapt}': CreateProcess error=2, The system cannot find the file specified.

Based on the documentation, the Ant build file allows you build 2 types of binary outputs:

1. debug - Builds the application and signs it with a debug key. The 'nodeps' target can be used to only build the current project and ignore the libraries using: 'ant nodeps debug'.

2. release - Builds the application. The generated apk file must be signed before it is published. The 'nodeps' target can be used to only build the current project and ignore the libraries using: 'ant nodeps release'

Let me try to build the "debug" binary output first.

```
C:\>cd \herong\HelloAndroid
```

```
C:\herong\HelloAndroid>\local\apache-ant-1.9.5\bin\ant debug


Buildfile: C:\herong\HelloAndroid\build.xml


-set-mode-check:


-set-debug-files:


-check-env:
 [checkenv] Android SDK Tools Revision 24.3.2
 [checkenv] Installed at C:\local\android-sdk-windows


-setup:
     [echo] Project Name: HelloAndroid
  [gettype] Project Type: Application


-set-debug-mode:


-debug-obfuscation-check:


-pre-build:


-build-setup:
[getbuildtools] Using latest Build Tools: 22.0.1
     [echo] Resolving Build Target for HelloAndroid...
[gettarget] Project Target:   Android 5.1.1
[gettarget] API level:        22
[gettarget] WARNING: No minSdkVersion value set.
          Application will install on all Android versions.
     [echo] ----------
     [echo] Creating output directories if needed...
    [mkdir] Created dir: C:\herong\HelloAndroid\bin\res
    [mkdir] Created dir: C:\herong\HelloAndroid\bin\rsObj
    [mkdir] Created dir: C:\herong\HelloAndroid\bin\rsLibs
    [mkdir] Created dir: C:\herong\HelloAndroid\gen
    [mkdir] Created dir: C:\herong\HelloAndroid\bin\classes
```

```
    [mkdir] Created dir: C:\herong\HelloAndroid\bin\dexedLibs
     [echo] ----------
     [echo] Resolving Dependencies for HelloAndroid...
[dependency] Library dependencies:
[dependency] No Libraries
[dependency]
[dependency] ------------------
     [echo] ----------
     [echo] Building Libraries with 'debug'...
   [subant] No sub-builds to iterate on

-code-gen:
[mergemanifest] Merging AndroidManifest files into one.
[mergemanifest] Manifest merger disabled. Using project manifest only.
     [echo] Handling aidl files...
     [aidl] No AIDL files to compile.
     [echo] ----------
     [echo] Handling RenderScript files...
     [echo] ----------
     [echo] Handling Resources...
     [aapt] Generating resource IDs...

BUILD FAILED
C:\local\android-sdk-windows\tools\ant\build.xml:649: The following
 error occurred while executing this line:
C:\local\android-sdk-windows\tools\ant\build.xml:694: Execute failed:
 java.io.IOException: Cannot run program
 "C:\herong\HelloAndroid\${aapt}": CreateProcess error=2, The system
 cannot find the file specified
  at java.lang.ProcessBuilder.start(ProcessBuilder.java:1048)
  at java.lang.Runtime.exec(Runtime.java:620)
  at org.apache.tools.ant.taskdefs.launcher.Java13CommandLauncher.exec
     (Java13CommandLauncher.java:58)
  ...
Total time: 0 seconds
```

Too bad, the build process failed. It looks like the "${aapt}" expression was not resulting to a path name for the "aapt" command. In other words, "aapt" was not a defined variable in the build.xml file.

I compared the Android SDK R24 installation with the old R17 installation, and found the following differences:

1. ${aapt} is no longer explicitly defined in R24 .\tools\ant\build.xml file:

```
In Android SDK R24:
    <property name="adb"
      location="${android.platform.tools.dir}/adb${exe}" />
    <property name="lint"
      location="${android.tools.dir}/lint${bat}" />


In Android SDK R17:
    <property name="adb"
      location="${android.platform.tools.dir}/adb${exe}" />
    <property name="zipalign"
      location="${android.tools.dir}/zipalign${exe}" />
    <property name="aidl"
      location="${android.platform.tools.dir}/aidl${exe}" />
    <property name="aapt"
      location="${android.platform.tools.dir}/aapt${exe}" />
    <property name="dx"
      location="${android.platform.tools.dir}/dx${bat}" />
    <property name="renderscript"
      location="${android.platform.tools.dir}/llvm-rs-cc${exe}"/>
```

2. Location of "aapt.exe" is changed:

```
In Android SDK R24:
    C:\local\android-sdk-windows\build-tools\22.0.1\aapt.exe

In Android SDK R17:
    C:\local\android-sdk-windows-R17\platform-tools\aapt.exe
```

Searching on the Internet does not get any good information. So I decided reinstall "Android SDK Tools 24.3.3" and "Android SDK Build-tools 22.0.1" with Android SDK Manager.

See next tutorial on the result of "ant debug".

Building the Debug Binary Package

This section provides a tutorial example on how to build the debug binary package of the HelloAndroid application using the Apache Ant tool and the build.xml file.

After reinstalling "Android SDK Tools 24.3.3" and "Android SDK Build-tools 22.0.1" with Android SDK Manager, I tried the "ant debug" command again. It worked this time:

```
C:\>cd \herong\HelloAndroid

C:\herong\HelloAndroid>\local\apache-ant-1.9.5\bin\ant debug

Buildfile: C:\herong\HelloAndroid\build.xml

-set-mode-check:

-set-debug-files:

-check-env:
  [checkenv] Android SDK Tools Revision 24.3.3
  [checkenv] Installed at C:\local\android-sdk-windows

-setup:
     [echo] Project Name: HelloAndroid
   [gettype] Project Type: Application

-set-debug-mode:

-debug-obfuscation-check:

-pre-build:

-build-setup:
[getbuildtools] Using latest Build Tools: 22.0.1
```

```
     [echo] Resolving Build Target for HelloAndroid...
[gettarget] Project Target:    Android 5.1.1
[gettarget] API level:         22
[gettarget] WARNING: No minSdkVersion value set. Application will
   install on all Android versions.
     [echo] ----------
     [echo] Creating output directories if needed...
    [mkdir] Created dir: C:\herong\HelloAndroid\bin
    [mkdir] Created dir: C:\herong\HelloAndroid\bin\res
    [mkdir] Created dir: C:\herong\HelloAndroid\bin\rsObj
    [mkdir] Created dir: C:\herong\HelloAndroid\bin\rsLibs
    [mkdir] Created dir: C:\herong\HelloAndroid\gen
    [mkdir] Created dir: C:\herong\HelloAndroid\bin\classes


    [mkdir] Created dir: C:\herong\HelloAndroid\bin\dexedLibs
     [echo] ----------
     [echo] Resolving Dependencies for HelloAndroid...
[dependency] Library dependencies:
[dependency] No Libraries
[dependency]
[dependency] ------------------
     [echo] ----------
     [echo] Building Libraries with 'debug'...
  [subant] No sub-builds to iterate on


-code-gen:
[mergemanifest] Merging AndroidManifest files into one.
[mergemanifest] Manifest merger disabled. Using project manifest only.
     [echo] Handling aidl files...
     [aidl] No AIDL files to compile.
     [echo] ----------
     [echo] Handling RenderScript files...
     [echo] ----------
     [echo] Handling Resources...
     [aapt] Generating resource IDs...
     [echo] ----------
     [echo] Handling BuildConfig class...
```

```
[buildconfig] Generating BuildConfig class.

-pre-compile:

-compile:
    [javac] Compiling 3 source files to
        C:\herong\HelloAndroid\bin\classes
    [javac] warning: [options] source value 1.5 is obsolete and will
        be removed in a future release
    [javac] warning: [options] To suppress warnings about obsolete
        options, use -Xlint:-options.
    [javac] 3 warnings

-post-compile:

-obfuscate:

-dex:
        [dex] input: C:\herong\HelloAndroid\bin\classes
        [dex] Converting compiled files and external libraries into
            C:\herong\android_20120000\raw\HelloAndroid\bin\classes.dex...

-crunch:
    [crunch] Crunching PNG Files in source dir:
        C:\herong\HelloAndroid\res
    [crunch] To destination dir: C:\herong\HelloAndroid\bin\res
    [crunch] Processing image to cache:
        C:\herong\HelloAndroid\res\drawable-hdpi\ic_launcher.png
        => C:\herong\HelloAndroid\bin\res\drawable-hdpi\ic_launcher.png
    [crunch]    (processed image to cache entry
        C:\herong\HelloAndroid\bin\res\drawable-hdpi\ic_launcher.png:
        87% size of source)
    ...
    [crunch] Crunched 4 PNG files to update cache

-package-resources:
        [aapt] Creating full resource package...
```

```
-package:
[apkbuilder] Current build type is different than previous build:
   forced apkbuilder run.
[apkbuilder] Creating HelloAndroid-debug-unaligned.apk and signing it
   with a debug key...

-post-package:

-do-debug:
 [zipalign] Running zip align on final apk...
    [echo] Debug Package:
        C:\herong\HelloAndroid\bin\HelloAndroid-debug.apk
[propertyfile] Creating new property file:
   C:\herong\HelloAndroid\bin\build.prop
[propertyfile] Updating property file:
   C:\herong\HelloAndroid\bin\build.prop

-post-build:

debug:

BUILD SUCCESSFUL
Total time: 2 seconds
```

By looking at the output, I think my HelloAndroid binary package, HelloAndroid-debug-unaligned.apk, is ready to be tested on the Android emulator.

Installing the Debug Binary Package

This section provides a tutorial example on how to install the debug binary package to the Android emulator using the Apache Ant tool and the build file.

Now I need to install the debug build, HelloAndroid-debug-unaligned.apk, on the Android emulator. The Android documentation does not have detailed instructions on this step. But I did the following steps to make it happen:

1. Run the Android emulator, vTablet, through the AVD Manager and wait for the emulator to be fully booted.

2. Install HelloAndroid-debug-unaligned.apk to the Android emulator using the Ant tool:

```
C:\>cd \herong\HelloAndroid
C:\herong\HelloAndroid>\local\apache-ant-1.9.5\bin\ant installd


-set-mode-check:


-set-debug-files:


install:
     [echo] Installing
        C:\herong\HelloAndroid\bin\HelloAndroid-debug.apk onto default
        emulator or device...
     [exec] * daemon not running. starting it now on port 5037 *
     [exec] * daemon started successfully *
     [exec]     pkg: /data/local/tmp/HelloAndroid-debug.apk
     [exec] Success
     [exec] 385 KB/s (37850 bytes in 0.096s)


installd:


BUILD SUCCESSFUL
Total time: 12 seconds
```

3. Go to Android emulator, and click the "Apps" icon. The "HelloAndroid" application is listed on the screen!

HelloAndroid Application Installation - Android SDK R24

Running the Debug Binary Package

This section provides a tutorial example on how to run the debug binary package that has been installed on the Android emulator.

After installing it on the Android emulator, running the HelloAndroid application is easy:

1. Go to the Android emulator and click the "Application" icon. The list of applications will show up.

2. Click on "HelloAndroid". The "HelloAndroid" application screen will show up!

Cool. My first Android application, HelloAndroid, is working nicely!

HelloAndroid Application Screen - Android SDK R24

Android Application Package (APK) Files

This chapter provides tutorial notes on Android application package (APK) files. Topics include introduction to APK file; packaging application files into a single APK file; using 'adb' command to install APK files; using 'adb' command to copy file to Android emulator.

Takeaways:

- An APK file is a ZIP archive file that contains all code and data files of a single Android application.

- You can build the APK file for your own application with the "Apache Ant" tool.

- You can download APK files of some free Android applications from Internet.

- You can install applications packaged in APK files to the Android emulator with the "adb" command.

- You can copy files to the Android emulator with the "adb" command.

What Is APK File Format?

This section describes the Android application package (APK) file, which is really a ZIP archive file that holds all binary codes, resources and other data required by the Android application.

What Is APK File Format? APK file format is used for Android application package files to distribute and install application software and middleware onto Google's Android operating system.

APK files must have the .apk file extension.

The MIME type associated with APK files is application/vnd.android.package-archive.

APK files are really ZIP archive files. You can open APK files with WinZIP on Windows systems.

APK files are usually contains the following folders:

```
classes.dex - The DEX file containing program classes compiled in the
    DEX file format understandable by the Dalvik virtual machine


resources.arsc - The ARSC file containing pre-compiled resources


AndroidManifest.xml - An additional Android manifest file, describing
    the name, version, access rights, referenced library files for the
    application.

META-INF - Folder with the following 3 files:
    MANIFEST.MF: the Manifest file
    CERT.RSA: The certificate of the application.
    CERT.SF: The list of resources and SHA-1 digest;


res - Folder containing resources not compiled into resources.arsc
```

Android PDF Viewer APK File Contents

This section provides a tutorial example on how to download the APK file of the Android PDF Viewer project from sourceforge.net. The APK file contents can be viewed by the WinZIP tool.

To help understand the APK file format, let's download the APK file of the Android PDF Viewer project from sourceforge.net.

1. Go to the Android PDF Viewer project download page, http://sourceforge.net/projects/andpdf/.

2. Click the "Download" button and save the downloaded APK file to C:\download\AndroidPdfViewer_1_0_1.apk.

3. Open the downloaded APK file with WinZIP. You can see all files and folders in the downloaded APK file:

```
AndroidManifest.xml 2,924 bytes
classes.dex 391,240 bytes
com <DIR>
    sun <DIR>
        pdfview <DIR>
            decode <DIR>
                CCITTCodes 4,152 bytes
            font <DIR>
                res <DIR>
                    BaseFonts.properties 955 bytes
                    d0500001.pfb 45,955 bytes
                    n0190031.pfb 68,590 bytes
                    n0190041.pfb 72,400 bytes
                    n0190231.pfb 71,719 bytes
                    n0190241.pfb 73,879 bytes
                    n0210031.pfb 113,206 bytes
                    n0210041.pfb 108,822 bytes
                    n0210231.pfb 108,217 bytes
                    n0210241.pfb 96,211 bytes
                    n0220031.pfb 96,263 bytes
                    n0220041.pfb 120,373 bytes
                    n0220231.pfb 101,133 bytes
                    n0220241.pfb 114,228 bytes
                    s0500001.pfb 32,213 bytes
                ttf <DIR>
                    resource <DIR>
                        glyphlist.txt 82,524 bytes
META-INF <DIR>
    CERT.RSA 844 bytes
    CERT.SF 2,791 bytes
```

```
    MANIFEST.MF 2,738 bytes
res <DIR>
    drawable <DIR>
        back01.png 1,566 bytes
        back02.png 1,342 bytes
        doc.png 1,552 bytes
        folder.png 942 bytes
        icon.png 3,022 bytes
        pdf.png 1,079 bytes
    layout <DIR>
        dialog_pagenumber.xml 1,388 bytes
        file_explorer.xml 976 bytes
        file_row.xml 948 bytes
        pdf_file_password.xml 1,712 bytes
        pdf_file_select.xml 3,336 bytes
        scroll_layout.xml 792 bytes
resources.arsc 3,112 bytes
```

Installing Android PDF Viewer APK File

This section provides a tutorial example on how to install the Android PDF Viewer APK file to the Android emulator using the 'adb' tool provided in the SDK package.

If you want to try the Android PDF Viewer on the emulator, you can install the downloaded APK file with the "adb" tool provided in the Android SDK package.

1. Run the Android emulator through the AVD Manager and wait for the emulator to be fully booted.

2. Install AndroidPdfViewer_1_0_1.apk to the Android emulator using the "adb" tool:

```
C:\local\android-sdk-windows\platform-tools>adb install \
    \download\AndroidPdfViewer_1_0_1.apk


1019 KB/s (1433355 bytes in 1.373s)
        pkg: /data/local/tmp/AndroidPdfViewer_1_0_1.apk
Success
```

3. Go to Android emulator and click the "Applications" icon. The "Android PDF Viewer" application is listed in the application list.

4. Click on "Android PDF Viewer" in the application list to run the application:

Android PDF Viewer Start Screen - Android SDK R24

Copy PDF File to Android Emulator's File System

This section provides a tutorial example on how to copy PDF files to the Android emulator's file system using the 'adb' tool provided in the SDK package.

To test the Android PDF Viewer, I need to copy PDF files into the emulator's file system. This can also be done with the "adb" command tool.

1. Run the Android emulator through the AVD Manager and wait for the emulator to be fully booted.

2. Copy a PDF file to the Android emulator using the "adb" tool:

```
C:\local\android-sdk-windows\platform-tools>adb push \
    \herong\herong_book_Android.pdf /sdcard/Download


908 KB/s (3356636 bytes in 3.606s)
```

3. Go to Android emulator and run "Android PDF Viewer" again.

4. Click the "Browse" icon next to the "PDF File" field. herong_book_Android.pdf is listed in the /sdcard/Download folder on the emulator.

5. Click "herong_book_Android.pdf" to select the PDF file and click the "Show" button. My PDF book will be displayed on the Android PDF Viewer:

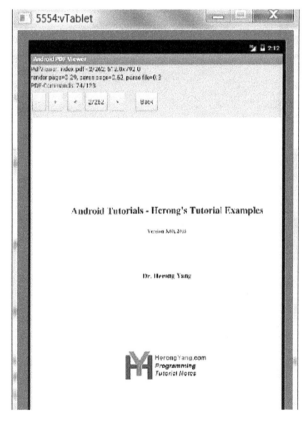

Android PDF Viewer on Herong's Book - Android SDK R24

Installing Adobe Reader APK File

This section provides a tutorial example on how to install the Adobe Reader APK file to the Android emulator using the 'adb' tool provided in the SDK package. Adobe Reader runs ok on the emulator. But it failed to show PDF files in the /sdcard/Download folder.

Let's repeat the process to download and install another APK file of Adobe Reader

1. Run the Android emulator through the AVD Manager and wait for the emulator to be fully booted.

2. Go to http://www.freewarelovers.com/android/app/adobe-reader and click "Download".

3. Click on " Adobe Reader 10.0.0" in the "Download" section and save the downloaded file to C:\download\Adobe_Reader_9.0.2.apk.

4. Install Adobe_Reader_9.0.2.apk to the Android emulator using the "adb" tool:

```
C:\local\android-sdk-windows\platform-tools>adb install \
   \download\Adobe_Reader_10.0.0.apk

1003 KB/s (1565975 bytes in 1.524s)
       pkg: /data/local/tmp/Adobe_Reader_9.0.2.apk
Success
```

5. Go to Android emulator and click the "Applications" icon. The "Adobe Reader" application is listed in the application list.

6. Click on "Adobe Reader" in the application list to run the application, and click "Agree" on the End User License Agreement. "Adobe Reader" will show up with no PDF files listed.

7. Click "herong_book_Android.pdf" to view the content. My PDF book will be displayed on the Android PDF Viewer:

Adobe Reader with No PDF Files - Android SDK R24

I don't know what is the problem. I do have "herong_book_Android.pdf" listed in the / sdcard/Download folder. On Android 4.0.3, Adobe Reader was able to see PDF files in the /sdcard/Download folder.

Android Debug Bridge (adb) Tool

This chapter provides tutorial notes on the Android Debug Bridge (adb) tool. Topics include quick introduction of Android Debug Bridge (adb); creating debugging connections to Android devices/emulators; running 'adb' commands over debugging connections; using 'adb install/uninstall' commands to install applications; using 'adb shell' command to manage the device; using 'adb push/pull' commands to copy files.

Takeaways:

- Android Debug Bridge (adb) is an Android developer tool to manage a connected emulator or device over Android debugging connections.

- Android debugging connections can be established with the USB debugging option, Wireless debugging option, or TCP port option.

- "adb" acts as a debugging client. It sends commands to the debugging daemon on the connected device, through the debugging server process.

- "adb install" allows you to install an Android application package on the connected emulator or device.

- "adb shell" allows you to manage the connected emulator or device with a Unix shell interface.

- "adb push/pull" allows you to copy files or folders to or from the connected emulator or device.

What Is Android Debug Bridge (adb)

This section describes the Android Debug Bridge (adb) tool, which allows you to manage an Android emulators or connected Android devices.

What Is Android Debug Bridge (adb)? "adb" is the command line tool provided in the Android SDK Platform Tools package. "adb" stands for Android Debug Bridge which allows you to communicate with an emulator instance or connected Android-powered device to:

- Manage the state of an emulator or device.

- Run shell commands on a device.

- Manage port forwarding on an emulator or device.

- Copy files to/from an emulator or device.

In order for "adb" to communicate with a device (or emulator), it requires that:

1. The device must be connected to your desktop computer using these options:

- Over USB Cable - Connect your Android device directly with USB cable to desktop computer.

- Over Wi-Fi Router - Connect your Android device to the same Wi-Fi router as your desktop computer.

- Android Emulator - Run the Android Emulator on your desktop computer.

2. An Android debugging environment must be established between the connected device and you desktop computer. This environment requires 3 components:

- Client Component - This is the "adb" tool, which sends out Android debugging commands.

- Daemon Component - This is a background process (called "adbd") running on the connected device to execute Android debugging commands.

- Server Component - This is a background process running on your desktop computer to to manage communications between the client and the daemon.

Here is a diagram that shows you Android debugging connection options and communication components:

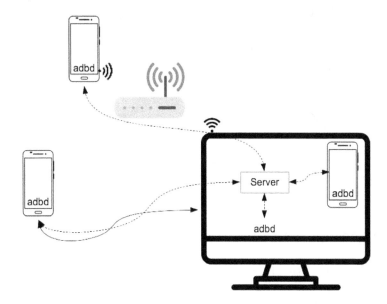

Android Debugging Connections and Components

In next tutorials, we will look at how to create Android debugging connections and manage related components.

Install "adb" as Part of SDK Platform Tools

This section provides a tutorial example on how to install the 'adb' tool as part of the Android SDK Platform Tools package.

What Is Android SDK Platform Tools? Android SDK Platform Tools is a sub-package of the Android SDK (also called Android Studio) package. It contains "adb", "fastboot" and other tools to interface with connected Android devices.

If you are an Android app developer, you probably have already installed the Android SDK package on your desktop computer. Android SDK Platform Tools related programs are located in the "platform-tools" sub-directory. No additional installation is needed.

If you are not an Android app developer and want to run "adb" tool, you can download and install the Android SDK Platform Tools package independently as shown in this tutorial.

1. Go to Android SDK Platform Tools Website at https://developer.android.com/tools/releases/platform-tools.

2. Click "Download SDK Platform-Tools for Mac" or other links depending on the platform of your desktop computer.

3. Save the downloaded file, platform-tools_r34.0.3-darwin.zip, in the ~/Downloads directory.

4. Unzip the downloaded file, you see all files are extracted into a sub-directory called "platform-tools".

5. Move "platform-tools" to the ~/Applications directory. The installation is done.

6. Test the installation by running the following command:

```
herong$ ~/Applications/platform-tools/adb version

Android Debug Bridge version 1.0.41
Version 34.0.3-10161052
Installed as /Users/herong/Applications/platform-tools/adb
Running on Darwin 16.7.0 (x86_64)
```

Cool, I have successfully installed the Android SDK Platform Tools package on my macOS computer.

Now I am ready to connect my Android phone and create the Android debugging environment as shown in the next tutorial.

USB Debugging Connection to Use "adb" Tool

This section provides a tutorial example on how to create a USB debugging connection to run debugging commands using the 'adb' tool.

The first option to connect an Android device to run "adb" debugging commands is to use a USB cable as shown in this tutorial.

1. Connect your Android phone with a USB cable to your desktop computer.

2. Turn on "Developer Options" on your Android phone by going to "Settings > About Phone > Software Information", and tapping "Build number" 7 times. Yes, 7 times!

3. Go back to "Settings". You will see "Developer Options" showing up at the end of the screen.

4. Turn on "USB Debugging" on your Android phone by going to "Settings > Developer Options", and turn on the "USB Debugging" option in the "DEBUGGING" section. You will see the following confirmation message:

```
Allow USB debugging?


USB debugging is intended for development purposes only. It can be
used to copy data between your computer and your device, install
applications on your device without notification, and read log data.
[OK] [Cancel]
```

5. Tap on "OK" to confirm. You will see an authorization request message.

```
Allow USB debugging?


The computer's RSA key fingerprint is "....".
[x] Always allow from this computer.
```

6. Check "Always allow..." and tap OK to authorize the connection.

7. Verify the USB debugging connection on your desktop computer by running the following "adb" command.

```
herong$ ~/Applications/platform-tools/adb devices


List of devices attached
988bdb3533534e4734 device
```

If you see a device listed in the output, you know that your Android phone is connected and ready to run "adb" commands.

If you see a device listed with an "unauthorized" status, you probably missed the authorization step. You can go back to Android phone, turn off and turn on "Settings > Developer Options > USB debugging". Then tap "OK" on the authorization message box.

8. Test the connection by running the following "adb" commands. The output confirms that the connected phone is running Android 8.0.0 based on Linux kernel 4.4.78.

```
herong$ ~/Applications/platform-tools/adb shell \
  getprop ro.build.version.release
8.0.0


herong$ ~/Applications/platform-tools/adb shell uname -a
Linux localhost 4.4.78-13052619 #1 SMP PREEMPT ... 2018 aarch64
```

9. Verify the "adbd" daemon process running on the connected device:

```
herong$ ~/Applications/platform-tools/adb shell

dream2qltecan:/ $ ps -elf | grep shell
shell   6866      1  0 13:03:53 ?      00:00:05 adbd --root_seclabel=...
shell  29977   6866  0 21:41:28 pts/0 00:00:00 sh -
shell  30029  29977 12 21:43:36 pts/0 00:00:00 ps -elf
shell  30030  29977  5 21:43:36 pts/0 00:00:00 grep shell

dream2qltecan:/ $ exit
herong$
```

The output confirms that "adbd" is running on the connected device as PID 6866, which runs the "sh" process (PID 29977) I requested. The "sh" process runs the "ps" process (PID 30029).

By default the "adbd" process runs under user "shell" with limited permissions. If you try the "adb root" command will restart it under user "root", you will get an error message:

```
herong$ ~/Applications/platform-tools/adb shell cat /system/build.prop
cat: /system/build.prop: Permission denied
```

```
herong$ ~/Applications/platform-tools/adb root
adbd cannot run as root in production builds
```

So the "adb shell" only gives you access limited to the user "shell", not unlimited as "root".

11. Verify the debugging server process running on the desktop computer. The server process manages the communication between the client "adb" and the daemon "adbd", as described in the previous tutorial.

```
herong$ ps -ef | grep adb

502 17323 1 0 22:20 adb -L tcp:5037 fork-server server --reply-fd 4
```

Cool, I have successfully created a USB debugging connection from my desktop computer to my Android phone and ready to run debugging command through the "adb" tool.

Wireless Debugging Connection to Use "adb" Tool

This section provides a tutorial example on how to create a wireless debugging connection to run debugging commands using the 'adb' tool.

If you are tired of use the USB debugging connection to run "adb" commands, you can try the wireless debugging connection as shown in this tutorial.

Option I - Using Wireless Pairing on Newer Android Phones - This option is for newer versions Android phones that support wireless pairing.

1. Connect your Android phone and your desktop computer to your home Wi-Fi router.

2. Turn on "Developer Options" on your Android phone by going to "Settings > About Phone > Software Inforrmation", and tapping "Build number" 7 times. Yes, 7 times!

3. Turn on "Wireless Debugging" on your Android phone by going to "Settings > Systems > Developer Options", and turn on the "Wireless Debugging" option in the "DEBUGGING" section. You will see the following confirmation message:

```
Allow wireless debugging on this network?
```

```
Network Name (SSID) "********"
[x] Always allow on this network


[Cancel] [Allow]
```

4. Check "Always allow..." and tap "Allow" to authorize the connection.

5. Tap "Wireless Debugging" to connection details:

```
Device name: moto g stylus


[Pair device with QR code]


[Pair device with pairing code]


(list of paired devices)
```

6. Tap "Pair device with pairing code". You see the paring code displayed:

```
Pair with device


Wi-Fi paring code: 123577
IP address & port: 10.0.0.150:45585
```

7. Pair phone on your desktop computer by running the following "adb" command with the above IP address/port and paring code:

```
herong$ ~/Applications/platform-tools/adb pair 10.0.0.150:45585


Enter pairing code: 123577


Successfully paired to 10.0.0.150:45585 [guid=adb-**********-XmxP3G]
```

8. List connected devices:

```
herong$ ~/Applications/platform-tools/adb devices


List of devices attached
adb-ZY22GWX96K-XmxP3G._adb-tls-connect._tcp. device
```

9. Test the connection by running the following "adb" commands. The output confirms that the connected phone is running Android 12 based on Linux kernel 4.19.191

```
herong$ ~/Applications/platform-tools/adb shell \
  getprop ro.build.version.release
12


herong$ ~/Applications/platform-tools/adb shell uname -a
Linux localhost 4.19.191+ #1 SMP PREEMPT ... 2023 aarch64
```

Option II - Using TCP Connection on Older Android Phones - This option is for Android 10 or older phones that do not support wireless pairing. You can also use this option, if you have problems with the above wireless pairing option.

1. Connect your Android phone and your desktop computer to your home Wi-Fi router. And connect the phone with a USB cable to create USB debugging connection.

2. Turn on "Developer Options" on your Android phone by going to "Settings > About Phone > Software Inforrmation", and tapping "Build number" 7 times. Yes, 7 times!

3. Turn on "USB Debugging" on your Android phone by going to "Settings > System > Developer Options", and turn on the "USB Debugging" option in the "DEBUGGING" section.

4. Tap on "OK" on the confirmation prompt and on the authorization prompt.

5. Verify the USB debugging connection,

```
herong$ ~/Applications/platform-tools/adb devices


List of devices attached
ZY22GWX96K device
```

6. Restart "adbd" to listen on a TCP port instead of the USB connection.

```
herong$ ~/Applications/platform-tools/adb tcpip 5555


restarting in TCP mode port: 5555
```

7. Disconnect the USB cable from your Android phone.

8. Find the IP address on the phone in "Settings > About Phone".

```
Device identifiers

IP address: 10.0.0.150
...
```

7. Reset the debugging connection to the TCP port.

```
herong$ ~/Applications/platform-tools/adb connect 10.0.0.150:5555

connected to 10.0.0.150:5555
```

8. Check the new debugging connection. You may see 2 connections: one established over the TCP port, and the other established over the wireless pairing.

```
herong$ ~/Applications/platform-tools/adb devices

List of devices attached
10.0.0.150:5555 device
adb-ZY22GWX96K-XmxP3G._adb-tls-connect._tcp. device
```

9. Test the TCP debugging connection with "-s 10.0.0.150:5555" option to specify the connection.

```
herong$ ~/Applications/platform-tools/adb -s 10.0.0.150:5555 shell ps

USER    PID  PPID    VSZ      RSS WCHAN   ADDR S NAME
root      1     0 2313104  10368 0          0 S init
root      2     0       0      0 0          0 S [kthreadd]
root      3     2       0      0 0          0 I [rcu_gp]
root      4     2       0      0 0          0 I [rcu_par_gp]
root      8     2       0      0 0          0 I [mm_percpu_wq]
...
```

Cool, I have successfully created 2 wireless debugging connections from my desktop computer to my Android phone and ready to run debugging command through the "adb" tool. One connection established over the TCP port, and the other established over the wireless pairing.

Debugging Connection to Android Device Emulators

This section provides a tutorial example on how to create a wireless debugging connection to run debugging commands using the 'adb' tool.

If you run debugging commands on Android device emulators, you can follow this tutorial to create debugging connections to emulators.

1. Launch the Android emulator through the AVD Manager and wait for the emulator to be fully booted.

2. Go to a Windows command window and run the following "adb" command.

```
> \local\android-sdk-windows\platform-tools\adb devices

* daemon not running. starting it now on port 5037 *
* daemon started successfully *


List of devices attached
emulator-5554    offline
```

3. Test the debugging connection with the following "adb" command.

```
> \local\android-sdk-windows\platform-tools\adb shell df
```

Filesystem	Size	Used	Free	Blksize
/dev	242.9M	24.0K	242.8M	4096
/sys/fs/cgroup	242.9M	12.0K	242.9M	4096
/mnt/asec	242.9M	0.0K	242.9M	4096
/mnt/obb	242.9M	0.0K	242.9M	4096

Cool, I have successfully created a debugging connection to my Android device emulator controlled by the AVD Manager.

Commands and Options Supported by "adb"

This section describes commands and options supported by the 'adb' tool. The 'adb help'
command can give you details on how to use other 'adb' commands and options.

If you want see what commands and options are supported by the "adb" (Android
Debug Bridge) tool, you run the "adb help" command:

```
C:\local\android-sdk-windows\platform-tools>adb help

Android Debug Bridge version 1.0.29

 -d            - directs command to the only connected USB device
                 returns an error if more than one USB device is present.
 -e            - directs command to the only running emulator.
                 returns an error if more than one emulator is running.
 -s <serial number> - directs command to the USB device or emulator
                 with the given serial number. Overrides ANDROID_SERIAL
                 environment variable.
 -p <product name or path> - simple product name like 'sooner', or
                 a relative/absolute path to a product
                 out directory like 'out/target/product/sooner'.
                 If -p is not specified, the ANDROID_PRODUCT_OUT
                 environment variable is used, which must
                 be an absolute path.
 devices       - list all connected devices
 connect <host>[:<port>] - connect to a device via TCP/IP
                 Port 5555 is used by default if no port number is
                 specified.
 disconnect [<host>[:<port>]] - disconnect from a TCP/IP device.
                 Port 5555 is used by default if no port number is
                 specified. Using this command with no additional
                 arguments will disconnect from all connected TCP/IP
                 devices.

device commands:
  adb push <local> <remote> - copy file/dir to device
  adb pull <remote> [<local>] - copy file/dir from device
  adb sync [ <directory> ] - copy host->device only if changed
               (-l means list but don't copy)
```

```
               (see 'adb help all')
adb shell - run remote shell interactively
adb shell <command> - run remote shell command
adb emu <command> - run emulator console command
adb logcat [ <filter-spec> ] - View device log
adb forward <local> <remote> - forward socket connections
            forward specs are one of:
                tcp:<port>
                localabstract:<unix domain socket name>
                localreserved:<unix domain socket name>
                localfilesystem:<unix domain socket name>
                dev:<character device name>
                jdwp:<process pid> (remote only)
adb jdwp  - list PIDs of processes hosting a JDWP transport
adb install [-l] [-r] [-s] <file> - push this package file to the
            device and install it
            ('-l' means forward-lock the app)
            ('-r' means reinstall the app, keeping its data)
            ('-s' means install on SD card instead of internal
            storage)
adb uninstall [-k] <package> - remove this app package from the device
            ('-k' means keep the data and cache directories)
adb bugreport - return all information from the device
            that should be included in a bug report.


adb backup [-f <file>] [-apk|-noapk] [-shared|-noshared] [-all]
            [-system|-nosystem] [<packages...>]
        - write an archive of the device's data to <file>.
          If no -f option is supplied then the data is written
          to "backup.ab" in the current directory.
          (-apk|-noapk enable/disable backup of the .apks
             themselves in the archive; the default is noapk.)
          (-shared|-noshared enable/disable backup of the device's
             shared storage / SD card contents; the default is
             noshared.)
          (-all means to back up all installed applications)
          (-system|-nosystem toggles whether -all automatically
```

```
                    includes system applications; the default is to
                    include system apps)
                (<packages...> is the list of applications to be backed
                    up. If the -all or -shared flags are passed, then the
                    package list is optional. Applications explicitly
                    given on the command line will be included even if
                    -nosystem would ordinarily cause them to be omitted.)


    adb restore <file> - restore device contents from the <file> backup
                archive
    adb keygen <file>  - generate adb public/private key. The private
                key is stored in <file>, and the public key is stored in
                <file>.pub. Any existing files are overwritten.


    adb help  - show this help message
    adb version - show version num


scripting:
    adb wait-for-device - block until device is online
    adb start-server - ensure that there is a server running
    adb kill-server - kill the server if it is running
    adb get-state - prints: offline | bootloader | device
    adb get-serialno - prints: <serial-number>
    adb status-window - continuously print device status for a specified
                device
    adb remount - remounts the /system partition on the device
                read-write
    adb reboot [bootloader|recovery] - reboots the device, optionally
                into the bootloader or recovery program
    adb reboot-bootloader - reboots the device into the bootloader
    adb root  - restarts the adbd daemon with root permissions
    adb usb   - restarts the adbd daemon listening on USB
    adb tcpip <port> - restarts the adbd daemon listening on TCP on the
                specified port


networking:
    adb ppp <tty> [parameters]   - Run PPP over USB.
```

```
Note: you should not automatically start a PPP connection.
<tty> refers to the tty for PPP stream. Eg. dev:/dev/omap_csmi_tty1
[parameters] - Eg. defaultroute debug dump local notty usepeerdns


adb sync notes: adb sync [ <directory> ]
  <localdir> can be interpreted in several ways:

  - If <directory> is not specified, both /system and /data partitions
            will be updated.


  - If it is "system" or "data", only the corresponding partition
    is updated.


environmental variables:
  ADB_TRACE - Print debug information. A comma separated list of the
              following values 1 or all, adb, sockets, packets, rwx,
              usb, sync, sysdeps, transport, jdwp
  ANDROID_SERIAL - The serial number to connect to. -s takes priority
              over this if given.
  ANDROID_LOG_TAGS - When used with the logcat option, only these
              debug tags are printed.
```

"adb install" and "adb uninstall" Commands

This section describes 'adb install' and 'adb uninstall' commands that allows you to install an application APK package and uninstall it on the connected emulator or device.

The most commonly used "adb" command is the "adb install" command that allows you to install an application stored in the specified APK file to the connect Android emulator or device:

```
adb install <path_to_apk>
```

You can also uninstall a package from the connected emulator or device by using the "adb uninstall" command:

```
adb uninstall <apk_name>
```

If you have downloaded the "Adobe Reader" APK file as described in the previous
chapter, you can play with the following "adb" install and uninstall commands:

```
C:\local\android-sdk-windows\platform-tools>adb install \
    \herong\down\Adobe_Reader_10.0.0.apk
1072 KB/s (1565975 bytes in 1.426s)
        pkg: /data/local/tmp/Adobe_Reader_9.0.2.apk
Success


C:\local\android-sdk-windows\platform-tools>adb install \
    \herong\down\Adobe_Reader_10.0.0.apk
1110 KB/s (1565975 bytes in 1.377s)
        pkg: /data/local/tmp/Adobe_Reader_9.0.2.apk
Failure [INSTALL_FAILED_ALREADY_EXISTS]


C:\local\android-sdk-windows\platform-tools>adb uninstall \
    com.adobe.reader
Success


C:\local\android-sdk-windows\platform-tools>adb uninstall \
    com.adobe.reader
Failure
```

Ok. Both "install" and "uninstall" command worked nicely.

"adb push" and "adb pull" Commands

*This section describes 'adb push' and 'adb pull' commands, which allows you to copy files to
and from the remote Android emulator or device.*

The "adb" tool also offers you commands to copy files into and from the connected
Android emulator or devices.

The "adb push <local> <remote>" copies a file or folder from the local system to the
remote emulator or device.

The "adb pull <remote> <local>" copies a file or folder from the remote emulator or device to the local system.

Example 1 - Copying "Silk-Road.jpg" to the /sdcard/Picture folder in the emulator:

```
C:\local\android-sdk-windows\platform-tools>adb push \
   \herong\Pictures\Silk-Road.jpg /storage/sdcard/Picture
258 KB/s (111019 bytes in 0.420s)
```

Example 2 - Copying "init.rc" from the / folder in the emulator:

```
C:\local\android-sdk-windows\platform-tools>adb pull \
   /init.rc \herong
573 KB/s (21728 bytes in 0.037s)
```

Example 3 - Copying all files from the /data/app folder in the emulator:

```
C:\local\android-sdk-windows\platform-tools>adb pull
   /data/app \herong\app
pull: building file list...
pull: /data/app/ApiDemos/ApiDemos.apk
   -> \herong\app/ApiDemos/ApiDemos.apk
pull: /data/app/CubeLiveWallpapers/CubeLiveWallpapers.apk
   -> \herong\app/CubeLiveWallpapers/CubeLiveWallpapers.apk
pull: /data/app/GestureBuilder/GestureBuilder.apk
   -> \herong\app/GestureBuilder/GestureBuilder.apk
pull: /data/app/SmokeTest/SmokeTest.apk
   -> \herong\app/SmokeTest/SmokeTest.apk
pull: /data/app/SmokeTestApp/SmokeTestApp.apk
   -> \herong\app/SmokeTestApp/SmokeTestApp.apk
pull: /data/app/SoftKeyboard/SoftKeyboard.apk
   -> \herong\app/SoftKeyboard/SoftKeyboard.apk
pull: /data/app/WidgetPreview/WidgetPreview.apk
   -> \herong\app/WidgetPreview/WidgetPreview.apk
pull: /data/app/com.herongyang-1/base.apk
   -> \herong\app/com.herongyang-1/base.apk
pull: /data/app/net.sf.andpdf.pdfviewer-1/base.apk
   -> \herong\app/net.sf.andpdf.pdfviewer-1/base.apk
pull: /data/app/com.adobe.reader-1/lib/arm/libAdobeReader.so
   -> \herong\app/com.adobe.reader-1/lib/arm/libAdobeReader.so
```

```
pull: /data/app/com.adobe.reader-1/base.apk
   -> \herong\app/com.adobe.reader-1/base.apk
11 files pulled. 0 files skipped.
1102 KB/s (11343777 bytes in 10.043s)
```

"adb shell" - Remote Shell Interface

This section describes the 'adb shell' command, which gives you a shell interface to the connected Android operating system. The shell interface allows you to manage the Android file system and invoke Android command line programs.

Another important command is the "adb shell" command, which gives you a shell interface to the connected Android operating system. The shell interface allows you to manage the Android file system and invoke Android command line programs.

Here is a "adb shell" command session I did on my Android 5.1.1 emulator:

```
> \local\android-sdk-windows\platform-tools\adb shell

root@generic:/ # pwd
pwd
/

root@generic:/ # ls -l
ls -l
drwxr-xr-x root    root              2015-06-21 acct
drwxrwx--- system cache             2015-06-21 cache
lrwxrwxrwx root    root              1969-12-31 charger -> /sbin/healthd
dr-x------ root    root              2015-06-21 config
lrwxrwxrwx root    root              2015-06-21 d -> /sys/kernel/debug
drwxrwx--x system system            2015-06-21 data
-rw-r--r-- root    root          281 1969-12-31 default.prop
drwxr-xr-x root    root              2015-06-21 dev
lrwxrwxrwx root    root              2015-06-21 etc -> /system/etc
-rw-r--r-- root    root        11166 1969-12-31 file_contexts
-rw-r----- root    root          922 1969-12-31 fstab.goldfish
```

```
-rwxr-x--- root    root      301452 1969-12-31 init
-rwxr-x--- root    root         944 1969-12-31 init.environ.rc
-rwxr-x--- root    root        2836 1969-12-31 init.goldfish.rc
-rwxr-x--- root    root       21728 1969-12-31 init.rc
-rwxr-x--- root    root        1927 1969-12-31 init.trace.rc
-rwxr-x--- root    root        3885 1969-12-31 init.usb.rc
-rwxr-x--- root    root         301 1969-12-31 init.zygote32.rc
drwxrwxr-x root    system              2015-06-21 mnt
dr-xr-xr-x root    root                1969-12-31 proc
-rw-r--r-- root    root        2771 1969-12-31 property_contexts
drwx------ root    root                2014-09-16 root
drwxr-x--- root    root                1969-12-31 sbin
lrwxrwxrwx root    root                2015-06-21 sdcard -> /storage/sdcard
-rw-r--r-- root    root         471 1969-12-31 seapp_contexts
-rw-r--r-- root    root          63 1969-12-31 selinux_version
-rw-r--r-- root    root      118317 1969-12-31 sepolicy
-rw-r--r-- root    root        9438 1969-12-31 service_contexts
drwxr-x--x root    sdcard_r            2015-06-21 storage
dr-xr-xr-x root    root                2015-06-21 sys
drwxr-xr-x root    root                1969-12-31 system
-rw-r--r-- root    root         323 1969-12-31 ueventd.goldfish.rc
-rw-r--r-- root    root        4464 1969-12-31 ueventd.rc
lrwxrwxrwx root    root                2015-06-21 vendor -> /system/vendor


root@generic:/ # cat default.prop
cat default.prop
#
# ADDITIONAL_DEFAULT_PROPERTIES
#
ro.secure=0
ro.allow.mock.location=1
ro.debuggable=1
ro.zygote=zygote32
dalvik.vm.dex2oat-Xms=64m
dalvik.vm.dex2oat-Xmx=512m
dalvik.vm.image-dex2oat-Xms=64m
dalvik.vm.image-dex2oat-Xmx=64m
```

```
ro.dalvik.vm.native.bridge=0
persist.sys.usb.config=adb

root@generic:/ # df
df
Filesystem              Size      Used      Free    Blksize
/dev                   242.9M    24.0K    242.8M    4096
/sys/fs/cgroup         242.9M    12.0K    242.9M    4096
/mnt/asec              242.9M     0.0K    242.9M    4096
/mnt/obb               242.9M     0.0K    242.9M    4096
/system                541.3M   363.9M   177.5M    4096
/data                  541.3M   147.2M   394.1M    4096
/cache                  65.0M     4.3M    60.6M    4096
/mnt/media_rw/sdcard    31.5M     8.0K    31.5M    512
/storage/sdcard         31.5M     8.0K    31.5M    512

root@generic:/ # ps
ps
USER     PID PPID VSIZE  RSS    NAME
root      1    0  8784   608    /init
root      2    0  0      0      kthreadd
root      3    2  0      0      ksoftirqd/0
root      5    2  0      0      kworker/u:0
root      6    2  0      0      khelper
root      7    2  0      0      sync_supers
root      8    2  0      0      bdi-default
root      9    2  0      0      kblockd
root     10    2  0      0      rpciod
root     11    2  0      0      kworker/0:1
root     12    2  0      0      kswapd0
root     13    2  0      0      fsnotify_mark
root     14    2  0      0      crypto
root     25    2  0      0      mtdblock0
root     26    2  0      0      mtdblock1
root     27    2  0      0      mtdblock2
root     29    2  0      0      binder
root     30    2  0      0      deferwq
```

```
root      31   2   0        0      kworker/u:2
root      32   2   0        0      mmcqd/0
root      33   1   8780     540    /sbin/ueventd
root      35   2   0        0      jbd2/mtdblock0-
root      36   2   0        0      ext4-dio-unwrit
root      37   2   0        0      kworker/0:2
root      42   2   0        0      jbd2/mtdblock1-
root      43   2   0        0      ext4-dio-unwrit
root      48   2   0        0      jbd2/mtdblock2-
root      49   2   0        0      ext4-dio-unwrit
logd      50   1   14148    2148   /system/bin/logd
root      51   1   9824     348    /sbin/healthd
root      52   1   10612    1252   /system/bin/lmkd
system    53   1   9448     680    /system/bin/servicemanager
root      54   1   13908    1948   /system/bin/vold
system    55   1   43032    12108  /system/bin/surfaceflinger
root      57   1   9244     568    /system/bin/qemud
shell     60   1   9312     744    /system/bin/sh
root      61   1   12876    384    /sbin/adbd
root      62   1   18708    1344   /system/bin/netd
root      63   1   10100    1336   /system/bin/debuggerd
radio     64   1   14436    1360   /system/bin/rild
drm       65   1   17608    3476   /system/bin/drmserver
media     66   1   109524   7932   /system/bin/mediaserver
install   67   1   9404     696    /system/bin/installd
keystore  68   1   12488    1912   /system/bin/keystore
root      71   1   484048   44420  zygote
root      77   2   0        0      kauditd
system    338  71  588008   75072  system_server
media_rw  438  1   11300    696    /system/bin/sdcard
u0_a30    579  71  504812   32876  com.android.inputmethod.latin
radio     603  71  515660   39356  com.android.phone
u0_a7     623  71  503688   41652  com.android.launcher
u0_a2     688  71  499452   29072  android.process.acore
u0_a6     728  71  486184   21872  com.android.externalstorage
u0_a39    765  71  488892   23004  com.android.printspooler
u0_a12    781  71  527564   60096  com.android.systemui
```

```
u0_a5     846  71 490584 29028 android.process.media
u0_a17    884  71 496092 26012 com.android.calendar
u0_a21    904  71 490620 25828 com.android.deskclock
u0_a1     919  71 488408 25572 com.android.providers.calendar
system    943  71 486212 21820 com.android.keychain
u0_a4     963  71 492372 23060 com.android.dialer
u0_a8     984  71 487204 21920 com.android.managedprovisioning
u0_a9     1003 71 496916 26748 com.android.mms
system    1031 71 497660 23332 com.android.settings
u0_a25    1054 71 502344 30300 com.android.email
u0_a27    1070 71 493348 24456 com.android.exchange
u0_a33    1093 71 488056 24708 com.android.music
root      1126 61 9312   752   /system/bin/sh
root      1132 2  0      0     flush-31:1
root      1134 2  0      0     flush-179:0

root@generic:/ # exit
exit
```

This is nice. With this shell interface, I have full control of my Android emulator system now.

See "Android Command Line Shell" chapter for more tutorials on using the "adb shell" interface.

Android File Systems

This chapter provides tutorial notes on Android file systems. Topics include introduction of file systems or partitions; common directories in the file system hierarchy; 'df -H' and 'mount' commands to display file systems, and and space usages; 'find -L . -name' command to search files.

Takeaways:

- A file system is partition of a storage device formatted in a specific way to store data.

- The file system hierarchy is the logical representation of multiple file systems organized in a tree structure.

- Each file system (or partition) is attached (or mounted) to a specific named node (referred as director or folder) in the tree.

- /system/app is the directory for pre-installed application packages.

- /product/app is the directory for user-installed application packages.

- /storage/sdcard is the directory for user files like, Downloads, Movie, Music, Pictures and Ringtones.

- "df -H" to display mounted file systems and their space usages.

- "mount" to display all file systems with their types and mount options.

- "find -L . -name" to search for files on Android systems.

File System Hierarchy and Common Directories

This section describes file systems, file system hierarchy and common directories used on Android systems.

What Is a File System? A file system is a large chunk (referred as partition) of a storage device formatted in a specific way to store data.

What Is the File System Hierarchy? The File System Hierarchy is the logical representation of multiple file systems organized in a tree structure. Each file system (or partition) is attached (or mounted) to a specific named node (referred as director or folder) in the tree. The file system attached to the root node is called the root partition.

One advantage of the File System Hierarchy is that any directory or file in any attached partition can be identified in a uniform path name format: /directory/directory/.../ directory(file).

For example, the following diagram illustrates how file systems (partitions) created on a storage device are attached to different nodes in the file system hierarchy.

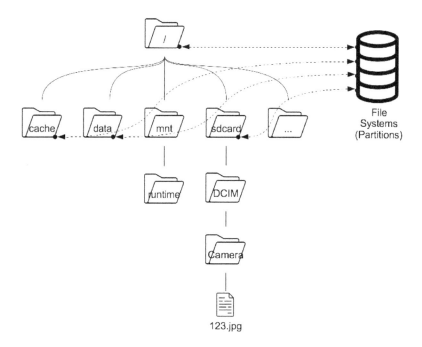

Partitions and File System Hierarchy

File "123.jpg" as shown in the file system hierarchy can be identified as "/sdcard/DCIM/ Camera/123.jpg", which is picture file created by the camera on the device.

Different Android devices produced by different vendors all have similar file system hierarchies with the following common top level directories:

```
/          - Mounting point of the root partition
|- acct    - Mounting point for the acct cgroup (control group)
|            partition to store user account information
|- cache   - Mounting point for the cache partition used as
|            a scratch pad by the system
|- data    - Mounting point for the data partition to store apps data
|  |- media    -
|  |- ...
|
|- dev     - Directory contains pseudo files representing devices
|- etc     - Directory to store system configurations
|- mnt     - Directory contains mounting points of other file systems
|  |- runtime   -
|  |- vendor    -
|  |- ...
|
|- proc    - Mounting point for the proc pseudo file system to access
|  |    system kernel data structures.
|  |- cpuinfo    - File linked to current CPU information
|  |- diskstats - File linked to disk statuses
|  |- version    - File linked to system kernel version
|  |- ...
|- product - Directory for product specific system files
|- root    - Home directory for the root user
|- sbin    - Directory for system binary executable programs
|- sdcard - Directory as a logical SD (Secure Digital) card
|  |- Alarms     - Directory for custom ringtone audio files
|  |- Android    - Directory as a shared storage for all apps
|  |  |- data
|  |  |- media
|  |  |- obb
|  |- Audiobooks
```

```
|   |- DCIM        - Directory for Digital Camera IMage files
|   |- Documents - Directory for user documents
|   |- Download   - Directory for downloaded files
|   |- Movies     - Directory for video files
|   |- Music      - Directory for audio files
|   |- Notifications - Directory for custom ringtone audio files
|   |- Pictures   - Directory for pictures
|   |- Podcasts   - Directory for post cast files
|   |- Recordings
|   |- Ringtones - Directory for custom ringtone audio files
|
|- storage - Directory contains mounting points external storages
|   |- emulated  - Directory contains emulated external storages
|   |- sdcard0   - Symbolic link to /sdcard
|   |- self      -
|
|- sys     - Mounting point for sysfs pseudo file system to access
|             system kernel objects
|
|- system - Directory for Android operating system files
|   |- app        - Directory for pre-installed application packages
|   |- bin        - Directory for system binary executable codes
|   |- build.prop - File containing configuration settings
|   |- fonts      - Directory for font files
|   |- framework - Directory for JAR and ODEX files of Android framework
|   |- lib        - Directory contains binary code libraries like libc.so
|   |- media      - Directory for system media files
|   |- ...
|
|- vendor - Directory for vendor specific system files
```

"df -H" - Display Mounted File Systems

This section provides a tutorial example on how to use the 'df -H' command on the 'adb shell' interface to display mounted file systems and their space usages.

To list file systems on your Android device, you can use the "df -H" command on the
"adb shell" interface. It displays mounted file systems and their space usages.

Here is an example on my Motorola phone, which runs on the Android 12 system with a
total storage of 128GB.

```
herong$ adb shell getprop ro.build.version.release
12


herong$ adb shell df -H
Filesystem              Size Used Avail Use% Mounted on
/dev/block/dm-8         1.0G 1.0G     0 100% /
tmpfs                   2.9G 2.8M  2.9G   1% /dev
tmpfs                   2.9G    0  2.9G   0% /mnt
/dev/block/dm-9         884M 881M     0 100% /system_ext
/dev/block/dm-10        591M 590M     0 100% /vendor
/dev/block/dm-11        3.8G 3.8G     0 100% /product
tmpfs                   2.9G  29k  2.9G   1% /apex
/dev/block/mmcblk0p14   3.9M  98k  3.5M   3% /mnt/product/persist
/dev/block/dm-12        110G 8.7G  101G   8% /data
/dev/block/loop5        8.6M 8.6M     0 100% /apex/com.android.runtime@1
/dev/block/loop10        37M  37M     0 100% /apex/com.android.i18n@1
/dev/block/dm-15        770k 741k   16k  98% /apex/com.android.ipsec@...
/dev/block/dm-18        5.9M 5.9M     0 100% /apex/com.android.media@...
/dev/fuse               110G 8.7G  101G   8% /storage/emulated

...
```

It seems that the same partition of 110GB is represented as 2 file systems: /dev/block/
dm-12 and /dev/fuse, which are mounted as 2 directories: /data and /storage/emulated.

As a comparison, here is what I got on my Samsung phone running Android 8.

```
herong$ adb shell getprop ro.build.version.release
8.0.0

herong$ adb shell df -H
Filesystem              Size  Used Avail Use% Mounted on
rootfs                  1.6G   11M  1.6G   1% /
tmpfs                   1.7G  766k  1.7G   1% /dev
/dev/block/dm-0         4.6G  4.1G  584M  88% /system
tmpfs                   1.7G     0  1.7G   0% /mnt
tmpfs                   1.7G     0  1.7G   0% /mnt/secure
/dev/block/sda16        100M   49M   51M  50% /firmware
/dev/block/sdd7          12M  4.6M  7.6M  38% /dsp
/dev/block/sda5          29M  188k   29M   1% /persist
/dev/block/sda20        609M  5.7M  604M   1% /cache
/dev/block/sda6          16M  922k   16M   6% /efs
```

```
/dev/block/sda15              100M   49M   51M  50% /firmware
/dev/block/sda16              115M   77M   39M  67% /firmware-modem
/dev/block/sda21               42M   12k   42M   1% /carrier
tmpfs                         1.7G     0  1.7G   0% /storage
/dev/block/dm-1                57G   36G   21G  63% /data
/data/knox/secure_fs/enc_user  57G   36G   21G  63% /data/enc_user
/data/knox/secure_fs/enc_media 57G   36G   21G  63% /data/knox/secure_fs/enc_media
/data/knox/secure_fs/enc_media 57G   36G   21G  63% /mnt/shell/enc_emulated
/data/media                    57G   36G   21G  64% /storage/emulated
```

Here is what I got on an Android 5.1.1 emulator.

```
herong> adb shell df
```

Filesystem	Size	Used	Free	Blksize
/dev	242.9M	24.0K	242.8M	4096
/sys/fs/cgroup	242.9M	12.0K	242.9M	4096
/mnt/asec	242.9M	0.0K	242.9M	4096
/mnt/obb	242.9M	0.0K	242.9M	4096
/system	541.3M	363.9M	177.5M	4096
/data	541.3M	158.0M	383.3M	4096
/cache	65.0M	4.3M	60.7M	4096
/mnt/media_rw/sdcard	31.5M	3.2M	28.3M	512
/storage/sdcard	31.5M	3.2M	28.3M	512

Here is what I got on an Android 4.0.3 emulator.

```
herong> adb shell df
```

Filesystem	Size	Used	Free	Blksize
/dev	252M	32K	252M	4096
/mnt/asec	252M	0K	252M	4096
/mnt/obb	252M	0K	252M	4096
/system	161M	161M	0K	4096
/data	124M	13M	110M	4096
/cache	64M	1M	62M	4096
/mnt/sdcard	126M	1016K	125M	512
/mnt/secure/asec	126M	1016K	125M	512

"mount" - Display Mounted File Systems

This section provides a tutorial example on how to use the 'mount' command on the 'adb shell' interface to display all file systems with their types and mount options.

The "df -H" command only displays mounted file systems as shown in the last tutorial. To list all file systems, mounted and not mounted, you can use the "mount" command on the "adb shell" interface. It displays all file systems configured on storage devices with their types and mount options.

Here is an example on my Motorola phone, which runs on the Android 12 system with a total storage of 128GB. I am not sure why it needs so many file systems.

```
herong$ adb shell getprop ro.build.version.release
12


herong$ adb shell mount


/dev/block/dm-8 on / type ext4 (ro,seclabel,relatime)
tmpfs on /dev type tmpfs (rw,seclabel,nosuid,relatime,mode=755)
devpts on /dev/pts type devpts (rw,seclabel,relatime,mode=600,...)
proc on /proc type proc (rw,relatime,gid=3009,hidepid=2)
sysfs on /sys type sysfs (rw,seclabel,relatime)
selinuxfs on /sys/fs/selinux type selinuxfs (rw,relatime)
tmpfs on /mnt type tmpfs (rw,seclabel,nosuid,nodev,noexec,...)
/dev/block/mmcblk0p19 on /metadata type ext4 (rw,seclabel,nosuid,...)
/dev/block/dm-9 on /system_ext type ext4 (ro,seclabel,relatime)
/dev/block/dm-10 on /vendor type ext4 (ro,seclabel,relatime)
/dev/block/dm-11 on /product type ext4 (ro,seclabel,relatime)
tmpfs on /apex type tmpfs (rw,seclabel,nosuid,nodev,noexec,...)
tmpfs on /linkerconfig type tmpfs (rw,seclabel,nosuid,nodev,...)
none on /dev/blkio type cgroup (rw,nosuid,nodev,noexec,relatime,blkio)
none on /sys/fs/cgroup type cgroup2 (rw,nosuid,nodev,noexec,relatime)
none on /dev/cpuctl type cgroup (rw,nosuid,nodev,noexec,relatime,cpu)
none on /dev/cpuset type cgroup (rw,nosuid,nodev,noexec,relatime,...)
none on /dev/memcg type cgroup (rw,nosuid,nodev,noexec,relatime,...)
none on /dev/stune type cgroup (rw,nosuid,nodev,noexec,relatime,...)
tracefs on /sys/kernel/tracing type tracefs (rw,seclabel,relatime)
none on /config type configfs (rw,nosuid,nodev,noexec,relatime)
binder on /dev/binderfs type binder (rw,relatime,max=1048576,...)
none on /sys/fs/fuse/connections type fusectl (rw,relatime)
```

```
bpf on /sys/fs/bpf type bpf (rw,nosuid,nodev,noexec,relatime)
pstore on /sys/fs/pstore type pstore (rw,seclabel,nosuid,nodev,...)
/dev/block/mmcblk0p21 on /mnt/vendor/protect_f type ext4 (rw,...)
/dev/block/mmcblk0p22 on /mnt/vendor/protect_s type ext4 (rw,...)
tmpfs on /storage type tmpfs (rw,seclabel,nosuid,nodev,noexec,...)
adb on /dev/usb-ffs/adb type functionfs (rw,relatime)
/dev/block/dm-12 on /data type f2fs (rw,lazytime,seclabel,nosuid,...)
tmpfs on /linkerconfig type tmpfs (rw,seclabel,nosuid,nodev,...)
/dev/block/dm-12 on /data/user/0 type f2fs (rw,lazytime,seclabel,...)
tmpfs on /data_mirror type tmpfs (rw,seclabel,nosuid,nodev,noexec,...)
/dev/block/dm-12 on /data_mirror/data_ce/null type f2fs (rw,...)
/dev/block/dm-12 on /data_mirror/data_ce/null/0 type f2fs (rw,...)
/dev/block/dm-12 on /data_mirror/data_de/null type f2fs (rw,...)
/dev/block/loop4 on /apex/com.android.vndk.v30@1 type ext4 (ro,...)
/dev/block/loop4 on /apex/com.android.vndk.v30 type ext4 (ro,...)
/dev/block/loop5 on /apex/com.android.runtime@1 type ext4 (ro,...)
/dev/block/dm-13 on /apex/com.android.mediaprovider@331011070 ...)
/dev/block/dm-13 on /apex/com.android.mediaprovider type ext4 (ro,...)
... (total of 59 lines)
```

As a comparison, here is what I got on my Samsung phone running Android 8.

```
herong$ adb shell getprop ro.build.version.release
8.0.0

herong$ adb shell mount

rootfs on / type rootfs (ro,seclabel,size=1627932k,nr_inodes=406983)
tmpfs on /dev type tmpfs (rw,seclabel,nosuid,relatime,size=...)
devpts on /dev/pts type devpts (rw,seclabel,relatime,mode=600)
proc on /proc type proc (rw,relatime,gid=3009,hidepid=2)
sysfs on /sys type sysfs (rw,seclabel,relatime)
selinuxfs on /sys/fs/selinux type selinuxfs (rw,relatime)
/dev/block/dm-0 on /system type ext4 (ro,seclabel,relatime)
debugfs on /sys/kernel/debug type debugfs (rw,seclabel,relatime)
none on /acct type cgroup (rw,relatime,cpuacct)
none on /dev/stune type cgroup (rw,relatime,schedtune)
tmpfs on /mnt type tmpfs (rw,seclabel,relatime,size=1698148k,...)
```

```
none on /config type configfs (rw,relatime)
tmpfs on /mnt/secure type tmpfs (rw,seclabel,relatime,size=...)
none on /dev/cpuctl type cgroup (rw,relatime,cpu)
none on /dev/cpuset type cgroup (rw,relatime,cpuset,noprefix,...)
pstore on /sys/fs/pstore type pstore (rw,seclabel,relatime)
/dev/block/sda16 on /firmware type vfat (ro,context=u:object_r:...)
/dev/block/sdd7 on /dsp type ext4 (ro,seclabel,nosuid,nodev,...)
/dev/block/sda5 on /persist type ext4 (rw,seclabel,nosuid,nodev,...)
... (total of 37 lines)
```

Here is what I got on an Android 5.1.1 emulator.

```
herong> adb shell mount

rootfs / rootfs ro,seclabel,relatime 0 0
tmpfs /dev tmpfs rw,seclabel,nosuid,relatime,mode=755 0 0
devpts /dev/pts devpts rw,seclabel,relatime,mode=600 0 0
proc /proc proc rw,relatime 0 0
sysfs /sys sysfs rw,seclabel,relatime 0 0
selinuxfs /sys/fs/selinux selinuxfs rw,relatime 0 0
debugfs /sys/kernel/debug debugfs rw,relatime 0 0
none /acct cgroup rw,relatime,cpuacct 0 0
none /sys/fs/cgroup tmpfs rw,seclabel,relatime,mode=750,gid=1000 0 0
tmpfs /mnt/asec tmpfs rw,seclabel,relatime,mode=755,gid=1000 0 0
tmpfs /mnt/obb tmpfs rw,seclabel,relatime,mode=755,gid=1000 0 0
none /dev/cpuctl cgroup rw,relatime,cpu 0 0
/dev/block/mtdblock0 /system ext4 ro,seclabel,relatime,data=ordered ...
/dev/block/mtdblock1 /data ext4 rw,seclabel,nosuid,nodev,noatime,nom...
/dev/block/mtdblock2 /cache ext4 rw,seclabel,nosuid,nodev,noatime,da...
/dev/block/vold/179:0 /mnt/media_rw/sdcard vfat rw,dirsync,nosuid,no...
/dev/fuse /storage/sdcard fuse rw,nosuid,nodev,noexec,relatime,user_...
```

Here is what I got on an Android 4.0.3 emulator.

```
herong> adb shell mount

rootfs / rootfs ro 0 0
tmpfs /dev tmpfs rw,nosuid,mode=755 0 0
devpts /dev/pts devpts rw,mode=600 0 0
```

```
proc /proc proc rw 0 0

sysfs /sys sysfs rw 0 0

none /acct cgroup rw,cpuacct 0 0

tmpfs /mnt/asec tmpfs rw,mode=755,gid=1000 0 0

tmpfs /mnt/obb tmpfs rw,mode=755,gid=1000 0 0

none /dev/cpuctl cgroup rw,cpu 0 0

/dev/block/mtdblock0 /system yaffs2 ro 0 0

/dev/block/mtdblock1 /data yaffs2 rw,nosuid,nodev 0 0

/dev/block/mtdblock2 /cache yaffs2 rw,nosuid,nodev 0 0

/dev/block/vold/179:0 /mnt/sdcard vfat rw,dirsync,nosuid,nodev,noe...

/dev/block/vold/179:0 /mnt/secure/asec vfat rw,dirsync,nosuid,node...

tmpfs /mnt/sdcard/.android_secure tmpfs ro,size=0k,mode=000 0 0
```

"find -L . -name" - Search Files on Android System

This section provides a tutorial example on how to use the 'find -L . -name' command on the 'adb shell' interface to search files on Android systems.

If you are looking for specific files on an Android system, you can use the "find -L . - name" command on the "adb shell" interface as shown in examples below.

1. Find a find with a given name under a given directory. I need to find the file "Resume.pdf" I saved from an email. The "-L" option is to follow symbolic links when searching sub-directories.

```
herong$ adb shell find -L /storage -name Resume.pdf

find: No /storage/emulated: Permission denied
/storage/self/primary/Download/Resume.pdf
```

2. Find all directories related to a keyword: "YouTube". The "2>/dev/null" pipe option is to trash "permission denied" and other error messages.

```
herong$ adb shell find -L / -name YouTube 2>/dev/null

/product/app/YouTube
/system/product/app/YouTube
```

This command may take a long time to finish, since it searches the entire file system hierarchy. You can terminate it by pressing Control-C.

3. Find files with a given pattern: "*.mp4".

```
herong$ adb shell find -L /storage -name *.mp4

/storage/self/primary/Movies/Messenger/received_892608415163156.mp4
  (Videos received from Messenger)
/storage/self/primary/DCIM/Camera/20230420_144750.mp4
/storage/self/primary/DCIM/Camera/20230513_121250.mp4
  (Videos recorded from Camera)
/storage/self/primary/Android/data/easy.sudoku.puzzle...xmrbwg.mp4
  (Videos used by the Sudoku app)
```

AboutAndroid - Application to Retrieve System Information

This chapter provides tutorial notes on AboutAndroid - An example application to retrieve system information. Topics include using java.lang.System class; displaying system properties and environment variables; using ScrollView and TextView classes; using android.os.Environment class.

Takeaways:

- java.lang.System.getProperties() method returns all system properties that are provided to Android applications.

- java.lang.System.getenv() method returns all environment variables defined in the operating system.

- android.widget.ScrollView and android.widget.TextView classes can be used together to provide a scrollable text screen.

- Android application environment is really a Dalvik Java Virtual Machine running on a Linux system.

- The android.os.Environment class allows you to access environment information.

- The android.content.Context class allows you access system information specific to the current application.

java.lang.System Class - Accessing System Information

This section describes the java.lang.System class on access system-related information and resources including standard input and output.

When writing applications for a new system, I usually want to find out information about that system first. This can be done easily by using the java.lang.System class, which provides access to system-related information and resources including standard input and output.

The java.lang.System class offers the following static methods:

- static Console console() - Returns the Console associated with this VM, or null.

- static long currentTimeMillis() - Returns the current system time in milliseconds since January 1, 1970 00:00:00 UTC.

- static Properties getProperties() - Returns the system properties.

- static Map<String, String> getenv() - Returns an unmodifiable map of all available environment variables.

- static void load(String pathName) - Loads and links the dynamic library that is identified through the specified path.

The java.lang.System class offers the following static fields:

- public static final PrintStream err - Default error output stream.

- public static final InputStream in - Default input stream.

- public static final PrintStream out - Default output stream.

See next tutorials on how to use java.lang.System class to find out Android system information.

Creating Android Project for Simple Application

This section provides tutorial example on how to create an Android project for a simple Android application using command line tools.

To build any Android applications, we need to create an Android project folder structure first.

Here is what I did to create a simple project called AboutAndroid in a command window:

```
C:\>cd \herong
C:\herong>JAVA_HOME=\Program Files\Java\jdk1.8.0_45\

C:\herong>\local\android-sdk-windows\tools\android create project \
    --package com.herongyang --activity AboutAndroid --target 2 \
    --path .\AboutAndroid
Created project directory: C:\herong\AboutAndroid
..
Added file C:\herong\AboutAndroid\build.xml


C:\herong>cd .\AboutAndroid
C:\herong\AboutAndroid>edit .\src\com\herongyang\AboutAndroid.java
/* AboutAndroid.java
 * Version 1.0 - Displaying text message
 * Copyright (c) 2015, HerongYang.com, All Rights Reserved.
 */
package com.herongyang;

import android.app.Activity;
import android.os.Bundle;
import android.widget.TextView;
public class AboutAndroid extends Activity {
    @Override
    public void onCreate(Bundle savedInstanceState) {
        super.onCreate(savedInstanceState);
        String msg = "";
```

```
    msg += "About Android\n";
    msg += "-------------\n";

    TextView tv = new TextView(this);
    tv.setText(msg);
    setContentView(tv);
  }
}


C:\herong\AboutAndroid>edit .\res\layout\main.xml
<?xml version="1.0" encoding="utf-8"?>
<LinearLayout
    xmlns:android="http://schemas.android.com/apk/res/android"
    android:orientation="vertical"
    android:layout_width="fill_parent"
    android:layout_height="fill_parent"
    >
<TextView
    android:layout_width="fill_parent"
    android:layout_height="wrap_content"
    />
</LinearLayout>
```

See next tutorial to build and install a simple Android application

Build, Install and Run Android Application

This section provides tutorial example on how to build, install and run an Android application. The Android application shows up automatically on the Android emulator.

Now I am ready to build, install and run the simple application on my Android emulator:

1. Run the Android emulator through the AVD Manager and wait for the emulator to be fully booted.

2. Build and install my application, AboutAndroid, using the Ant tool:

```
C:\>cd \herong\AboutAndroid

C:\herong\AboutAndroid>\local\apache-ant-1.9.5\bin\ant debug

...

C:\herong\AboutAndroid>\local\apache-ant-1.9.5\bin\ant installd

...
```

3. Go to the emulator and run "AboudAndroid" from the application list. The AboutAndroid start screen will show up:

AboutAndroid Start Screen

Ok. My application is working!

System.getProperties() - Retrieving System Properties

This section provides tutorial example on how to use the java.lang.System.getProperties() method to retrieve and display Android system properties.

After practiced the build, install and run Android application process, I want to obtain Android system properties through the java.lang.System class.

1. Enhance my application to print out system properties by editing .\src\com \herongyang\AboutAndroid.java

```
/* AboutAndroid.java
 * Version 2.0 - Displaying system properties
 * Copyright (c) 2015, HerongYang.com, All Rights Reserved.
 */
package com.herongyang;

import android.app.Activity;
import android.os.Bundle;
import android.widget.TextView;
public class AboutAndroid extends Activity {
    @Override
    public void onCreate(Bundle savedInstanceState) {
        super.onCreate(savedInstanceState);
        String msg = "";

        msg += "System properties\n";
        msg += "-------------\n";
        java.util.Properties props = System.getProperties();
        java.util.Enumeration e = props.propertyNames();
        while (e.hasMoreElements()) {
            String k = (String) e.nextElement();
            String v = props.getProperty(k);
            msg += k+": "+v+"\n";
        }

        TextView tv = new TextView(this);
        tv.setText(msg);
        setContentView(tv);
    }
}
```

2. Uninstall the previous version by running "ant uninstall" command.

3. Build, install and run the application again on the emulator. Some system properties are displayed:

AboutAndroid System Properties

But there is problem with the display, the screen does not have enough space to display all properties, and you can not scroll down screen to see more properties. In the next tutorial, I will try to design a scrollable view.

android.widget.ScrollView Class - Scrolling Text View

This section provides tutorial example on how to create a scrollable screen to view large contents of text using the android.widget.ScrollView Class.

According the Android reference document, "The TextView class also takes care of its own scrolling, so does not require a ScrollView, but using the two together is possible to achieve the effect of a text view within a larger container." But I don't know how to make TextView object to become scrollable. So I places the TextView object inside a ScrollView object to make it work.

1. Enhance my application to make the screen scrollable by editing .\src\com
\herongyang\AboutAndroid.java

```
/* AboutAndroid.java
 * Version 3.0 - Making the screen scrollable
 * Copyright (c) 2015, HerongYang.com, All Rights Reserved.
 */
package com.herongyang;

import android.app.Activity;
import android.os.Bundle;
import android.widget.TextView;
import android.widget.ScrollView;
public class AboutAndroid extends Activity {
    @Override
    public void onCreate(Bundle savedInstanceState) {
        super.onCreate(savedInstanceState);
        String msg = "";

        msg += "System properties\n";
        msg += "------------\n";
        java.util.Properties props = System.getProperties();
        java.util.Enumeration e = props.propertyNames();
        while (e.hasMoreElements()) {
            String k = (String) e.nextElement();
            String v = props.getProperty(k);
            msg += k+": "+v+"\n";
        }

        TextView tv = new TextView(this);
        tv.setText(msg);
        ScrollView sv = new ScrollView(this);
        sv.addView(tv);
        setContentView(sv);
    }
}
```

2. Uninstall the previous version, build, install and run this new version. Some system properties are displayed:

AboutAndroid System Properties

Very nice. I can scroll down to see all system properties now!

After reviewing the output, I see several interesting system properties on my Android emulator:

```
java.home: /system
java.vm.name: Dalvik
java.vm.version: 2.1.0
java.vm.vendor: The Android Project
java.runtime.name: Android Runtime
os.name: Linux
os.version: 3.4.67-01422-gd3ffcc7-dirty
```

Below was some system properties I got from my Android 4.0.3 emulator created with Android SDK R17:

```
java.home: /system
java.vm.name: Dalvik
```

```
java.vm.version: 1.6.0
java.vm.vendor: The Android Project
java.runtime.name: Android Runtime
os.name: Linux
os.version: 2.6.29-g46b05b2
os.arch.armv71
```

System.getenv() Method - System Environment Variables

This section provides tutorial example on how to display system environment variables using the java.lang.System.getenv() method.

With the ScrollView working, I can display more information about the system now with java.lang.System.getenv() method:

1. Enhance my application to display environment variables editing .\src\com\herongyang\AboutAndroid.java

```java
/* AboutAndroid.java
 * Version 4.0 - Adding environment variables
 * Copyright (c) 2015, HerongYang.com, All Rights Reserved.
 */
package com.herongyang;

import android.app.Activity;
import android.os.Bundle;
import android.widget.TextView;
import android.widget.ScrollView;
public class AboutAndroid extends Activity {
    @Override
    public void onCreate(Bundle savedInstanceState) {
        super.onCreate(savedInstanceState);
        String msg = "";


        msg += "System properties\n";
```

```
    msg += "-------------\n";
    java.util.Properties props = System.getProperties();
    java.util.Enumeration e = props.propertyNames();
    while (e.hasMoreElements()) {
        String k = (String) e.nextElement();
        String v = props.getProperty(k);
        msg += k+": "+v+"\n";
    }

    msg += "\n";
    msg += "Environment variables\n";
    msg += "-------------\n";
    java.util.Map envs = System.getenv();
    java.util.Set keys = envs.keySet();
    java.util.Iterator i = keys.iterator();
    while (i.hasNext()) {
        String k = (String) i.next();
        String v = (String) envs.get(k);
        msg += k+": "+v+"\n";
    }

    TextView tv = new TextView(this);
    tv.setText(msg);
    ScrollView sv = new ScrollView(this);
    sv.addView(tv);
    setContentView(sv);
    }
}
```

2. Uninstall the previous version, build, install and run this new version. Environment variables are displayed after system properties.

Some interesting environment variables on my Android emulator are:

```
ANDROID_ASSETS: /system/app
ANDROID_DATA: /data
ANDROID_ROOT: /system
ASEC_MOUNTPOINT: /mnt/asec
BOOTCLASSPATH: /system/framework/core.jar:/system/framework/core-...
```

```
EXTERNAL_STORAGE: /storage/sdcard
LOOP_MOUNTPOINT: /mnt/obb
PATH: /sbin:/vendor/bin:/system/sbin:/system/bin:/system/xbin
```

Below was some system properties I got from my Android 4.0.3 emulator created with Android SDK R17:

```
ANDROID_ASSETS: /system/app
ANDROID_DATA: /data
ANDROID_ROOT: /system
ASEC_MOUNTPOINT: /mnt/asec
BOOTCLASSPATH: /system/framework/core.jar:/system/framework/core-...
EXTERNAL_STORAGE: /mnt/sdcard
LD_LIBRARY_PATH: /vendor/lib:/system/lib
LOOP_MOUNTPOINT: /mnt/obb
PATH: /sbin:/vendor/bin:/system/sbin:/system/bin:/system/xbin
```

android.os.Environment Class - Environment Folders

This section provides tutorial example on how to display environment folders: data, external storage, download cache, and root folders using the android.os.Environment class.

Another Android class, android.os.Environment, can also be used to retrieve environment folder information as shown in the following example:

```
/* AboutAndroid.java
 * Version 5.0 - Adding environment folders
 * Copyright (c) 2015, HerongYang.com, All Rights Reserved.
 */
package com.herongyang;

import android.app.Activity;
import android.os.Bundle;
import android.widget.TextView;
import android.widget.ScrollView;
import android.os.Environment;
public class AboutAndroid extends Activity {
```

```java
@Override
public void onCreate(Bundle savedInstanceState) {
    super.onCreate(savedInstanceState);
    String msg = "";

    msg += "System properties\n";
    msg += "-------------\n";
    java.util.Properties props = System.getProperties();
    java.util.Enumeration e = props.propertyNames();
    while (e.hasMoreElements()) {
        String k = (String) e.nextElement();
        String v = props.getProperty(k);
        msg += k+": "+v+"\n";
    }

    msg += "\n";
    msg += "Environment variables\n";
    msg += "-------------\n";
    java.util.Map envs = System.getenv();
    java.util.Set keys = envs.keySet();
    java.util.Iterator i = keys.iterator();
    while (i.hasNext()) {
        String k = (String) i.next();
        String v = (String) envs.get(k);
        msg += k+": "+v+"\n";
    }

    msg += "\n";
    msg += "Environment folders\n";
    msg += "-------------\n";
    msg += "Data folder: "
        +Environment.getDataDirectory().getPath()+"\n";
    msg += "Download cache folder: "
        +Environment.getDownloadCacheDirectory().getPath()+"\n";
    msg += "External Storage folder: "
        +Environment.getExternalStorageDirectory().getPath()+"\n";
    msg += "Root folder: "
```

```
        +Environment.getRootDirectory().getPath()+"\n";


    TextView tv = new TextView(this);
    tv.setText(msg);
    ScrollView sv = new ScrollView(this);
    sv.addView(tv);
    setContentView(sv);
  }
}
```

2. Uninstall the previous version, build, install and run this new version. I get the following extra information at the end:

```
Data folder: /data
Download cache folder: /cache
External storage folder: /storage/sdcard
Root folder: /system
```

Below was some system properties I got from my Android 4.0.3 emulator created with Android SDK R17:

```
Data folder: /data
Download cache folder: /cache
External storage folder: /mnt/sdcard
Root folder: /system
```

android.content.Context - Application Context Information

This section provides tutorial example on how to display application context information using instance methods of the android.content.Context class like application package name, private file folder, private cache folder, etc.

For information about the running application itself, the android.app.Activity object inherits some useful instance methods from the android.content.Context class:

- abstract String[] fileList() - Returns an array of strings naming the private files associated with this Context's application package.

- abstract File getCacheDir() - Returns the absolute path to the application specific cache directory on the filesystem.

- abstract File getExternalCacheDir() - Returns the absolute path to the directory on the external filesystem (that is somewhere on Environment.getExternalStorageDirectory() where the application can place cache files it owns.

- abstract File getFilesDir() - Returns the absolute path to the directory on the filesystem where files created with openFileOutput(String, int) are stored.

- abstract File getObbDir() - Return the directory where this application's OBB (Opaque Binary Blob) files (if there are any) can be found.

- abstract String getPackageCodePath() - Return the full path to this context's primary Android package.

- abstract String getPackageName() - Return the name of this application's package.

- abstract String getPackageResourcePath() - Return the full path to this context's primary Android package.

I enhanced again my AboutAndroid application to display its context information using methods listed above:

```
/* AboutAndroid.java
 * Version 6.0 - Adding application context info
 * Copyright (c) 2015, HerongYang.com, All Rights Reserved.
 */
package com.herongyang;

import android.app.Activity;
import android.os.Bundle;
import android.widget.TextView;
import android.widget.ScrollView;
import android.os.Environment;
public class AboutAndroid extends Activity {
    @Override
    public void onCreate(Bundle savedInstanceState) {
```

```
super.onCreate(savedInstanceState);
String msg = "";

msg += "System properties\n";
msg += "-------------\n";
java.util.Properties props = System.getProperties();
java.util.Enumeration e = props.propertyNames();
while (e.hasMoreElements()) {
    String k = (String) e.nextElement();
    String v = props.getProperty(k);
    msg += k+": "+v+"\n";
}

msg += "\n";
msg += "Environment variables\n";
msg += "-------------\n";
java.util.Map envs = System.getenv();
java.util.Set keys = envs.keySet();
java.util.Iterator i = keys.iterator();
while (i.hasNext()) {
    String k = (String) i.next();
    String v = (String) envs.get(k);
    msg += k+": "+v+"\n";
}

msg += "\n";
msg += "Environment folders\n";
msg += "-------------\n";
msg += "Data folder: "
    +Environment.getDataDirectory().getPath()+"\n";
msg += "Download cache folder: "
    +Environment.getDownloadCacheDirectory().getPath()+"\n";
msg += "External Storage folder: "
    +Environment.getExternalStorageDirectory().getPath()+"\n";
msg += "Root folder: "
    +Environment.getRootDirectory().getPath()+"\n";
```

```
        msg += "\n";
        msg += "Application context info\n";
        msg += "-------------\n";
        msg += "Cache folder: "
            +getCacheDir().getPath()+"\n";
        msg += "External cache folder: "
            +getExternalCacheDir().getPath()+"\n";
        msg += "File folder: "
            +getFilesDir().getPath()+"\n";
        msg += "OBB folder: "
            +getObbDir().getPath()+"\n";
        msg += "Package name: "
            +getPackageName()+"\n";
        msg += "Package code path: "
            +getPackageCodePath()+"\n";
        msg += "Package resource path: "
            +getPackageResourcePath()+"\n";

        TextView tv = new TextView(this);
        tv.setText(msg);
        ScrollView sv = new ScrollView(this);
        sv.addView(tv);
        setContentView(sv);
    }
}
```

2. Uninstall the previous version, build, install and run this new version. I get the following extra information at the end:

```
Cache folder: /data/data/com.herongyang/cache
External cache folder: /storage/sdcard/Android/data/com.herongyang/cache
File folder: /data/data/com.herongyang/files
OBB folder: /storage/sdcard/Android/obb/com.herongyang
Package name: com.herongyang
Package code path: /data/app/com.herongyang-1/base.apk
Package resource path: /data/app/com.herongyang-1/base.apk
```

Below was some system properties I got from my Android 4.0.3 emulator created with Android SDK R17:

```
Cache folder: /data/data/com.herongyang/cache

External cache folder: /mnt/sdcard/Android/data/com.herongyang/cache

File folder: /data/data/com.herongyang/files

OBB folder: /mnt/sdcard/Android/obb/com.herongyang

Package name: com.herongyang

Package code path: /data/app/com.herongyang-1.apk

Package resource path: /data/app/com.herongyang-1.apk
```

android.app.Activity Class and Activity Lifecycle

This chapter provides tutorial notes on android.app.Activity class and activity lifecycle. Topics include introduction of activity states, lifetime periods and activity callback methods; creating log file in the application's private file folder; implementing activity callback methods; writing example application ActivityLog to test application lifecycle.

Takeaways:

- android.app.Activity class represents an activity you allow the user to interact with on the screen.

- An activity has 4 states: active, paused, stopped and destroyed.

- An activity has 3 lifetime periods: entire lifetime, visible lifetime and foreground lifetime.

- android.app.Activity class provides 7 callback methods to the application program to manage the activity lifecycle.

- The normal calling sequence of callback methods is: onCreate(), onStart(), onResume(), onPause(), onStop() and onDestroy().

• Application's private file folder is located at /data/data/<package-name>/files.

Introduction of Activity Lifecycle

This section describes the android.app.Activity class which represents an activity you allow the user to interact with on the screen. An activity has 4 states: Active, Paused, Stopped and Destroyed.

In the last chapter, we learned how to access the Android application environment information using the java.lang.System and android.os.Environment classes. Now let's take a closer look at the starting class of our simple applications created so far: android.app.Activity.

The android.app.Activity class represents an activity you allow the user to interact with on the screen. The android.app.Activity class takes care of creating an empty window for you to place visual content using the setContentView() method.

An Activity object has four states:

• Active - If an activity in the foreground of the screen (at the top of the stack), it is active or running.

• Paused - If an activity has lost focus but is still visible (that is, a new non-full-sized or transparent activity has focus on top of your activity), it is paused. A paused activity is completely alive (it maintains all state and member information and remains attached to the window manager), but can be killed by the system in extreme low memory situations.

• Stopped - If an activity is completely obscured by another activity, it is stopped. It still retains all state and member information, however, it is no longer visible to the user so its window is hidden and it will often be killed by the system when memory is needed elsewhere.

• Destroyed - If an activity is paused or stopped, the system can drop the activity from memory by either asking it to finish, or simply killing its process. When it is displayed again to the user, it must be completely restarted and restored to its previous state.

Android reference document provides the following diagram to illustrate the lifecycle of an Activity object:

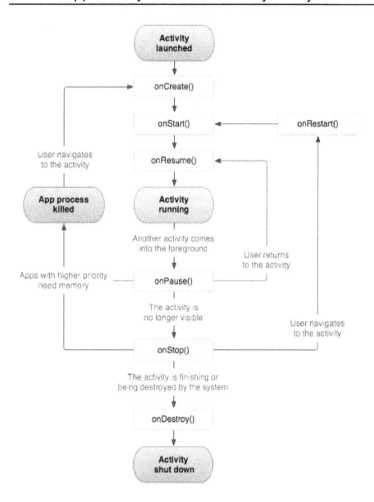

The entire lifecycle of Activity object is divided into 3 nested lifetime periods:

- Entire lifetime - The period between the moment the activity is created and the moment the activity is destroyed.

- Visible lifetime - The period between the moment the activity is started showing on the screen and the moment the activity is stopped showing on the screen.

- Foreground lifetime - The period between the moment the user resumes interaction with this activity and the moment the user switches to other activities leaving this activity paused.

See next tutorials on you can add code logics when the activity entering or leaving a lifetime period.

onCreate() and Other Callback Methods

This section describes activity callback methods: onCreate(), onStart(), onResume(), onPause(), onStop(), onDestroyed(), and onRestart().

As mentioned in the previous section, the lifecycle of an activity has 4 states and 3 lifetime periods. If you want to monitor and adding your own code logics to an activity, you can use the following 7 basic callback methods provided by the android.app.Activity class:

- onCreate() - Called when the activity is first created. This is where you should do all of your normal static set up: create views, bind data to lists, etc. This method also provides you with a Bundle containing the activity's previously frozen state, if there was one. onCreate() is always followed by onStart().

- onRestart() - Called after your activity has been stopped and prior to it being started again. onRestart() is always followed by onStart().

- onStart() - Called when the activity is becoming visible to the user. onStart() is followed by onResume() if the activity comes to the foreground, or onStop() if it becomes hidden.

- onResume() - Called when the activity will start interacting with the user. At this point your activity is at the top of the activity stack, with user input going to it. onResume() is always followed by onPause().

- onPause() - Called when the system is about to start resuming a previous activity. This is typically used to commit unsaved changes to persistent data, stop animations and other things that may be consuming CPU, etc. Implementations of this method must be very quick because the next activity will not be resumed until this method returns. onPause() is followed by either onResume() if the activity returns back to the front, or onStop() if it becomes invisible to the user.

- onStop() - Called when the activity is no longer visible to the user, because another activity has been resumed and is covering this one. This may happen either because a new activity is being started, an existing one is being brought in front of this one, or this one is being destroyed. onStop() is followed by either onRestart() if this activity is coming back to interact with the user, or onDestroy() if this activity is going away.

- onDestroy() - The final call you receive before your activity is destroyed. This can happen either because the activity is finishing (someone called finish() on it, or because the system is temporarily destroying this instance of the activity to save space. You can distinguish between these two scenarios with the isFinishing() method.

The following diagram shows the 4 states, 3 lifetime periods and 7 callback methods are related:

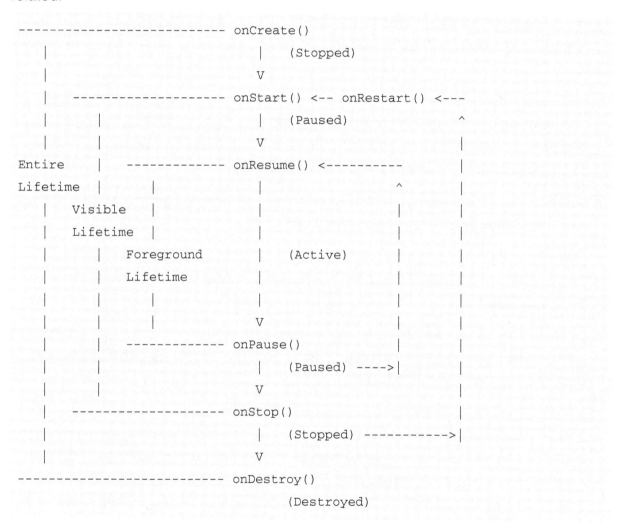

```
-------------------------- onCreate()
      |                             |    (Stopped)
      |                             V
      |    -------------------- onStart() <-- onRestart() <---
      |    |                        |    (Paused)                ^
      |    |                        V                            |
Entire |    ------------- onResume() <----------              |
Lifetime |    |                    |                    ^        |
      |  Visible   |               |                    |        |
      |  Lifetime  |               |                    |        |
      |    |   Foreground   |   (Active)    |        |
      |    |   Lifetime     |               |        |
      |    |    |           |               |        |
      |    |    |           V               |        |
      |    |    ------------- onPause()      |        |
      |    |                    |    (Paused) ---->|        |
      |    |                    V                            |
      |    -------------------- onStop()                     |
      |                             |    (Stopped) ----------->|
      |                             V
-------------------------- onDestroy()
                                    (Destroyed)
```

See next tutorials to implement callback methods.

ActivityLog - Application to Create Log File

This section provides a tutorial example on how to create application, ActivityLog, to create a log file to monitor activity lifecycle using the android.content.Context.openFileOutput() method.

The best way to monitor the lifecycle of an activity is to write messages into a log file. For that, we need to learn how to open a file and write text messages to the file on an Android system.

According to the Android reference document, the android.content.Context class provides you methods to interface with the data folder assigned to your application in the file system.

- abstract FileOutputStream openFileOutput(String name, int mode) - Open a private file associated with this Context's application package for writing.

- abstract FileInputStream openFileInput(String name) - Open a private file associated with this Context's application package for reading.

Now I am ready to create a new application, ActivityLog, with a new package, com.herongyang.activity:

```
C:\>cd \herong
C:\herong>set JAVA_HOME=\Program Files\Java\jdk1.8.0_45\

C:\herong>\local\android-sdk-windows\tools\android create project \
   --package com.herongyang.activity --activity ActivityLog --target 2 \
   --path .\ActivityLog
Created project directory: C:\herong\ActivityLog
..
Added file C:\herong\ActivityLog\build.xml

C:\herong>cd ActivityLog
C:\herong\ActivityLog>del .\res\layout\main.xml
```

Modify the Activity Java class, .\src\com\herongyang\activity\ActivityLog.java, to write a short message to a log file:

```
/* ActivityLog.java
 * Version 1.0 - Creating the log file
 * Copyright (c) 2015, HerongYang.com, All Rights Reserved.
 */
```

```
package com.herongyang.activity;

import android.app.Activity;
import android.os.Bundle;
import android.widget.TextView;
import android.content.Context;
import java.io.*;
public class ActivityLog extends Activity {
    @Override
    public void onCreate(Bundle savedInstanceState) {
        super.onCreate(savedInstanceState);
        String msg = "";

        msg += "Activity created\n";
        msg += "----------------\n";

        try {
            FileOutputStream fos =
                openFileOutput("Activity.log", Context.MODE_APPEND);
            OutputStreamWriter out = new OutputStreamWriter(fos);
            out.write(msg);
            out.close();
            fos.close();
        } catch (Exception e) {
            e.printStackTrace(System.err);
        }

        TextView tv = new TextView(this);
        tv.setText(msg);
        setContentView(tv);
    }
}
```

Note that:

- I removed the .\res\layout\main.xml file, because I am creating my own TextView object and using the default layout to manage the view in my activity Java code.

- I am using Context.MODE_APPEND when opening the log file so that new log messages will be appended to the end of the log file.

See the next tutorial on how to test this ActivityLog application.

Viewing Activity Log File with "cat" Command in "adb shell"

This section provides a tutorial example on how to test ActivityLog application, find the log file with the 'adb shell' window, and view the log file content with the 'cat' shell command.

Continue from the previous tutorial, I did the following to test my ActivityLog application:

1. Build and install ActivityLog on my Android emulator using the Apache Ant tool.

2. Run the ActivityLog on the emulator. The "Activity created" message displayed on the screen. So the user interface behaves as I expected.

3. Run "adb shell" in a command window to find the log file, which should be located in the application's private file folder, /data/data/<package-name>/files, based what we learned from the previous chapter:

```
C:\herong>\local\android-sdk-windows\platform-tools\adb shell
# cd /data/data/com.herongyang.activity/files
cd /data/data/com.herongyang.activity/files
# ls -l
ls -l
-rw-rw---- u0_a61   u0_a61   34 2015-03-01 22:46 Activity.log
```

4. Verify the log file content with "cat" shell command:

```
# cat Activity.log
cat Activity.log
Activity created
----------------
```

This confirms that ActivityLog has created the log file correctly. See a similar "adb shell" screenshot below:

adb shell - Viewing Activity Log File

Of course, you can delete the log file with "rm Activity.log" shell command, if needed.

See next tutorials on adding other activity callback methods to monitor the activity object lifecycle.

Implementing Activity Callback Methods

This section provides a tutorial example on how to implement activity callback methods using ActivityLog application as an example to log a short message from each callback method in a log file.

In this tutorial, I am going to enhance my ActivityLog application to implement other callback methods. See the ActivityLog.java source code below:

```
/* ActivityLog.java
 * Version 2.0 - Adding more callback methods
 * Copyright (c) 2015, HerongYang.com, All Rights Reserved.
 */
package com.herongyang.activity;

import android.app.Activity;
import android.os.Bundle;
import android.widget.TextView;
import android.content.Context;
import java.io.*;
public class ActivityLog extends Activity {
    @Override
    public void onCreate(Bundle savedInstanceState) {
```

```
      super.onCreate(savedInstanceState);
      String msg = "";
      msg += "Activity created\n";
      msg += "----------------\n";
      TextView tv = new TextView(this);
      tv.setText(msg);
      setContentView(tv);


      logLine("Checkpoint #1 - onCreate() called");
   }
   public void onStart() { //working
      super.onStart();
      logLine("Checkpoint #2 - onStart() called");
   }
   public void onResume() {
      super.onResume();
      logLine("Checkpoint #3 - onResume() called");
   }
   public void onPause() {
      super.onPause();
      logLine("Checkpoint #4 - onPause() called");
   }
   public void onStop() {
      super.onStop();
      logLine("Checkpoint #5 - onStop() called");
   }
   public void onRestart() {
      super.onRestart();
      logLine("Checkpoint #6a - onRestart() called");
   }
   public void onDestroy() {
      super.onDestroy();
      logLine("Checkpoint #6b - onDestroyed() called");
   }
   public void logLine(String msg) {
      try {
         FileOutputStream fos =
```

```
        openFileOutput("Activity.log", Context.MODE_APPEND);
      OutputStreamWriter out = new OutputStreamWriter(fos);
      out.write((new java.util.Date()).toString()+": "+msg+"\n");
      out.close();
      fos.close();
   } catch (Exception e) {
      e.printStackTrace(System.err);
   }
  }
}
```

Some notes on the enhanced ActivityLog.java code:

- When implementing your own callback methods, onStart(), onResume(), onPause(), onStop(), onRestart() and onDestroy(), you have to call the super class's implementation of the same method. Otherwise, an execution exception will be thrown.

- A checkpoint number is used in the log to help showing the sequence of when each callback method is called.

Now build and install the enhanced version of ActivityLog to the emulator. Then follow next tutorials on how to test the activity lifecycle by running ActivityLog in different ways.

ActivityLog Test - Activity Terminated by User

This section provides a tutorial example on how to test activity lifecycle with the ActivityLog application in case user terminates the activity by clicking the return icon.

ActivityLog Test #1 - Run ActivityLog and terminate it immediately.

1. Click on the application icon on the emulator's home screen. "ActivityLog" is listed in the application list.

2. Click on "ActivityLog" to start the application. Message "Activity created" is displayed on the screen.

3. Click on the "return" button on the emulator control panel. The application list is displayed again.

4. Run "adb shell" to view the log file:

```
# cat Activity.log
cat Activity.log
Sun Mar 01 19:03:56 2015: Checkpoint #1 - onCreate() called
Sun Mar 01 19:03:56 2015: Checkpoint #2 - onStart() called
Sun Mar 01 19:03:57 2015: Checkpoint #3 - onResume() called
Sun Mar 01 19:03:58 2015: Checkpoint #4 - onPause() called
Sun Mar 01 19:04:00 2015: Checkpoint #5 - onStop() called
Sun Mar 01 19:04:00 2015: Checkpoint #6b - onDestroyed() called
```

Takeaways:

- My ActivityLog application is working!

- Clicking the "return" button on the emulator control panel terminates the current application

- The callback methods are called in a simple lifecycle in this sequence: onStart(), onStart(), onResume(), onPause(), onStop(), and onDestroy().

ActivityLog Test - Activity Stopped and Restarted

This section provides a tutorial example on how to test activity lifecycle with the ActivityLog application in case user stops the activity by clicking the home icon and restart it again by clicking its name in the application list.

ActivityLog Test #2 - Run ActivityLog and restart it later.

1. Click on the application icon on the emulator's home screen. "ActivityLog" is listed in the application list.

2. Click on "ActivityLog" to start the application. Message "Activity created" is displayed on the screen.

3. Click on the "home" button on the emulator control panel. The emulator home screen is displayed again.

4. Click on the application icon on the emulator's home screen. Then click on "ActivityLog" in the application list again. Message "Activity created" is displayed again.

5. Run "adb shell" to view the log file:

```
# cat Activity.log
cat Activity.log
Sun Mar 01 19:15:28 2015: Checkpoint #1 - onCreate() called
Sun Mar 01 19:15:28 2015: Checkpoint #2 - onStart() called
Sun Mar 01 19:15:28 2015: Checkpoint #3 - onResume() called
Sun Mar 01 19:15:35 2015: Checkpoint #4 - onPause() called
Sun Mar 01 19:15:37 2015: Checkpoint #5 - onStop() called
Sun Mar 01 19:15:47 2015: Checkpoint #6a - onRestart() called
Sun Mar 01 19:15:47 2015: Checkpoint #2 - onStart() called
Sun Mar 01 19:15:47 2015: Checkpoint #3 - onResume() called
```

Takeaways:

- Clicking the "home" button on the emulator control panel puts the application in the stopped state.

- When clicking the name of the stopped application in the application list, Android will restart the application by-passing the onCreate() step.

- The calling sequence of callback methods on a stopped-and-restarted activity is: onStart(), onStart(), onResume(), onPause(), onStop(), onRestart(), onStart(), and onResume().

ActivityLog Test - Activity Paused and Resumed

This section tries to test activity lifecycle with the ActivityLog application in case user pauses the activity and resumes it later.

ActivityLog Test #3 - Run ActivityLog and resume it later.

Unfortunately, I could not find any way to pause and resume an application on my Android emulator. I will leave this section empty for now.

View Objects and Layout Resource Files

This chapter provides tutorial notes on View objects and Layout resource files. Topics include the android.view.View base class; View, ViewGroup and layout objects; creating view objects in Java code; defining layouts in Layout Resource Files; identifying and referring layouts; Inserting view objects in the layout hierarchy.

Takeaways:

- android.view.View class is the base class for all view and layout classes.

- android.view.ViewGroup class is the base class for all view layout classes that can contain other View objects as children.

- View and layout objects can be defined in layout resource files.

- View and layout objects can be created in Java code.

- View object hierarchy can be constructed to represent complex UI representation.

android.view.View Class - Base of User Interface Components

This section describes the android.view.View class which is the basic building block for all user interface components. Android SDK provides over 50 different specific views based on the android.view.View class to help you develop GUI (Graphical User Interface) applications.

android.view.View class is the basic building block for user interface components. A android.view.View object occupies a rectangular area on the screen and is responsible for drawing and event handling.

android.view.View class is the base class for other user interface components like buttons, text areas, etc.

Multiple android.view.View objects can be arranged on the screen based on layouts.

Multiple android.view.View objects can be nested into trees.

One application usually has a single android.view.View tree.

A android.view.View object has the following basic properties:

- Size - The width and height of the view in unit of pixels.

- Position - The horizontal and vertical coordinates of the top-left corner of the view in its parent view.

- Padding - The empty space between edges and the content of the view.

- Parent - The parent view.

- Visibility - Indicator of view's visibility.

- Background - View's background.

The Android SDK provides a number of specific view objects as subclasses of the android.view.View class. Some commonly used view subclasses are:

- ImageView - Displays an arbitrary image, such as an icon.

- KeyboardView - Renders a virtual Keyboard.

- ProgressBar - Displays a visual indicator of progress in some operation.

- Space - Displays an empty space that may be used to create gaps between components in general purpose layouts.

- SurfaceView - Provides a dedicated drawing surface embedded inside of a view hierarchy.

- TextView - Displays text to the user and optionally allows them to edit it.

- TextureView - Displays a content stream, such as a video.

- ViewGroup - Represents a special view that can contain other views as children. The view group is the base class for layouts and views containers.

- ViewStub - Represents a special view that is initially invisible with zero size, and can inflated later at runtime.

- AutoCompleteTextView - Displays an editable text view that shows completion suggestions automatically while the user is typing.

- Button - Represents a push-button widget.

- CalendarView - Represents a calendar widget for displaying and selecting dates.

- CheckBox - Represents a checkbox with two-states that can be either checked or unchecked.

- Chronometer - Represents a simple timer.

- DatePicker - Represents a widget for selecting a date.

- EditText - Represents a thin veneer over TextView that configures itself to be editable.

- ExpandableListView - Represents a view that shows items in a vertically scrolling two-level list.

- FragmentBreadCrumbs - Displays "bread crumbs" representing the fragment stack in an activity.

- FrameLayout - Blocks out an area on the screen to display a single item.

- Gallery - Shows items in a center-locked, horizontally scrolling list.

- GestureOverlayView - Represents a transparent overlay for gesture input that can be placed on top of other widgets or contain other widgets.

- GridLayout - Places its children in a rectangular grid.

- GridView - Shows items in two-dimensional scrolling grid.

- HorizontalScrollView - Represents a layout container for a view hierarchy that can be scrolled by the user, allowing it to be larger than the physical display.

- ImageButton - Displays a button with an image (instead of text) that can be pressed or clicked by the user.

- LinearLayout - Represents a layout that arranges its children in a single column or a single row.

- ListView - Represents a view that shows items in a vertically scrolling list.

- MediaController - Represents a view containing controls for a MediaPlayer.

- NumberPicker - Represents a widget that enables the user to select a number form a predefined range.

- PagerTitleStrip - Represents a non-interactive indicator of the current, next, and previous pages of a ViewPager.

- RadioButton - Represents a radio button is a two-states button that can be either checked or unchecked.

- RadioGroup - Creates a multiple-exclusion scope for a set of radio buttons.

- RelativeLayout - Represents a layout where the positions of the children can be described in relation to each other or to the parent.

- ScrollView - Represents a layout container for a view hierarchy that can be scrolled by the user, allowing it to be larger than the physical display.

- SearchView - Represents a widget that provides a user interface for the user to enter a search query and submit a request to a search provider.

- SeekBar - Represents an extension of ProgressBar that adds a draggable thumb.

- SlidingDrawer - Hides content out of the screen and allows the user to drag a handle to bring the content on screen.

- Spinner - Displays one child at a time and lets the user pick among them.

- StackView - Displays items as a stack.

- Switch - Represents a two-state toggle switch widget that can select between two options.

- TabHost - Represents a container for a tabbed window view.

- TabWidget - Displays a list of tab labels representing each page in the parent's tab collection.

- TableLayout - Represents a layout that arranges its children into rows and columns.

- TableRow - Represents a layout that arranges its children horizontally.

- TimePicker - Represents a view for selecting the time of day, in either 24 hour or AM/PM mode.

- ToggleButton - Displays checked/unchecked states as a button with a "light" indicator and by default accompanied with the text "ON" or "OFF".

- VideoView - Displays a video file.

- ViewAnimator - Represents a FrameLayout container that will perform animations when switching between its views.

- ViewFlipper - Animates between two or more views that have been added to it.

- ViewPager - Represents a layout manager that allows the user to flip left and right through pages of data.

- ViewSwitcher - Switches between two views, and has a factory from which these views are created.

- WebView - Displays web pages.

- ZoomButton - Displays a button with zoom in and zoom options.

- ZoomControls - Displays a simple set of controls used for zooming and provides callbacks to register for events.

View, ViewGroup, Layout, and Widget

This section describes UI class and object terminologies used in Android SDK documentation. View and ViewGroup are base classes serving as UI building blocks.

Widget and Layout are classes extended from View or ViewGroup class providing specific UI functions.

In the Android SDK documentation, there are 4 terms used to refer to different parts of the user interface (UI) class hierarchy:

- View - Refer to the android.view.View class, which is the base class of all UI classes. android.view.View class is the root of the UI class hierarchy. So from an object point of view, all UI objects are View objects.

- ViewGroup - Refer to the android.view.ViewGroup class, which is the base class of some special UI classes that can contain other View objects as children. Since ViewGroup objects are also View objects, multiple ViewGroup objects and View objects can be organized into an object tree to build complex UI structure.

- Widget - Refer to any UI class that provides a specific simple or complex UI function. A simple Widget can use single View object. A complex Widget can use a View object tree with many ViewGroup objects and View objects.

- Layout - Refer to any UI class that is specially designed to place child View objects into a UI pattern. Obviously, a Layout has to be a subclass of the android.view.View.ViewGroup.

Examples of UI classes:

- The android.widget.Button class is a Widget class that represents a simple UI component with a single View object.

- The android.widget.LinearLayout class is a Widget class and also a Layout class that represents a complex UI component with a ViewGroup object containing other View objects as children. Child View objects in a LinearLayout object are placed on the UI in a linear pattern.

- The android.widget.DatePicker class is a Widget class that represents a very complex UI component with a ViewGroup object containing year, month, and day spinners. Each spinner is a ViewGroupd object containing years, months, or days as View objects for users to select.

When building your own UI, you can search and find a Widget class provided in the Android SDK that matches your UI structure. Then you extend a new class from that Widget class to add your own customizations.

If you want build your UI from scratch, you can just start with a ViewGroup object, add child ViewGroup or View objects repeatedly to build a View object tree, then customize each View or ViewGroup object to complete the UI structure.

What Is Layout Resource File?

This section describes a Layout Resource File, which is XML file that defines a view hierarchy of nested view groups and views to provide a user interface layout on the Android device screen.

What Is Layout Resource File? A Layout Resource File is an XML file that defines a view hierarchy of nested view groups and views to provide a user interface layout on the Android device screen.

Here is an example of Layout Resource File:

```
<?xml version="1.0" encoding="utf-8"?>
<LinearLayout
    xmlns:android="http://schemas.android.com/apk/res/android"
    android:orientation="vertical"
    android:layout_width="fill_parent"
    android:layout_height="fill_parent">
    <TextView
        android:layout_width="fill_parent"
        android:layout_height="wrap_content"
        android:text="Hello World, HelloAndroid"
    />
</LinearLayout>
```

Note that:

- The namespace, http://schemas.android.com/apk/res/android, defines the XML schema of layout resource files.

- Each XML element in the layout resource file defines a view object for the layout.

- Each attribute of each XML element defines a property of the view object.

- This layout one has two view objects in the view hierarchy: a LinearLayout view object and a TextView view object.

- The LinearLayout view object is used as the root view and a container of other view objects

- The TextView view object is used to display a text message on the screen to the user.

With the introduction of Layout Resource Files, Android developers now have 3 options to created layout and view objects:

- "Layout Resource File only" - All UI layouts and views are defined in layout resource files only. The advantage of using layout resource files is that layouts and views can be easily customized without changing the Java source code.

- "Java Class Code only" - All UI layouts and views are created in Java class code only. The advantage of using Java code is that layouts and views can be dynamically managed based on the execution time situation.

- "Mixed of Layout Resource File and Java Class Code" - Major UI layouts and views are defined layout resource files and minor ones are created in Java class code. This is probably the best option.

AndroidView v1.0 - Creating a Layout in Java Class

This section provides a tutorial example on how to create a LinearLayout object with 2 Button objects in the activity Java class. Layout resource XML file is not used in this example.

To help playing with Android views, I want to start another new Android application called AndroidView using the "android create project" command:

```
C:\herong>\local\android-sdk-windows\tools\android create project \
   --package com.herongyang.view --activity AndroidView --target 2 \
   --path .\AndroidView

Created project directory: C:\herong\AndroidView

...
```

```
Added file C:\herong\AndroidView\build.xml
```

In the first version of AndroidView, I want to create a LinearLayout with two buttons:

```java
/* AndroidView.java
 * Version 1.0 - Starting with 1 LinearLayout and 2 buttons
 * Copyright (c) 2015, HerongYang.com, All Rights Reserved.
 */
package com.herongyang.view;

import android.app.Activity;
import android.os.Bundle;
import android.widget.LinearLayout;
import android.widget.Button;
public class AndroidView extends Activity {
    @Override
    public void onCreate(Bundle savedInstanceState) {
        super.onCreate(savedInstanceState);

        // Create the layout
        LinearLayout l = new LinearLayout(this);

        // Create the left button
        Button bl = new Button(this);
        bl.setText("Yes");
        l.addView(bl);

        // Create the right button
        Button br = new Button(this);
        br.setText("No");
        l.addView(br);

        // Set the layout as the activity content
        setContentView(l);
    }
}
```

After building and installing the project, what I see when running AndroidView on the emulator is similar to this:

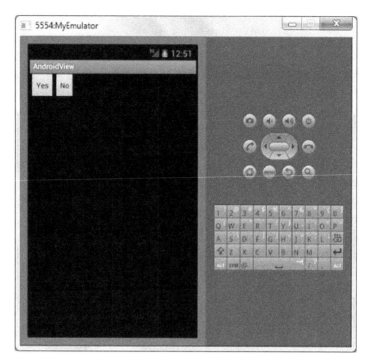

AndroidView - Using Java Objects

The output looks good to me. 1 LinearLayout holding 2 Buttons horizontally.

Notice that in this version of AndroidView, I created the LinearLayout object from the Java program without using the layout resource file. The next tutorial will show you how to create layout objects from the layout resource files.

AndroidView v2.0 - Creating a Layout in Resource File

This section provides a tutorial example on how to create a LinearLayout object with 2 Button objects in the layout resource file. No layout objects are create in this example.

As I mentioned earlier, UI components can also be defined in layout resource files. Now let's try to build AndroidView version 2 with the LinearLayout and Button objects defined in a layout resource file.

First modify the main layout resource file, .\res\layout\main.xml:

```
<?xml version="1.0" encoding="utf-8"?>
```

```
<!-- AndroidView_layout.xml
 - Version 2.0 - Using layout resource file
 - Copyright (c) 2015, HerongYang.com, All Rights Reserved.
-->
<LinearLayout
    xmlns:android="http://schemas.android.com/apk/res/android"
    android:layout_width="wrap_content"
    android:layout_height="wrap_content"
    >
    <Button
        android:layout_width="wrap_content"
        android:layout_height="wrap_content"
        android:text="Submit"
    />
    <Button
        android:layout_width="wrap_content"
        android:layout_height="wrap_content"
        android:text="Cancel"
    />
</LinearLayout>
```

Then modify the Java class code, .\src\com\herongyang\view\AndroidView.java:

```
/* AndroidView.java
 * Version 2.0 - Using layout resource file
 * Copyright (c) 2015, HerongYang.com, All Rights Reserved.
 */
package com.herongyang.view;

import android.app.Activity;
import android.os.Bundle;
public class AndroidView extends Activity {
    @Override
    public void onCreate(Bundle savedInstanceState) {
        super.onCreate(savedInstanceState);

        // Set the layout as the activity content
        setContentView(R.layout.main);
```

```
      }
   }
```

Things to remember when using layout resource files:

- Each XML element in the layout resource file represents a View subclass object.

- Child XML elements represent child View objects of a ViewGroup object.

- "layout_width" and "layout_height" are required attributes for each XML element to specify the size of the view object.

- "wrap_content" wrap the size of the view object just enough to cover the content of the view.

- Like other Java resource files, layout resource files are automatically loaded when you request it using the "R.*" format.

- The setContentView() method has two versions: setContentView(View layoutObject) for setting layout objects created in the Java code; setContentView(int layoutID) for setting layouts defined in layout resource files.

After building and installing the project, what I see when running AndroidView on the emulator is similar to this:

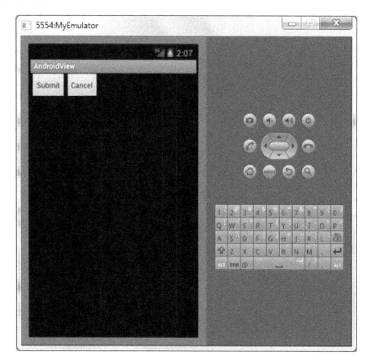

AndroidView - Using Layout Resource Files

AndroidView v3.0 - Referencing Views in Resource Files

This section provides a tutorial example on how to identify and reference layouts or views defined the layout resource file. This is needed to mix layouts and views created in Java code with those defined in the resource file.

With AndroidView version 3, I want to try the mixed approach to develop the UI layout, where major UI layouts and views are defined layout resource files and minor ones are created in Java class code.

In order to mix UI layouts and views defined in the layout resource file to those created in the Java code, I need to learn two 2 new features provided in the Android SDK:

1. Assigning a ID to the layout or view defined in the layout resource file. This can be done using the "id" attribute as shown in the following example:

```
<someView android:id="@+id/someID"/>
```

2. Obtaining the reference to the layout or view object defined in the layout resource file. This can be done using the findviewById() method as shown in the following example:

```
findViewById(R.id.someID);
```

The next question is what layouts and views should be defined in the layout resource file and what should be created in the Java code. The answer depends on the nature of the application. For my AndroidView version 3, here is what I want:

- The screen should display an input form with three blocks: a contact information block, an address block, and an action button block.

- The layout of these blocks should be defined in the layout resource file so I can re-arrange it easily later.

- Detail fields in each block should be created in the Java code so I can control them with program logics.

So I enhanced .\src\com\herongyang\view\AndroidView.java as follows:

```
/* AndroidView.java
```

```
 * Version 3.0 - Mixing View objects with Layouts from resource file
 * Copyright (c) 2015, HerongYang.com, All Rights Reserved.
 */
package com.herongyang.view;

import android.app.Activity;
import android.os.Bundle;
import android.widget.LinearLayout;
import android.widget.Button;
import android.widget.TextView;
public class AndroidView extends Activity {
   @Override
   public void onCreate(Bundle savedInstanceState) {
      super.onCreate(savedInstanceState);

      // Set the top layout as the activity content
      setContentView(R.layout.main);

      // Build detail fields
      LinearLayout l;
      l = (LinearLayout) findViewById(R.id.lContact);
      buildContact(l);
      l = (LinearLayout) findViewById(R.id.lAddress);
      buildAddress(l);
      l = (LinearLayout) findViewById(R.id.lAction);
      buildAction(l);
   }
   public void buildContact(LinearLayout l) {
      TextView v = new TextView(this);
      v.setText("First name: Herong");
      l.addView(v);

      v = new TextView(this);
      v.setText("Last name: Yang");
      l.addView(v);
   }
   public void buildAddress(LinearLayout l) {
```

```
      TextView v = new TextView(this);

      v.setText("City: Paris");

      l.addView(v);


      v = new TextView(this);

      v.setText("Country: France");

      l.addView(v);

   }

   public void buildAction(LinearLayout l) {

      Button b = new Button(this);

      b.setText("Submit");

      l.addView(b);


      b = new Button(this);

      b.setText("Cancel");

      l.addView(b);

   }

}
```

See next tutorials on how to create layout resource file to display the final form. The resource file will define 3 layouts identified as lContact, lAddress and lAction.

AndroidView v3.1 - Layouts with Vertical Orientation

This section provides a tutorial example on how to develop a layout resource file to display all fields in all blocks in vertical orientation.

To finish the AndroidView project, I will create a new layout resource file, which defines a top layout and three sub layouts to host detail fields that are created in AndroidView.java.

Here is my first try with .\res\layout\main.xml:

```
<?xml version="1.0" encoding="utf-8"?>
<!-- AndroidView_layout.xml
  - Version 3.1 - Showing blocks vertically
  - Copyright (c) 2015, HerongYang.com, All Rights Reserved.
```

```
-->
<LinearLayout
    xmlns:android="http://schemas.android.com/apk/res/android"
    android:layout_width="wrap_content"
    android:layout_height="wrap_content"
    android:orientation="vertical"
>
    <LinearLayout
        android:id="@+id/lContact"
        android:layout_width="wrap_content"
        android:layout_height="wrap_content"
        android:orientation="vertical"
    />
    <LinearLayout
        android:id="@+id/lAddress"
        android:layout_width="wrap_content"
        android:layout_height="wrap_content"
        android:orientation="vertical"
    />
    <LinearLayout
        android:id="@+id/lAction"
        android:layout_width="wrap_content"
        android:layout_height="wrap_content"
        android:orientation="vertical"
    />
</LinearLayout>
```

Build, install and run the application again on the emulator. My form shows up on the screen:

AndroidView - Vertical Layout Orientation

What do you think about this layout? I don't like it. See next tutorial for my second try.

AndroidView v3.2 - Layouts with Horizontal Orientation

This section provides a tutorial example on how to develop a layout resource file to display all fields in blocks in horizontal orientation.

Here is my second try with .\res\layout\main.xml:

```
<?xml version="1.0" encoding="utf-8"?>
<!-- AndroidView_layout.xml
  - Version 3.2 - Putting two blocks side-by-side
  - Copyright (c) 2012, HerongYang.com, All Rights Reserved.
-->
<LinearLayout
    xmlns:android="http://schemas.android.com/apk/res/android"
    android:layout_width="wrap_content"
```

```
        android:layout_height="wrap_content"
        android:orientation="vertical"
        >
        <LinearLayout
            android:layout_width="wrap_content"
            android:layout_height="wrap_content"
            android:orientation="horizontal"
            >
            <LinearLayout
                android:id="@+id/lContact"
                android:layout_width="wrap_content"
                android:layout_height="wrap_content"
                android:orientation="vertical"
            />
            <LinearLayout
                android:id="@+id/lAddress"
                android:layout_width="wrap_content"
                android:layout_height="wrap_content"
                android:orientation="vertical"
            />
        </LinearLayout>
        <LinearLayout
            android:id="@+id/lAction"
            android:layout_width="wrap_content"
            android:layout_height="wrap_content"
            android:orientation="horizontal"
        />
    </LinearLayout>
```

With this layout resource file, I am expecting that the Contact block and Address block will be displayed side. The Action block will be displayed below them.

Without any changes in the Java code, I rebuild, install and run the application again on the emulator. I see this on the emulator:

AndroidView - Horizontal Layout Orientation

The layout does not look so nice. But it matches what the resource is asking. Additional borders, spaces and colors can be added to make it better.

AndroidView v4.0 - Inserting Views to Parent Layout

This section provides a tutorial example on how to identify and reference layouts or views defined the layout resource file. This is needed to mix layouts and views created in Java code with those defined in the resource file.

As the last tutorial on View objects, I am going to follow the view tree to find the parent layout and insert a DatePicker view in the Java code:

```
/* AndroidView.java
 * Version 4.0 - Inserting views into the parent layout
 * Copyright (c) 2012, HerongYang.com, All Rights Reserved.
 */

package com.herongyang.view;
```

```
import android.app.Activity;
import android.os.Bundle;
import android.widget.LinearLayout;
import android.widget.Button;
import android.widget.TextView;
import android.widget.DatePicker;
public class AndroidView extends Activity {
    @Override
    public void onCreate(Bundle savedInstanceState) {
        super.onCreate(savedInstanceState);

        // Set the top layout as the activity content
        setContentView(R.layout.main);

        // Build detail fields
        LinearLayout l;
        l = (LinearLayout) findViewById(R.id.lContact);
        buildContact(l);
        l = (LinearLayout) findViewById(R.id.lAddress);
        buildAddress(l);
        l = (LinearLayout) findViewById(R.id.lAction);
        buildAction(l);

        // Insert a new child to the parent
        LinearLayout p = (LinearLayout) l.getParent();
        addDatePicker(p);
    }
    public void addDatePicker(LinearLayout l) {
        DatePicker v = new DatePicker(this);
        l.addView(v);
    }
    public void buildContact(LinearLayout l) {
        TextView v = new TextView(this);
        v.setText("First name: Herong");
        l.addView(v);

        v = new TextView(this);
```

```
        v.setText("Last name: Yang");
        l.addView(v);
    }
    public void buildAddress(LinearLayout l) {
        TextView v = new TextView(this);
        v.setText("City: Paris");
        l.addView(v);


        v = new TextView(this);
        v.setText("Country: France");
        l.addView(v);
    }
    public void buildAction(LinearLayout l) {
        Button b = new Button(this);
        b.setText("Submit");
        l.addView(b);


        b = new Button(this);
        b.setText("Cancel");
        l.addView(b);
    }
}
```

Rebuild, install and run the application again on the emulator. I see this on the emulator:

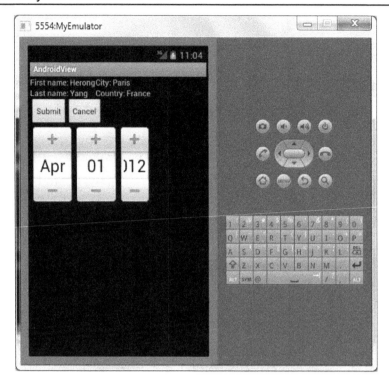

AndroidView - Date Picker

It works! I am able to use the getParent() method in the view tree to get hold of the parent layout and insert a DatePicker view into the layout.

Using "adb logcat" Command for Debugging

This chapter provides tutorial notes on the 'adb logcat' command. Topics include using 'adb logcat' command options and arguments; viewing log buffers: main, events, and radio; creating rotated log files; control log format as 'brief' or 'long'; filtering out log entries by priority and process tag; retrieving Java exceptions from AndroidRuntime logs.

Takeaways:

* "adb logcat" command dumps log entries from 3 log buffers: main, events and radio.

* "adb logcat -v long" command dumps log entries in long format.

* "adb logcat -f /sdcard/Download/Android.log -r 1024 -n 8" commands dumps log entries into rotated log files on the device.

* "adb logcat AndroidRuntime:E *:S" dumps only error log entries generated from the "AndroidRuntime" process, including Java exceptions.

"adb logcat" Command - Displaying System Logs

This section describes the 'adb logcat' command that can be used to print out Android system log data for debugging purpose.

When developing new Android applications, you have to learn some tools to help you to debug the code. The primary debugging tool provided in the Android SDK is the Android Debug Bridge (ADB) program.

In previous tutorials, we learned how to use the following ADB commands:

* "adb install/uninstall" - To install or uninstall an Android application package on the connected emulator or device.

* "adb shell" - To provide a Unix shell interface to the connected emulator or device.

* "adb push/pull" - To copy files or folders to or from the connected emulator or device.

ADB also has another very useful command that can be used to debug applications:

* "adb logcat" - To print out log data from the connected emulator or device.

Let's starts the Android emulator and run the "adb logcat" command to see what can get:

```
C:\herong\>\local\android-sdk-windows\platform-tools\adb logcat


W/Zygote  (   37): Preloaded drawable resource #0x108022c \
   (res/drawable-hdpi/dialog_top_holo_dark.9.png) that varies with \
   configuration!!
D/dalvikvm(   37): GC_EXPLICIT freed 3K, 1% free 8601K/8643K, \
   paused 3ms+4ms
...
I/Zygote  (   37): ...preloaded 31 resources in 50ms.
D/dalvikvm(   37): GC_EXPLICIT freed 29K, 1% free 9028K/9091K, ...
...
I/dalvikvm(   37): System server process 77 has been created
I/Zygote  (   37): Accepting command socket connections
E/BatteryService(   77): usbOnlinePath not found
...
I/sysproc (   77): Entered system_init()
I/sysproc (   77): ServiceManager: 0x1e4ad0
D/SensorService(   77): nuSensorService starting...
I/SensorService(   77): Goldfish 3-axis Accelerometer
...
I/SystemServer(   77): Activity Manager
```

```
I/ActivityManager(    77): Memory class: 48
F/BatteryStatsImpl(    77): problem reading network stats
F/BatteryStatsImpl(    77): java.lang.IllegalStateException: \
   problem parsing idx 1
F/BatteryStatsImpl(    77):  at com.android.internal.net. \
   NetworkStatsFactory.readNetworkStatsDetail \
   (NetworkStatsFactory.java:300)
F/BatteryStatsImpl(    77):  at com.android.internal.net. \
   NetworkStatsFactory.readNetworkStatsDetail
   (NetworkStatsFactory.java:250) \
...
F/BatteryStatsImpl(    77): Caused by: java.io.FileNotFoundException: \
   /proc/net/xt_qtaguid/stats: open failed: ENOENT \
   (No such file or directory)
F/BatteryStatsImpl(    77):  at libcore.io.IoBridge.open \
   (IoBridge.java:406)
F/BatteryStatsImpl(    77):  at java.io.FileInputStream.<init> \
   (FileInputStream.java:78)
...
E/AndroidRuntime(    77): Error reporting WTF
E/AndroidRuntime(    77): java.lang.NullPointerException
E/AndroidRuntime(    77):  at com.android.internal.os. \
   RuntimeInit.wtf(RuntimeInit.java:345)
E/AndroidRuntime(    77):  at android.util.Log$1. \
   onTerribleFailure(Log.java:103)
E/AndroidRuntime(    77):  at android.util.Log.wtf(Log.java:278)
...

^C
```

Note that:

- It looks like the "adb logcat" command is printing all log data from the entire Android system.

- Some log entries are providing general information like "W/Zygote (37): Preloaded drawable resource #0x108022c Preloaded drawable resource #0x108022c (res/ drawable-hdpi/dialog_top_holo_dark.9.png"

- Some log entries are reporting Java exceptions like "F/BatteryStatsImpl(77): java.lang.IllegalStateException: problem parsing idx 1"

- And there is even a null pointer exception in the AndroidRuntime code. See these 2 log entries: "E/AndroidRuntime(77): java.lang.NullPointerException" and "E/AndroidRuntime(77): at com.android.internal.os.RuntimeInit.wtf(RuntimeInit.java:345)"

- You need to press "<Ctrl>-C" to stop "adb logcat" command. Otherwise it will continuously print new log data on the screen.

Actually, "logcat" is also available as shell command on the connected the device. You can run it directly in a shell interface window.

See the next tutorial on how to use "adb logcat" command options.

"adb logcat" Command Options and Log Buffers

This section describes the 'adb logcat' command options to dump and manage log buffers: main, events, and radio. An example is given to dump logs into a set of rotated log files.

To better use the "adb logcat" command, we need to look at its options:

- "adb logcat -b <buffer>" - Loads an alternate log buffer for viewing, such as event or radio. The main buffer is used by default. There are 3 log buffers on the Android system: "main", "events", and "radio". The default buffer is "main".

- "adb logcat -c" - Clears (flushes) the entire log and exits.

- "adb logcat -d" - Dumps the log to the screen and exits.

- "adb logcat -f <filename>" - Writes log message output to a file. The default is the "stdout - Standard Output".

- "adb logcat -g" - Prints the size of the specified log buffer and exits.

- "adb logcat -n <count>" - Sets the maximum number of rotated logs to <count>. The default value is 4. Requires the -r option.

- "adb logcat -r <kbytes>" - Rotates the log file every <kbytes> of output. The default value is 16. Requires the -f option.

- "adb logcat -s" - Sets the default filter spec to silent.

- "adb logcat -v <format>" - Sets the output format for log messages. The default is brief format.

Here are two examples of using "adb logcat" options:

1. To show the size of the default log buffer (main) and clear it on the connected device:

```
C:\herong\>\local\android-sdk-windows\platform-tools\adb logcat -g
main: ring buffer is 256Kb (212Kb consumed), max entry is 5120b, ...
system: ring buffer is 256Kb (70Kb consumed), max entry is 5120b,...
crash: ring buffer is 256Kb (0b consumed), max entry is 5120b, ma...


C:\herong\>\local\android-sdk-windows\platform-tools\adb logcat -c


C:\herong\>\local\android-sdk-windows\platform-tools\adb logcat -g
main: ring buffer is 256Kb (98b consumed), max entry is 5120b, ma...
system: ring buffer is 256Kb (0b consumed), max entry is 5120b, m...
crash: ring buffer is 256Kb (0b consumed), max entry is 5120b, ma...
```

2. To continuously dump log entries to a set of 8 rotated log files of 1 MB each on the file system of the connected device:

```
C:\herong\>\local\android-sdk-windows\platform-tools\adb logcat \
   -f /sdcard/Download/Android.log -r 1024 -n 8


(leave it running)
```

See next tutorials on how to control the format of the "adb logcat" output.

"adb logcat -v" Command - Log Format Control

This section describes how to use the 'adb logcat -v' command option to control the format of log entries. 'adb logcat -v long' dumps all data elements of each log entry.

If you want to control the format of each log entry is dumped, you need to use the "adb logcat -v <format>" option, which supports the following formats:

- "adb logcat -v brief" - Display priority/tag and the PID of process issuing the message (the default format).

- "adb logcat -v process" - Display PID only.

- "adb logcat -v tag" - Display the priority/tag only.

- "adb logcat -v raw" - Display the raw log message, with no other metadata fields.

- "adb logcat -v time" - Display the date, invocation time, priority/tag, and PID of the process issuing the message.

- "adb logcat -v thread" - Display the priority, tag, and the PID and TID of the thread issuing the message.

- "adb logcat -v threadtime" - Display the date, invocation time, priority, tag, and the PID and TID of the thread issuing the message.

- "adb logcat -v long" - Display all metadata fields and separate messages with a blank lines.

Here are 2 examples of using "adb logcat -v" format options:

1. To show all data elements of the log entry with the "-v long" format:

```
C:\herong>\local\android-sdk-windows\platform-tools\adb logcat -v long

...
[ 04-01 16:00:00.278   172:0xb0 D/dalvikvm ]
GC_CONCURRENT freed 3840K, 19% free 18438K/22727K, paused 6ms+6ms


[ 04-01 16:04:07.239    77:0x5e F/BatteryStatsImpl ]
problem reading network stats
java.lang.IllegalStateException: problem parsing idx 1
        at com.android.internal.net.NetworkStatsFactory.readNetwor...
        at com.android.internal.net.NetworkStatsFactory.readNetwor...
        at com.android.internal.os.BatteryStatsImpl.getNetworkStat...
        at com.android.internal.os.BatteryStatsImpl.access$100(Bat...
...
```

2. To show all data elements of the log entry with the "-v threadtime" format:

```
C:\herong>\local\android-sdk-windows\platform-tools\adb logcat \
```

```
   -v threadtime


...
04-01 16:05:35.099     158     163 D dalvikvm: GC_CONCURRENT freed 384...
04-01 16:06:41.048      77     153 W ThrottleService: unable to find s...
04-01 16:06:41.228      77      80 D dalvikvm: GC_CONCURRENT freed 489...
04-01 16:11:35.339      77      91 V BackupManagerService: Running a b...
...
```

See next tutorial on how to filtering log entries.

"adb logcat" Command Arguments - Output Filters

*This section describes how to use the 'adb logcat' command arguments to filter out unwanted log entries. 'adb logcat dalvikvm:V *:S' means dump all log entries from the Java Virtual Machine, dalvikvm, and nothing from all other processes.*

If you look carefully in the output of the "logcat" command, you will that each log entry is associated with a priority code and a process tag name.

In the output of the "brief" format, the first field is the priority code and the second field is the process tag name. For example, the following "brief" log output shows that the priority code is "E" for Error and the process tag name is "AndroidRuntime":

```
E/AndroidRuntime(   77): java.lang.NullPointerException
```

As another example, the following "long" log output shows that the priority code is "F" for Fatal and the process tag name is "BatteryStatsImpl"

```
[ 04-01 16:04:07.239     77:0x5e F/BatteryStatsImpl ]
problem reading network stats
java.lang.IllegalStateException: problem parsing idx 1
        at com.android.internal.net.NetworkStatsFactory.readNetwor...
        at com.android.internal.net.NetworkStatsFactory.readNetwor...
        at com.android.internal.os.BatteryStatsImpl.getNetworkStat...
        at com.android.internal.os.BatteryStatsImpl.access$100(Bat...
...
```

In order to help you to focus on log entries that interested to your debugging goal, "adb logcat" command allows you to specify filters as command arguments as:

```
adb logcat <options> <process-tag>:<priority-code> ...
```

When filters are provided, the "logcat" command will dump log entries that are generated from specified processes with priorities higher than the specified code, plus all log entries that generated from unspecified processes.

A wildcard character, "*", can be used to represent all processes

Below is a list of all priority codes that can be used in the "logcat" command:

- V - Verbose (lowest priority)

- D - Debug

- I - Info (default priority)

- W - Warning

- E - Error

- F - Fatal

- S - Silent (highest priority, on which nothing is ever printed)

Here are 2 examples of using filters with the "adb logcat" command:

1. To dump all log entries with "I (for Info)" priority and higher from all processes - The default behavior of the logcat command:

```
C:\herong>\local\android-sdk-windows\platform-tools\adb logcat \
   *:I


...
W/ThrottleService(   77): unable to find stats for iface rmnet0
F/NetworkStats(   77): problem reading network stats
F/NetworkStats(   77): java.lang.IllegalStateException: problem pa...
F/NetworkStats(   77):  at com.android.internal.net.NetworkStatsFa...
F/NetworkStats(   77):  at com.android.server.NetworkManagementSer...
...
```

2. To dump all log entries from "dalvikvm (the Java Virtual Machine)" and nothing from all other processes:

```
C:\herong>\local\android-sdk-windows\platform-tools\adb logcat \
   dalvikvm:V *:S


...

D/dalvikvm(   77): GC_CONCURRENT freed 516K, 14% free 11320K/13063K...
D/dalvikvm(  158): GC_CONCURRENT freed 384K, 6% free 9529K/10119K, ...
D/dalvikvm(  172): GC_FOR_ALLOC freed 2288K, 22% free 17742K/22727K...
D/dalvikvm(  172): GC_FOR_ALLOC freed 388K, 18% free 18734K/22727K,...
D/dalvikvm(  172): GC_CONCURRENT freed 2795K, 22% free 17941K/22727...
D/dalvikvm(  172): GC_CONCURRENT freed 1307K, 19% free 18629K/22727...

...
```

Using "adb logcat" Command to Track the Lifecycle of an Application

This section provides a tutorial example how to use the 'adb logcat' command to track the lifecycle of an application. The 'events' log buffer provides log entries for each Activity callback method.

In previous tutorials, we have learned how to use the "adb logcat" command options and arguments filter out log entries and control the output format. Now let's try to use the "adb logcat" to watch how my applications get executed on the device.

1. Run the "adb logcat" command to dump all log entries from "ActivityManager" in the "main" log buffer and leave it there running:

```
C:\herong>\local\android-sdk-windows\platform-tools\adb logcat -c

C:\herong>\local\android-sdk-windows\platform-tools\adb logcat \
   ActivityManager:V *:S
```

2. Go to the emulator. Launch my 2 example applications, "AboutAndroid" and "AndroidView".

3. Look at the "adb logcat" window. The following log entries are printed out:

```
I/ActivityManager(   77): START {act=android.intent.action.MAIN \
```

```
    cat=[android.intent.category.LAUNCHER] flg=0x10200000 \
    cmp=com.herongyang/.AboutAndroid} from pid 172
I/ActivityManager(   77): START {act=android.intent.action.MAIN \
    cat=[android.intent.category.HOME] flg=0x10200000 \
    cmp=com.android.launcher/com.android.launcher2.Launcher} from \
    pid 77
I/ActivityManager(   77): START {act=android.intent.action.MAIN \
    cat=[android.intent.category.LAUNCHER] flg=0x10200000 \
    cmp=com.herongyang.view/.AndroidView} from pid 172
I/ActivityManager(   77): Displayed com.herongyang.view/.AndroidView: \
    +1s334ms
```

4. Run the "adb logcat" command to dump all log entries in the "events" buffer and leave it there running:

```
C:\herong>\local\android-sdk-windows\platform-tools\adb logcat \
    -b events -c


C:\herong>\local\android-sdk-windows\platform-tools\adb logcat \
    -b events *:V
```

5. Go to the emulator. Launch my 2 example applications, "AboutAndroid" and "AndroidView". Also click some buttons on "AndroidView".

6. Look at the "adb logcat" window. The following log entries are printed out:

```
I/am_create_activity(   77): [1095000544,13, \
    com.herongyang/.AboutAndroid,android.intent.action.MAIN,NULL,NULL,\
    270532608]
I/am_pause_activity(   77): [1095117944, \
    com.android.launcher/com.android.launcher2.Launcher]
I/am_on_paused_called(  172): com.android.launcher2.Launcher
I/am_restart_activity(   77): [1095000544,13, \
    com.herongyang/.AboutAndroid]
I/binder_sample(  172): [android.app.IActivityManager,19,82, \
    com.android.launcher,16]
I/am_on_resume_called(  506): com.herongyang.AboutAndroid
I/activity_launch_time(   77): [1095000544, \
    com.herongyang/.AboutAndroid,903,903]
```

```
I/am_pause_activity(    77): [1095000544,com.herongyang/.AboutAndroid]
I/am_on_paused_called(  506): com.herongyang.AboutAndroid
I/am_task_to_front(    77): 2
I/am_new_intent(    77): [1095234520,2, \
   com.android.launcher/com.android.launcher2.Launcher, \
   android.intent.action.MAIN,NULL,NULL,274726912]
I/am_resume_activity(    77): [1095117944,2, \
   com.android.launcher/com.android.launcher2.Launcher]
I/am_on_resume_called(  172): com.android.launcher2.Launcher
I/am_create_task(    77): 14
I/am_create_activity(    77): [1095317016,14, \
   com.herongyang.view/.AndroidView,android.intent.action.MAIN,NULL, \
   NULL,270532608]
I/am_pause_activity(    77): [1095117944, \
   com.android.launcher/com.android.launcher2.Launcher]
I/am_on_paused_called(  172): com.android.launcher2.Launcher
I/am_restart_activity(    77): [1095317016,14, \
   com.herongyang.view/.AndroidView]
I/am_on_resume_called(  488): com.herongyang.view.AndroidView
I/activity_launch_time(    77): [1095317016,
   com.herongyang.view/.AndroidView,974,974]
I/binder_sample(  172): [android.app.IActivityManager,19,1189, \
   com.android.launcher,100]
I/am_finish_activity(    77): [1095317016,14, \
   com.herongyang.view/.AndroidView,app-request]
I/am_pause_activity(    77): [1095317016, \
   com.herongyang.view/.AndroidView]
I/am_on_paused_called(  488): com.herongyang.view.AndroidView
I/am_resume_activity(    77): [1095117944,2, \
   com.android.launcher/com.android.launcher2.Launcher]
I/am_on_resume_called(  172): com.android.launcher2.Launcher
I/am_destroy_activity(    77): [1095317016,14, \
   com.herongyang.view/.AndroidView,finish-imm]
I/binder_sample(  488): [android.view.IWindowSession,3,275, \
   com.herongyang.view,55]
```

Those "am_on_*" log entries from the "events" log buffer record clearly the lifecycle of both applications, com.herongyang.AboutAndroid and com.herongyang.view.AndroidView.

What do you think? Are those log entries from the "main" and "events" log buffers useful to you?

Java Exceptions in AndroidRuntime Error Log

This section provides a tutorial on how use the 'adb logcat' command to retrieve Java exceptions from the AndroidRuntime error log entries.

In order to see what will happen if an Android application runs into a problem, I wrote another new application called "AndroidDebug" with this Java code:

```java
/* AndroidDebug.java
 * Version 1.0 - Set activity content to a child view
 * Copyright (c) 2015, HerongYang.com, All Rights Reserved.
 */
package com.herongyang.debug;

import android.app.Activity;
import android.os.Bundle;
import android.widget.LinearLayout;
import android.widget.Button;
public class AndroidDebug extends Activity {
    @Override
    public void onCreate(Bundle savedInstanceState) {
        super.onCreate(savedInstanceState);

        // Create the layout
        LinearLayout l = new LinearLayout(this);

        // Create the left button
        Button bl = new Button(this);
        bl.setText("Yes");
        l.addView(bl);
```

```
      // Create the right button
      Button br = new Button(this);
      br.setText("No");
      l.addView(br);

      // Set the left button as the activity content
      setContentView(bl);
   }
}
```

Build the new application project and install it on the emulator.

Go to the emulator and try to launch "AndroidDebug". I see this error message on the screen: "Unfortunately, AndroidDebug has stopped".

Android View Problem

The application crashed. But don't worry. We can use the "adb logcat" command to find out more information about the crash.

```
C:\herong\AndroidDebug>\local\android-sdk-windows\platform-tools\adb \
```

```
    logcat -b crash AndroidRuntime:E *:S


...

E/AndroidRuntime(  812): FATAL EXCEPTION: main
E/AndroidRuntime(  812): java.lang.RuntimeException: Unable to start \
    activity ComponentInfo{com.herongyang.debug \
    /com.herongyang.debug.AndroidDebug}: \
    java.lang.IllegalStateException: The specified child already has \
    a parent. You must call removeView() on the child's parent first.
E/AndroidRuntime(  812):     at android.app.ActivityThread.performL...
E/AndroidRuntime(  812):     at android.app.ActivityThread.handleLa...
E/AndroidRuntime(  812):     at android.app.ActivityThread.access$6...
E/AndroidRuntime(  812):     at android.app.ActivityThread$H.handle...
E/AndroidRuntime(  812):     at android.os.Handler.dispatchMessage(...
E/AndroidRuntime(  812):     at android.os.Looper.loop(Looper.java:...
E/AndroidRuntime(  812):     at android.app.ActivityThread.main(Act...
E/AndroidRuntime(  812):     at java.lang.reflect.Method.invokeNati...
E/AndroidRuntime(  812):     at java.lang.reflect.Method.invoke(Met...
E/AndroidRuntime(  812):     at com.android.internal.os.ZygoteInit$...
E/AndroidRuntime(  812):     at com.android.internal.os.ZygoteInit....
E/AndroidRuntime(  812):     at dalvik.system.NativeStart.main(Nati...
E/AndroidRuntime(  812): Caused by: java.lang.IllegalStateException: \
    The specified child already has a parent. You must call \
    removeView() on the child's parent first.
E/AndroidRuntime(  812):     at android.view.ViewGroup.addViewInner...
E/AndroidRuntime(  812):     at android.view.ViewGroup.addView(View...
E/AndroidRuntime(  812):     at android.view.ViewGroup.addView(View...
E/AndroidRuntime(  812):     at com.android.internal.policy.impl.Ph...
E/AndroidRuntime(  812):     at com.android.internal.policy.impl.Ph...
E/AndroidRuntime(  812):     at android.app.Activity.setContentView \
    (Activity.java:1855)                                        ...
E/AndroidRuntime(  812):     at com.herongyang.debug.AndroidDebug.\
    onCreate(AndroidDebug.java:30)                              ...
E/AndroidRuntime(  812):     at android.app.Activity.performCreate(...
E/AndroidRuntime(  812):     at android.app.Instrumentation.callAct...
E/AndroidRuntime(  812):     at android.app.ActivityThread.performL...
E/AndroidRuntime(  812):     ... 11 more
```

...

Do you see what is the cause of the problem? The statement, "setContentView(bl);" is trying to set View object "bl" as the Activity content view. But it already have a parent view, the layout "l".

Fixing the problem is easy. I will leave it you.

By the way, on Android 4.0.3, the AndroidRuntime log is in the "main" buffer. You need to run the following command to see the RuntimeException:

```
C:\herong\AndroidDebug>\local\android-sdk-windows\platform-tools\adb \
    logcat -b main AndroidRuntime:E *:S
```

Build Process and Package File Content

This chapter provides tutorial notes on the Android project build process. Topics include Android project folder structure; project build process; Ant automated build command; Android Asset Packaging Tool (aapt); Java compiler (javac); Dalvik Executable (dex) conversion; 'apkbuilder' command for packaging and signing; .apk package file content; digests and signature of .apk file.

Takeaways:

- There are 7 steps involved in building an Android application package: Resource code generation, Interface code generation, Java compilation, Byte code conversion, Packaging, Signing the package, Aligning the package.

- The "ant debug/release" command does all 7 steps of the build process automatically.

- "aapt (Android Asset Packaging Tool)" is a nice tool that can be used to perform resource code generation and packaging.

- "javac (Java Compiler)" is a tool provided by the JDK (Java Development Kit).

- "dx.bat" is a batch file that invokes the "dex" tool to convert Java byte code to DEX (Dalvik Executable) code.

- "apkbuilder.bat" is a batch file that performs the packaging and signing steps.

- "zipalign" is a command that aligns files in an .apk package file properly to improve performance.

- An .apk package file is really a ZIP file.

- The debug version of an Android application package is signed by a debug private-public key pair, which is self-signed and can not be verified with any root certificate authorities.

- The package signature is stored in the META-INFO\CERT.RSA file in the package. The signature is really the SHA1 signature of the digest file, META-INFO\CERT.SF.

"android create project" Command Options

This section describes 'android create project' command options that you need to use to specify Java class package name, starting activity class name, project folder and Android platform target.

In previous tutorials, we have been following these steps to create some simple Android applications and test them on the emulator:

- Use the "android create project" command to create a new application project.

- Use a text editor to modify the activity Java source code in the .\src folder

- Use a text editor to modify the layout resource file in the .\res folder

- Use the "ant debug" command to build the project into a Debug package .apk file

- Use the "ant installd" command to install the Debug package to the emulator.

- Test the Debug package on the emulator.

Now let's take closer look at some of these steps starting with the "android create project" command.

Here is the command I used to create my first Android application HelloAndroid:

```
C:\>cd \herong
C:\herong>\local\android-sdk-windows\tools\android create project \
   --package com.herongyang --activity HelloAndroid --target 2 \
   --path .\HelloAndroid
```

4 options are used in this command to help defining my application project:

- "--package com.herongyang" same as "-k com.herongyang" - Required option to specify the Java package name for application Java classes and resources.

- "--activity HelloAndroid" same as "-a HelloAndroid" - Required option to specify the starting activity class name for the application.

- "--target 2" same as "-t 2" - Required option to specify which target (Android platform and version) the application is going to run on. You may have multiple targets installed in your Android SDK environment and referred by target IDs. I have 2 targets installed in my SDK environment. Target #2 is "Android 4.0.3 - API Level 15".

- "--path .\HelloAndroid" same as "-p .\HelloAndroid" - Required option to specify the root folder to hold application files.

You can try to create another application project with the short option names:

```
C:\herong>\local\android-sdk-windows\tools\android create project \
   -k com.test -a AndroidTest -t 2 -p .\AndroidTest

Created project directory: C:\herong\AndroidTest
Created directory C:\herong\AndroidTest\src\com\test
Added file C:\herong\AndroidTest\src\com\test\AndroidText.java
Created directory C:\herong\AndroidTest\res
Created directory C:\herong\AndroidTest\bin
Created directory C:\herong\AndroidTest\libs
Created directory C:\herong\AndroidTest\res\values
Added file C:\herong\AndroidTest\res\values\strings.xml
Created directory C:\herong\AndroidTest\res\layout
```

```
Added file C:\herong\AndroidTest\res\layout\main.xml
Created directory C:\herong\AndroidTest\res\drawable-hdpi
Created directory C:\herong\AndroidTest\res\drawable-mdpi
Created directory C:\herong\AndroidTest\res\drawable-ldpi
Added file C:\herong\AndroidTest\AndroidManifest.xml
Added file C:\herong\AndroidTest\build.xml
Added file C:\herong\AndroidTest\proguard-project.txt
```

You can delete the project folder C:\herong\AndroidTest and try it again with different option values.

In the next tutorial, we will review files and folders created by the "android create project" command.

Android Project Folder Structure

This section describes the Android project folder structure, which has a source folder, a resource folder, a generated-code folder, and a binary folder.

In this tutorial, let's look at the Android application project folder structure using the HelloAndroid application as an example. If you have not created the project yet, run the following command now:

```
C:\herong>\local\android-sdk-windows\tools\android create project \
   -k com.herongyang -a HelloAndroid -t 2 -p .\HelloAndroid
```

Now open the project folder \herong\HelloAndroid using the "dir /s \herong \HelloAndroid" command. You will see the following folder structure:

```
C:\herong\HelloAndroid
   AndroidManifest.xml
   ant.properties
   bin - Binary folder to hold build output
      build.prop
      classes - Binary class files
         com
            herongyang
               BuildConfig.class
```

```
                    HelloAndroid.class
                    R$attr.class
                    R$drawable.class
                    R$layout.class - Layout resource file
                    R$string.class
                    R.class
        classes.dex
        classes.dex.d
        HelloAndroid-debug-unaligned.apk
        HelloAndroid-debug-unaligned.apk.d
        HelloAndroid-debug.apk
        HelloAndroid.ap_
        HelloAndroid.ap_.d
        jarlist.cache
        res
            drawable-hdpi - High resolution icon
                ic_launcher.png
            drawable-ldpi - Low resolution icon
                ic_launcher.png
            drawable-mdpi - Medium resolution icon
                ic_launcher.png
    build.xml
    gen
        com
            herongyang
                BuildConfig.java
                R.java
    libs - Empty folder
    local.properties
    proguard-project.txt
    project.properties
    res
        drawable-hdpi - High resolution icon
            ic_launcher.png
        drawable-ldpi - Low resolution icon
            ic_launcher.png
        drawable-mdpi - Medium resolution icon
```

```
            ic_launcher.png
      layout - Layout resource files
         main.xml
      values
         strings.xml - String resource file
  src
      com
         herongyang
            HelloAndroid.java
```

Some detailed explanations of key folders and files in an Android project folder structure based on the Android document:

- .\src\ - The source folder which contains your stub Activity file, which is stored at src/your/package/namespace/ActivityName.java. All other source code files (such as .java or .aidl files) go here as well.

- .\bin\ - The binary folder which contains output files of the build process. This is where you can find the final .apk file and other compiled resources.

- .\jni\ - The JNI (Java Native Interface) folder which contains native code sources developed using the Android NDK (Native Development Kit). You will not have this folder, if you don't have any native code.

- .\gen\ - The generated-code folder which contains Java source files generated by ADT (Android Developer Tools), such as your R.java file and interfaces created from AIDL files.

- .\assets\ - The asset folder which constrain raw asset files. Files that you save here are compiled into an .apk file as-is, and the original filename is preserved. You can navigate this directory in the same way as a typical file system using URIs and read files as a stream of bytes using the the AssetManager. For example, this is a good location for textures and game data.

- .\res\ - The resource folder which contains application resources, such as drawable files, layout files, and string values.

- .\res\anim\ - The animation resource folder which contains resource XML files that are compiled into animation objects.

- .\res\color\ - The color resource folder which contains resource XML files that describe colors.

- .\res\drawable\ - The drawable resource folder which contains bitmap files (PNG, JPEG, or GIF), 9-Patch image files, and XML files that describe Drawable shapes or a Drawable objects that contain multiple states (normal, pressed, or focused).

- .\res\layout\ - The layout resource folder which contains XML files that are compiled into screen layouts (or part of a screen).

- .\res\menu\ - The menu resource folder which contains XML files that define application menus.

- .\res\raw\ - The raw resource folder which contains arbitrary raw asset files. Saving asset files here instead of in the assets/ directory only differs in the way that you access them. These files are processed by aapt and must be referenced from the application using a resource identifier in the R class. For example, this is a good place for media, such as MP3 or Ogg files.

- .\res\values\ - The value resource folder that contains XML files that are compiled into many kinds of resource. Unlike other resources in the res/ directory, resources written to XML files in this folder are not referenced by the file name. Instead, the XML element type controls how the resources is defined within them are placed into the R class.

- .\res\xml\ - The XML resource folder which contains miscellaneous XML files that configure application components. For example, an XML file that defines a PreferenceScreen, AppWidgetProviderInfo, or Searchability Metadata.

- .\libs\ - The library folder which contains private external libraries.

- .\AndroidManifest.xml - The project manifest file that describes the nature of the application and each of its components. For instance, it describes: certain qualities about the activities, services, intent receivers, and content providers; what permissions are requested; what external libraries are needed; what device features are required, what API Levels are supported or required; and others.

- .\project.properties - The project properties files which contains project settings, such as the build target. This file is integral to the project, so maintain it in a source revision control system. To edit project properties in Eclipse, right-click the project folder and select Properties.

- .\local.properties - The local properties file which contains customizable computer-specific properties for the build system. If you use Ant to build the project, this contains the path to the SDK installation. Because the content of the file is specific to the local installation of the SDK, the local.properties should not be maintained in a source revision control system. If you use Eclipse, this file is not used.

- .\ant.properties - The Ant properties file which contains customizable properties for the build system. You can edit this file to override default build settings used by Ant and also provide the location of your keystore and key alias so that the build tools can sign your application when building in release mode. This file is integral to the project, so maintain it in a source revision control system. If you use Eclipse, this file is not used.

- .\build.xml - The Ant build file for your project. This is only applicable for projects that you build with Ant.

Android Application Project Build Process

This section describes the Android application project build process which consists of 7 steps: Resource code generation, Interface code generation, Java Compilation, Byte code conversion, Packaging, Signing, and Package optimization.

Before going into details of the Android project build process, let's look this build process diagram provided in the Android document:

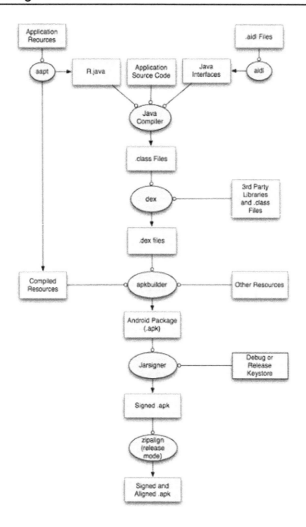

Android Project Build Process Diagram

The build process can be summarized as below:

- Resource code generation - The aapt (Android Asset Packaging Tool) tool takes your application resource files, such as the AndroidManifest.xml file and the XML files for your Activities, and compiles them. An R.java is also produced so you can reference your resources from your Java code.

- Interface code generation - The aidl (Android Interface Definition Language) tool converts any .aidl interfaces that you have into Java interfaces.

- Java compilation - The javac (Java Compiler) tool compiles all of your Java code, including the R.java and .aidl files, into .class files.

- Byte code conversion - The dex tool converts the .class files to Dalvik byte code. Any 3rd party libraries and .class files that you have included in your project are also converted into .dex files so that they can be packaged into the final .apk file.

- Packaging - The apkbuilder tool packages all non-compiled resources (such as images), compiled resources, and the .dex files into an .apk file.

- Signing the package - The jarsigner tool signs the .apk file with a debug key or a release key it can be installed to a device.

- Package optimization - The zipalign tool aligns the files in the .apk package to decreases memory usage when the application is running on a device.

See next tutorials on how use those build tools.

Project Build Process Done by "ant debug" Command

This section describes the Android project build process done by the 'ant debug' command defined in the Ant build file. It performs 'aidl', 'aapt', 'javac', 'dex', 'apkbuilder' and 'zipalign' all together automatically.

With the use of Ant build file, those 7 project build steps are all performed automatically by a single Ant task, "debug" or "release", defined in the build file. Let's exam the "ant debug" output on the "HelloAndroid" project to see how those build steps are performed:

```
C:\herong\HelloAndroid>\local\apache-ant-1.9.5\bin\ant debug

Buildfile: C:\herong\HelloAndroid\build.xml

-set-mode-check:

-set-debug-files:

-check-env:
 [checkenv] Android SDK Tools Revision 24.3.3
 [checkenv] Installed at C:\local\android-sdk-windows

-setup:
```

```
        [echo] Project Name: HelloAndroid
    [gettype] Project Type: Application


-set-debug-mode:


-debug-obfuscation-check:


-pre-build:


-build-setup:
[getbuildtools] Using latest Build Tools: 22.0.1
        [echo] Resolving Build Target for HelloAndroid...
  [gettarget] Project Target:    Android 5.1.1
  [gettarget] API level:         22
  [gettarget] WARNING: No minSdkVersion value set. Application will
              install on all Android versions.
        [echo] ----------
        [echo] Creating output directories if needed...
       [mkdir] Created dir: C:\herong\HelloAndroid\bin\rsObj
       [mkdir] Created dir: C:\herong\HelloAndroid\bin\rsLibs
        [echo] ----------
        [echo] Resolving Dependencies for HelloAndroid...
 [dependency] Library dependencies:
 [dependency] No Libraries
 [dependency]
 [dependency] ------------------
        [echo] ----------
        [echo] Building Libraries with 'debug'...
     [subant] No sub-builds to iterate on


-code-gen:
[mergemanifest] Found Deleted Target File
[mergemanifest] Merging AndroidManifest files into one.
[mergemanifest] Manifest merger disabled. Using project manifest only.
        [echo] Handling aidl files...
        [aidl] No AIDL files to compile.
        [echo] ----------
```

```
     [echo] Handling RenderScript files...
     [echo] ----------
     [echo] Handling Resources...
     [aapt] Found Deleted Target File
     [aapt] Generating resource IDs...
     [echo] ----------
     [echo] Handling BuildConfig class...
[buildconfig] No need to generate new BuildConfig.

-pre-compile:

-compile:
    [javac] Compiling 1 source file to
            C:\herong\HelloAndroid\bin\classes

-post-compile:

-obfuscate:

-dex:
      [dex] input: C:\herong\HelloAndroid\bin\classes
      [dex] Found Deleted Target File
      [dex] Converting compiled files and external libraries into
            C:\herong\HelloAndroid\bin\classes.dex...

-crunch:
   [crunch] Crunching PNG Files in source dir:
            C:\herong\HelloAndroid\res
   [crunch] To destination dir: C:\herong\HelloAndroid\bin\res
   [crunch] Crunched 0 PNG files to update cache

-package-resources:
     [aapt] Found Deleted Target File
     [aapt] Creating full resource package...

-package:
[apkbuilder] Found Deleted Target File
```

```
[apkbuilder] Creating HelloAndroid-debug-unaligned.apk and signing it
             with a debug key...

-post-package:


-do-debug:
 [zipalign] Running zip align on final apk...
     [echo] Debug Package:
            C:\herong\\HelloAndroid\bin\HelloAndroid-debug.apk
[propertyfile] Updating property file: C:\herong\HelloAndroid\bin\build.prop


-post-build:


debug:


BUILD SUCCESSFUL
Total time: 5 seconds
```

Here is what I see in the output:

- "[aidl] No AIDL files to compile." - This is the interface code generation step performed by the "aidl" tool. But there is no .aidl files in my project to process.

- "[aapt] Generating resource IDs..." - This is the resource code generation step performed by the "aapt" tool. This is only 1 resource file, .\res\layout\main.xml, that gets processed and 1 Java code generated at .\gen\com\herongyang\R.java.

- "[javac] Compiling 1 source file to C:\herong\HelloAndroid\bin\classes" - This is the Java compilation step performed by the "javac" tool. Compiled class files are stored in the .\bin\classes folder.

- "[dex] Converting compiled files and external libraries into C:\herong\HelloAndroid \bin\classes.dex" - This is the byte code conversion step performed by the "dex" tool.

- "[apkbuilder] Creating HelloAndroid-debug-unaligned.apk and signing it with a debug key..." - This is the packaging step and the signing step performed by the "apkbuilder" tool.

- "[zipalign] Running zip align on final apk..." - This is package optimization step performed by the "zipalign" tool.

Detailed Output of "ant -verbose debug" Command

This section describes the output of the 'ant -verbose debug' command, which provides more details how each of 'aidl', 'aapt', 'javac', 'dex', 'apkbuilder' and 'zipalign' tools are invoked in the Ant build process.

Looking at the default output of the "ant debug" command, we get the idea of what development tools are used in the Ant build file to finish the full build process of an Android project. But if you want to know how those tools are invoked, you need to use the "-verbose" option to see more details.

Let's remove all files generated by the previous build process and run "ant -verbose debug" command on the HelloAndroid project:

```
C:\herong\HelloAndroid>\local\apache-ant-1.9.5\bin\ant all clean


C:\herong\HelloAndroid>\local\apache-ant-1.9.5\bin\ant -verbose debug


Apache Ant(TM) version 1.9.5 compiled on May 31 2015
Trying the default build file: build.xml
Buildfile: C:\herong\HelloAndroid\build.xml
Detected Java version: 1.8 in: C:\Program Files\Java\jdk1.8.0_45\jre
Detected OS: Windows 7
parsing buildfile C:\herong\HelloAndroid\build.xml with
    URI = file:/C:/herong//HelloAndroid/build.xml
Project base dir set to: C:\herong\HelloAndroid
parsing buildfile jar:file:/C:/local/apache-ant-1.9.5/lib/ant.jar...
  [property] Loading C:\herong\HelloAndroid\local.properties
  [property] Loading C:\herong\HelloAndroid\ant.properties
  [property] Loading Environment env.
Property "env.ANDROID_HOME" has not been set
Importing file C:\herong\HelloAndroid\custom_rules.xml
    from C:\herong\HelloAndroid\build.xml
Cannot find C:\herong\HelloAndroid\custom_rules.xml imported
    from C:\herong\HelloAndroid\build.xml
Importing file C:\local\android-sdk-windows\tools\ant\build.xml
    from C:\herong\HelloAndroid\build.xml
```

```
Overriding previous definition of reference to ant.projectHelper
parsing buildfile C:\local\android-sdk-windows\tools\ant\build.xml
   with URI = file:/C:/local/android-sdk-windows/tools/ant/build.xml
Property "key.store" has not been set
 [macrodef] creating macro   do-only-if-not-library
 [macrodef] creating macro   do-only-if-manifest-hasCode
 [macrodef] creating macro   dex-helper
 [macrodef] creating macro   package-helper
 [macrodef] creating macro   zipalign-helper
 [macrodef] creating macro   run-tests-helper
 [macrodef] creating macro   record-build-key
 [macrodef] creating macro   record-build-info
 [macrodef] creating macro   uninstall-helper
Overriding previous definition of reference to ant.projectHelper
Build sequence for target(s) `debug' is [-set-mode-check, -set-d...
Complete build sequence is [-set-mode-check, -set-debug-files, -...


-set-mode-check:


-set-debug-files:


-check-env:
 [checkenv] Android SDK Tools Revision 24.3.3
 [checkenv] Installed at C:\local\android-sdk-windows


-setup:
    [echo] Project Name: HelloAndroid
 [gettype] Project Type: Application


-set-debug-mode:
Property "emma.enabled" has not been set


-debug-obfuscation-check:


-pre-build:


-build-setup:
```

```
[getbuildtools] Using latest Build Tools: 22.0.1
 [property] Loading C:\herong\HelloAndroid\bin\build.prop
Override ignored for property "build.last.target"
Override ignored for property "build.last.is.instrumented"
Override ignored for property "build.last.is.packaging.debug"
Override ignored for property "build.last.is.signing.debug"
    [echo] Resolving Build Target for HelloAndroid...
[gettarget] Project Target:   Android 5.1.1
[gettarget] API level:        22
[gettarget] WARNING: No minSdkVersion value set. Application will
            install on all Android versions.
    [echo] ----------
    [echo] Creating output directories if needed...
   [mkdir] Skipping C:\herong\HelloAndroid\res because it already ...
   [mkdir] Skipping C:\herong\HelloAndroid\libs because it already...
   [mkdir] Skipping C:\herong\HelloAndroid\bin because it already ...
   [mkdir] Skipping C:\herong\HelloAndroid\bin\res because it alre...
   [mkdir] Created dir: C:\herong\HelloAndroid\bin\rsObj
   [mkdir] Created dir: C:\herong\HelloAndroid\bin\rsLibs
   [mkdir] Skipping C:\herong\HelloAndroid\gen because it already ...
   [mkdir] Skipping C:\herong\HelloAndroid\bin\classes because it ...
   [mkdir] Skipping C:\herong\HelloAndroid\bin\dexedLibs because i...
    [echo] ----------
    [echo] Resolving Dependencies for HelloAndroid...
[dependency] Library dependencies:
[dependency] No Libraries
[dependency]
[dependency] ------------------
    [echo] ----------
    [echo] Building Libraries with 'debug'...
  [subant] No sub-builds to iterate on

-code-gen:
[mergemanifest] Found Deleted Target File
[mergemanifest] Merging AndroidManifest files into one.
[mergemanifest] Manifest merger disabled. Using project manifest only.
    [echo] Handling aidl files...
```

```
    [aidl] No AIDL files to compile.
    [echo] ----------
    [echo] Handling RenderScript files...
    [echo] ----------
    [echo] Handling Resources...
Property "android.library" has not been set
    [aapt] Found Deleted Target File
    [aapt] Generating resource IDs...
    [aapt] Current OS is Windows 7
    [aapt] Executing
'C:\local\android-sdk-windows\build-tools\22.0.1\aapt.exe'
with arguments:
    [aapt] 'package'
    [aapt] '-f'
    [aapt] '-m'
    [aapt] '-0'
    [aapt] 'apk'
    [aapt] '-M'
    [aapt] 'C:\herong\HelloAndroid\bin\AndroidManifest.xml'
    [aapt] '-S'
    [aapt] 'C:\herong\HelloAndroid\bin\res'
    [aapt] '-S'
    [aapt] 'C:\herong\HelloAndroid\res'
    [aapt] '-I'
 [aapt] 'C:\local\android-sdk-windows\platforms\android-22\android.jar'
    [aapt] '-J'
    [aapt] 'C:\herong\HelloAndroid\gen'
    [aapt] '--generate-dependencies'
    [aapt] '-G'
    [aapt] 'C:\herong\HelloAndroid\bin\proguard.txt'
    [aapt]
    [aapt] The ' characters around the executable and arguments are
    [aapt] not part of the command.
    [echo] ----------
    [echo] Handling BuildConfig class...
[buildconfig] No need to generate new BuildConfig.
```

```
-pre-compile:

-compile:
    [javac] com\herongyang\HelloAndroid.java omitted as
C:\herong\HelloAndroid\bin\classes\com\herongyang\HelloAndroid.cla...
    [javac] C:\herong\HelloAndroid\gen\R.java.d skipped - don't kn...
    [javac] com\herongyang\BuildConfig.java omitted as
C:\herong\HelloAndroid\bin\classes\com\herongyang\BuildConfig.clas...
    [javac] com\herongyang\R.java added as com\herongyang\R.class ...
[javac] Compiling 1 source file to C:\herong\HelloAndroid\bin\classes
    [javac] Using modern compiler
    [javac] Compilation arguments:
    [javac] '-d'
    [javac] 'C:\herong\HelloAndroid\bin\classes'
    [javac] '-classpath'
    [javac] 'C:\herong\HelloAndroid\bin\classes'
    [javac] '-sourcepath'
    [javac] 'C:\herong\HelloAndroid\src;C:\herong\HelloAndroid\gen'
    [javac] '-target'
    [javac] '1.5'
    [javac] '-bootclasspath'
[javac] 'C:\local\android-sdk-windows\platforms\android-22\android.jar'
    [javac] '-encoding'
    [javac] 'UTF-8'
    [javac] '-g'
    [javac] '-source'
    [javac] '1.5'
    [javac]
    [javac] The ' characters around the executable and arguments are
    [javac] not part of the command.
    [javac] File to be compiled:
    [javac]     C:\herong\HelloAndroid\gen\com\herongyang\R.java

-post-compile:

-obfuscate:
```

```
-dex:
      [dex] input: C:\herong\HelloAndroid\bin\classes
      [dex] Found Deleted Target File
      [dex] Converting compiled files and external libraries into
            C:\herong\HelloAndroid\bin\classes.dex...
       [dx] Current OS is Windows 7
       [dx] Executing
'C:\local\android-sdk-windows\build-tools\22.0.1\dx.bat'
with arguments:
       [dx] '--dex'
       [dx] '--output'
       [dx] 'C:\herong\HelloAndroid\bin\classes.dex'
       [dx] 'C:\herong\HelloAndroid\bin\classes'
       [dx]
       [dx] The ' characters around the executable and arguments are
       [dx] not part of the command.


-crunch:
   [crunch] Current OS is Windows 7
   [crunch] Executing
'C:\local\android-sdk-windows\build-tools\22.0.1\aapt.exe'
with arguments:
   [crunch] 'crunch'
   [crunch] '-v'
   [crunch] '-S'
   [crunch] 'C:\herong\HelloAndroid\res'
   [crunch] '-C'
   [crunch] 'C:\herong\HelloAndroid\bin\res'
   [crunch]
   [crunch] The ' characters around the executable and arguments are
   [crunch] not part of the command.
   [crunch] Crunching PNG Files in source dir:
            C:\herong\HelloAndroid\res
   [crunch] To destination dir: C:\herong\HelloAndroid\bin\res
   [crunch] Crunched 0 PNG files to update cache


-package-resources:
```

```
     [aapt] Found Deleted Target File
     [aapt] Creating full resource package...
     [aapt] Current OS is Windows 7
     [aapt] Executing
'C:\local\android-sdk-windows\build-tools\22.0.1\aapt.exe'
with arguments:
     [aapt] 'package'
     [aapt] '--no-crunch'
     [aapt] '-f'
     [aapt] '--debug-mode'
     [aapt] '-0'
     [aapt] 'apk'
     [aapt] '-M'
     [aapt] 'C:\herong\HelloAndroid\bin\AndroidManifest.xml'
     [aapt] '-S'
     [aapt] 'C:\herong\HelloAndroid\bin\res'
     [aapt] '-S'
     [aapt] 'C:\herong\HelloAndroid\res'
     [aapt] '-I'
[aapt] 'C:\local\android-sdk-windows\platforms\android-22\android.jar'
     [aapt] '-F'
     [aapt] 'C:\herong\HelloAndroid\bin\HelloAndroid.ap_'
     [aapt] '--generate-dependencies'
     [aapt]
     [aapt] The ' characters around the executable and arguments are
     [aapt] not part of the command.

-package:
[apkbuilder] Found Deleted Target File
[apkbuilder] Creating HelloAndroid-debug-unaligned.apk and signing it
             with a debug key...

-post-package:

-do-debug:
 [zipalign] Running zip align on final apk...
[zip-align] Current OS is Windows 7
```

```
[zip-align] Executing
'C:\local\android-sdk-windows\build-tools\22.0.1\zipalign.exe'
with arguments:
[zip-align] '-f'
[zip-align] '4'
[zip-align]
'C:\herong\HelloAndroid\bin\HelloAndroid-debug-unaligned.apk'
[zip-align] 'C:\herong\HelloAndroid\bin\HelloAndroid-debug.apk'
[zip-align]
[zip-align] The ' characters around the executable and arguments are
[zip-align] not part of the command.
      [echo] Debug Package:
            C:\herong\HelloAndroid\bin\HelloAndroid-debug.apk
[propertyfile] Updating property file:
            C:\herong\HelloAndroid\bin\build.prop

-post-build:

debug:

BUILD SUCCESSFUL
Total time: 2 seconds
```

Wow! I can see more useful information in the output now:

- "aapt package" command is used in the resource code generation step. Command options and arguments are clearly printed out in the output. We can actually try it yourself without use "ant".

- Command options and arguments of "javac" command are also printed in the output for the Java compilation step.

- The "dex" tool is actually invoked from the dx.bat batch file for the byte code conversion step.

- The "aapt crunch" tool is actually used in the packaging step.

- There are no details about the "apkbuilder" in package signing step.

- Command options and arguments of "zipalign" command are also printed in the output for the package optimization step.

Output of "ant -verbose debug" - Android SDK R17

This section describes the output of the 'ant -verbose debug' command, which provides more details how each of 'aidl', 'aapt', 'javac', 'dex', 'apkbuilder' and 'zipalign' tools are invoked in the Ant build process in Android SDK R17.

The output of "ant -verbose debug" command on the HelloAndroid project in Android SDK R17 is listed below as a reference:

```
C:\herong\HelloAndroid>\local\apache-ant-1.8.3\bin\ant -verbose debug


Apache Ant(TM) version 1.8.3 compiled on February 26 2012
Trying the default build file: build.xml
Buildfile: C:\herong\HelloAndroid\build.xml
Detected Java version: 1.7 in: C:\Progra~1\Java\jdk1.7.0_03\jr
Detected OS: Windows 7
parsing buildfile C:\herong\HelloAndroid\build.xml with URI = file...
Project base dir set to: C:\herong\HelloAndroid
parsing buildfile jar:file:/C:/local/apache-ant-1.8.3/lib/ant.jar!...
 [property] Loading C:\herong\HelloAndroid\local.properties
 [property] Loading C:\herong\HelloAndroid\ant.properties
Importing file C:\herong\HelloAndroid\custom_rules.xml from C:\her...
Cannot find C:\herong\HelloAndroid\custom_rules.xml imported from ...
Importing file C:\local\android-sdk-windows\tools\ant\build.xml fr...
Overriding previous definition of reference to ant.projectHelper
parsing buildfile C:\local\android-sdk-windows\tools\ant\build.xml...
Property "key.store" has not been set
 [macrodef] creating macro  do-only-if-not-library
 [macrodef] creating macro  do-only-if-manifest-hasCode
 [macrodef] creating macro  dex-helper
 [macrodef] creating macro  package-helper
 [macrodef] creating macro  zipalign-helper
 [macrodef] creating macro  run-tests-helper
 [macrodef] creating macro  record-build-key
 [macrodef] creating macro  record-build-info
 [macrodef] creating macro  uninstall-helper
```

```
Overriding previous definition of reference to ant.projectHelper
Build sequence for target(s) `debug' is [-set-mode-check, -set-deb...
Complete build sequence is [-set-mode-check, -set-debug-files, -se...


-set-mode-check:


-set-debug-files:


-set-debug-mode:


-debug-obfuscation-check:


-setup:
     [echo] Creating output directories if needed...
    [mkdir] Skipping C:\herong\HelloAndroid\res because it already...
    [mkdir] Skipping C:\herong\HelloAndroid\libs because it alread...
    [mkdir] Created dir: C:\herong\HelloAndroid\bin
    [mkdir] Created dir: C:\herong\HelloAndroid\bin\res
     [echo] Gathering info for HelloAndroid...
    [setup] Android SDK Tools Revision 17
    [setup] Project Target: Google APIs
    [setup] Vendor: Google Inc.
    [setup] Platform Version: 4.0.3
    [setup] API level: 15
    [setup]
    [setup] ------------------
    [setup] Resolving library dependencies:
    [setup] No library dependencies.
    [setup]
    [setup] ------------------
    [setup] API<=15: Adding annotations.jar to the classpath.
    [setup]
    [setup] ------------------
    [setup] WARNING: No minSdkVersion value set. Application will ...

-build-setup:
  [property] Loading C:\herong\HelloAndroid\bin\build.prop
```

```
 [property] Unable to find property file: C:\herong\HelloAndroid\b...
    [mkdir] Created dir: C:\herong\HelloAndroid\gen
    [mkdir] Created dir: C:\herong\HelloAndroid\bin\classes


-pre-build:


-code-gen:
     [echo] ----------
     [echo] Handling aidl files...
     [aidl] No AIDL files to compile.
     [echo] ----------
     [echo] Handling RenderScript files...
[renderscript] No RenderScript files to compile.
     [echo] ----------
     [echo] Handling Resources...
Property "android.library" has not been set
     [aapt] Generating resource IDs...
     [aapt] Current OS is Windows 7
     [aapt] Executing \
'C:\local\android-sdk-windows\platform-tools\aapt.exe' with arguments:
     [aapt] 'package'
     [aapt] '-f'
     [aapt] '-m'
     [aapt] '-M'
     [aapt] 'C:\herong\HelloAndroid\AndroidManifest.xml'
     [aapt] '-S'
     [aapt] 'C:\herong\HelloAndroid\bin\res'
     [aapt] '-S'
     [aapt] 'C:\herong\HelloAndroid\res'
     [aapt] '-I'
     [aapt] \
'C:\local\android-sdk-windows\platforms\android-15\android.jar'
     [aapt] '-J'
     [aapt] 'C:\herong\HelloAndroid\gen'
     [aapt] '--generate-dependencies'
     [aapt]
     [aapt] The ' characters around the executable and arguments are
```

```
        [aapt] not part of the command.
        [echo] ----------
        [echo] Handling BuildConfig class...
[buildconfig] Generating BuildConfig class.


-pre-compile:


-compile:
Property "tested.project.absolute.dir" has not been set
Property "tested.project.absolute.dir" has not been set
       [javac] com\herongyang\HelloAndroid.java added as com\herongya...
       [javac] C:\herong\HelloAndroid\gen\R.java.d skipped - don't kn...
       [javac] com\herongyang\BuildConfig.java added as com\herongyan...
       [javac] com\herongyang\R.java added as com\herongyang\R.class ...
       [javac] Compiling 3 source files to \
C:\herong\HelloAndroid\bin\classes
       [javac] Using modern compiler
       [javac] Compilation arguments:
       [javac] '-d'
       [javac] 'C:\herong\HelloAndroid\bin\classes'
       [javac] '-classpath'
       [javac] 'C:\herong\HelloAndroid\bin\classes; \
C:\herong\HelloAndroid; \
C:\local\android-sdk-windows\tools\support\annotations.jar'
       [javac] '-sourcepath'
       [javac] 'C:\herong\HelloAndroid\src;C:\herong\HelloAndroid\gen'
       [javac] '-target'
       [javac] '1.5'
       [javac] '-bootclasspath'
       [javac] 'C:\local\android-sdk-windows\platforms\android-15\and...
       [javac] '-encoding'
       [javac] 'UTF-8'
       [javac] '-g'
       [javac] '-source'
       [javac] '1.5'
       [javac]
       [javac] The ' characters around the executable and arguments are
```

```
    [javac] not part of the command.
    [javac] Files to be compiled:
    [javac] \herong\HelloAndroid\src\com\herongyang\HelloAndroid.java
    [javac] \herong\HelloAndroid\gen\com\herongyang\BuildConfig.java
    [javac] \herong\HelloAndroid\gen\com\herongyang\R.java


-post-compile:


-obfuscate:


-dex:
[dex] Converting compiled files and external libraries into \
C:\herong\HelloAndroid\bin\classes.dex...
 [dx] Current OS is Windows 7
 [dx] Executing \
'C:\local\android-sdk-windows\platform-tools\dx.bat' with arguments:
 [dx] '--dex'
 [dx] '--output'
 [dx] 'C:\herong\HelloAndroid\bin\classes.dex'
 [dx] 'C:\herong\HelloAndroid\bin\classes'
 [dx] 'C:\local\android-sdk-windows\tools\support\annotations.jar'
 [dx]
 [dx] The ' characters around the executable and arguments are
 [dx] not part of the command.


-crunch:
   [crunch] Current OS is Windows 7
   [crunch] Executing \
'C:\local\android-sdk-windows\platform-tools\aapt.exe' with arguments:
   [crunch] 'crunch'
   [crunch] '-v'
   [crunch] '-S'
   [crunch] 'C:\herong\HelloAndroid\res'
   [crunch] '-C'
   [crunch] 'C:\herong\HelloAndroid\bin\res'
   [crunch]
   [crunch] The ' characters around the executable and arguments are
```

```
    [crunch] not part of the command.
    [crunch] Crunching PNG Files in source dir: \
C:\herong\HelloAndroid\res
    [crunch] To destination dir: C:\herong\HelloAndroid\bin\res
    [crunch] Processing image to cache: \
C:\herong\HelloAndroid\res\drawable-hdpi\ic_launcher.png => \
C:\herong\HelloAndroid\bin\res\drawable-hdpi\ic_launcher.png
    [crunch]    (processed image to cache entry C:\herong\HelloAndro...
    [crunch] Processing image to cache: \
C:\herong\HelloAndroid\res\drawable-ldpi\ic_launcher.png => \
C:\herong\HelloAndroid\bin\res\drawable-ldpi\ic_launcher.png
    [crunch]    (processed image to cache entry C:\herong\HelloAndro...
    [crunch] Processing image to cache: \
C:\herong\HelloAndroid\res\drawable-mdpi\ic_launcher.png => \
C:\herong\HelloAndroid\bin\res\drawable-mdpi\ic_launcher.png
    [crunch]    (processed image to cache entry C:\herong\HelloAndro...
    [crunch] Crunched 3 PNG files to update cache

-package-resources:
[aapt] Creating full resource package...
[aapt] Current OS is Windows 7
[aapt] Executing \
'C:\local\android-sdk-windows\platform-tools\aapt.exe' with arguments:
[aapt] 'package'
[aapt] '--no-crunch'
[aapt] '-f'
[aapt] '--debug-mode'
[aapt] '-M'
[aapt] 'C:\herong\HelloAndroid\AndroidManifest.xml'
[aapt] '-S'
[aapt] 'C:\herong\HelloAndroid\bin\res'
[aapt] '-S'
[aapt] 'C:\herong\HelloAndroid\res'
[aapt] '-I'
[aapt] 'C:\local\android-sdk-windows\platforms\android-15\android.jar'
[aapt] '-F'
[aapt] 'C:\herong\HelloAndroid\bin\HelloAndroid.ap_'
```

```
[aapt] '--generate-dependencies'
[aapt]
[aapt] The ' characters around the executable and arguments are
[aapt] not part of the command.


-package:
[apkbuilder] Current build type is different than previous build: \
forced apkbuilder run.
[apkbuilder] Creating HelloAndroid-debug-unaligned.apk and signing \
it with a debug key...


-post-package:


-do-debug:
 [zipalign] Running zip align on final apk...
[zip-align] Current OS is Windows 7
[zip-align] Executing \
'C:\local\android-sdk-windows\tools\zipalign.exe' with arguments:
[zip-align] '-f'
[zip-align] '4'
[zip-align] \
'C:\herong\HelloAndroid\bin\HelloAndroid-debug-unaligned.apk'
[zip-align] 'C:\herong\HelloAndroid\bin\HelloAndroid-debug.apk'
[zip-align]
[zip-align] The ' characters around the executable and arguments are
[zip-align] not part of the command.
    [echo] Debug Package: \
C:\herong\HelloAndroid\bin\HelloAndroid-debug.apk
[propertyfile] Creating new property file: \
C:\herong\HelloAndroid\bin\build.prop
[propertyfile] Updating property file: \
C:\herong\HelloAndroid\bin\build.prop
[propertyfile] Updating property file: \
C:\herong\HelloAndroid\bin\build.prop
[propertyfile] Updating property file: \
C:\herong\HelloAndroid\bin\build.prop
```

```
-post-build:


debug:


BUILD SUCCESSFUL
Total time: 4 seconds
```

"aapt" - Android Asset Packaging Tool

*This section describes 'aapt', the Android Asset Packaging Tool, which can be used to list,
add and remove files in an APK file, package resources, crunching PNG files, etc.*

Based on the "ant -verbose debug" output, "aapt package" is the tool used by Ant to do
resource code generation.

If you run the "aapt" command with no argument, you will get the command usage
description:

```
C:\herong\HelloAndroid>\local\android-sdk-windows\platform-tools\aapt


Android Asset Packaging Tool


Usage:
aapt l[ist] [-v] [-a] file.{zip,jar,apk}
  List contents of Zip-compatible archive.


aapt d[ump] [--values] WHAT file.{apk} [asset [asset ...]]
  badging         Print the label and icon for the app declared in APK.
  permissions     Print the permissions from the APK.
  resources       Print the resource table from the APK.
  configurations  Print the configurations in the APK.
  xmltree         Print the compiled xmls in the given assets.
  xmlstrings      Print the strings of the given compiled xml assets.


aapt p[ackage] [-d][-f][-m][-u][-v][-x][-z][-M AndroidManifest.xml]
  [-0 extension [-0 extension ...]] [-g tolerance] [-j jarfile]
```

```
[--debug-mode] [--min-sdk-version VAL] [--target-sdk-version VAL]
[--app-version VAL] [--app-version-name TEXT] [--custom-package VAL]
[--rename-manifest-package PACKAGE]
[--rename-instrumentation-target-package PACKAGE]
[--utf16] [--auto-add-overlay]
[--max-res-version VAL]
[-I base-package [-I base-package ...]]
[-A asset-source-dir]  [-G class-list-file]
[-P public-definitions-file]
[-S resource-sources [-S resource-sources ...]]
[-F apk-file] [-J R-file-dir]
[--product product1,product2,...]
[-c CONFIGS] [--preferred-configurations CONFIGS]
[-o]
[raw-files-dir [raw-files-dir] ...]


Package the android resources.  It will read assets and resources
that are supplied with the -M -A -S or raw-files-dir arguments.
The -J -P -F and -R options control which files are output.

aapt r[emove] [-v] file.{zip,jar,apk} file1 [file2 ...]
  Delete specified files from Zip-compatible archive.


aapt a[dd] [-v] file.{zip,jar,apk} file1 [file2 ...]
  Add specified files to Zip-compatible archive.


aapt c[runch] [-v] -S resource-sources ... -C output-folder ...
  Do PNG preprocessing and store the results in output folder.


aapt v[ersion]
  Print program version.


Modifiers:
  -a print Android-specific data (resources, manifest) when listing
  -c specify which configurations to include.  The default is all
     configurations.  The value of the parameter should be a comma
     separated list of configuration values.  Locales should be
```

```
    specified as either a language or language-region pair.
    Some examples:
        en
        port,en
        port,land,en_US
    If you put the special locale, zz_ZZ on the list, it will perform
    pseudolocalization on the default locale, modifying all of the
    strings so you can look for strings that missed the
    internationalization process.  For example:
        port,land,zz_ZZ
-d one or more device assets to include, separated by commas
-f force overwrite of existing files
-g specify a pixel tolerance to force images to grayscale, default 0
-j specify a jar or zip file containing classes to include
-k junk path of file(s) added
-m make package directories under location specified by -J
-o create overlay package (ie only resources; expects
    <overlay-package> in manifest)
-u update existing packages (add new, replace older, remove deleted
    files)
-v verbose output
-x create extending (non-application) resource IDs
-z require localization of resource attributes marked with
    localization="suggested"
-A additional directory in which to find raw asset files
-G A file to output proguard options into.
-F specify the apk file to output
-I add an existing package to base include set
-J specify where to output R.java resource constant definitions
-M specify full path to AndroidManifest.xml to include in zip
-P specify where to output public resource definitions
-S directory in which to find resources.  Multiple directories will
    be scanned and the first match found (left to right) will take
    precedence.
-0 specifies an additional extension for which such files will not
    be stored compressed in the .apk.  An empty string means to not
    compress any files at all.
```

```
--debug-mode
    inserts android:debuggable="true" in to the application node of
    the manifest, making the application debuggable even on
    production devices.
--min-sdk-version
    inserts android:minSdkVersion in to manifest.  If the version is
    7 or higher, the default encoding for resources will be in UTF-8.
--target-sdk-version
    inserts android:targetSdkVersion in to manifest.
--max-res-version
    ignores versioned resource directories above the given value.
--values
    when used with "dump resources" also includes resource values.
--version-code
    inserts android:versionCode in to manifest.
--version-name
    inserts android:versionName in to manifest.
--custom-package
    generates R.java into a different package.
--extra-packages
    generate R.java for libraries. Separate libraries with ':'.
--generate-dependencies
    generate dependency files in the same directories for R.java and
    resource package
--auto-add-overlay
    Automatically add resources that are only in overlays.
--preferred-configurations
    Like the -c option for filtering out unneeded configurations, but
    only expresses a preference.  If there is no resource available
    with the preferred configuration then it will not be stripped.
--rename-manifest-package
    Rewrite the manifest so that its package name is the package name
    given here.  Relative class names (for example .Foo) will be
    changed to absolute names with the old package so that the code
    does not need to change.
--rename-instrumentation-target-package
    Rewrite the manifest so that all of its instrumentation
```

```
          components target the given package.  Useful when used in
          conjunction with --rename-manifest-package to fix tests against
          a package that has been renamed.
     --product
          Specifies which variant to choose for strings that have
          product variants
     --utf16
          changes default encoding for resources to UTF-16.  Only useful
          when API level is set to 7 or higher where the default encoding
          is UTF-8.
     --non-constant-id
          Make the resources ID non constant. This is required to make an R
          java class that does not contain the final value but is used to
          make reusable compiled libraries that need to access resources.
```

Ok. "aapt" is a generic Android asset package tool that be used as:

- "aapt list" - Listing contents of a ZIP, JAR or APK file.

- "aapt dump" - Dumping specific information from an APK file.

- "aapt package" - Packaging Android resources.

- "aapt remove" - Removing files from a ZIP, JAR or APK file.

- "aapt add" - Adding files to a ZIP, JAR or APK file.

- "aapt crunch" - Crunching PNG files.

In the next tutorial, we will try to run an "aapt package" command example.

"aapt package" Command - Resource Code Generation

This section describes the 'aapt package' command to perform the resource code generation step in the Android project build process. The main output is the R.java file in the .\gen folder.

Looking at the output of "ant -verbose debug", I have created this "aapt package" command to perform the resource code generation step of the build process. This is how the command works on the HelloAndroid project:

```
C:\herong\HelloAndroid>
   \local\android-sdk-windows\build-tools\22.0.1\aapt
   package -v -f -m -M AndroidManifest.xml -S .\bin\res -S .\res
   -I C:\local\android-sdk-windows\platforms\android-22\android.jar
   -J .\gen --generate-dependencies

Configurations:
 (default)
 hdpi
 ldpi
 mdpi

Files:
  drawable\ic_launcher.png
    Src: (hdpi) .\res\drawable-hdpi\ic_launcher.png
    Src: (ldpi) .\res\drawable-ldpi\ic_launcher.png
    Src: (mdpi) .\res\drawable-mdpi\ic_launcher.png
  layout\main.xml
    Src: () .\res\layout\main.xml
  values\strings.xml
    Src: () .\res\values\strings.xml
  AndroidManifest.xml
    Src: () AndroidManifest.xml

Resource Dirs:
  Type drawable
    drawable\ic_launcher.png
      Src: (hdpi) .\res\drawable-hdpi\ic_launcher.png
      Src: (ldpi) .\res\drawable-ldpi\ic_launcher.png
      Src: (mdpi) .\res\drawable-mdpi\ic_launcher.png
  Type layout
    layout\main.xml
      Src: () .\res\layout\main.xml
  Type values
```

```
      values\strings.xml
        Src: () .\res\values\strings.xml
Including resources from package: \
C:\local\android-sdk-windows\platforms\android-15\android.jar
applyFileOverlay for drawable
trying overlaySet Key=ic_launcher.png
baseFile 0 has flavor ,,,,,,,,,,,hdpi,,,,,,,
baseFile 1 has flavor ,,,,,,,,,,,ldpi,,,,,,,
baseFile 2 has flavor ,,,,,,,,,,,mdpi,,,,,,,
overlayFile 0 has flavor ,,,,,,,,,,,hdpi,,,,,,,
overlayFile 1 has flavor ,,,,,,,,,,,ldpi,,,,,,,
overlayFile 2 has flavor ,,,,,,,,,,,mdpi,,,,,,,
found a match (0) for overlay file ic_launcher.png, \
for flavor ,,,,,,,,,,,hdpi,,,,,,,
found a match (1) for overlay file ic_launcher.png, \
for flavor ,,,,,,,,,,,ldpi,,,,,,,
found a match (2) for overlay file ic_launcher.png, \
for flavor ,,,,,,,,,,,mdpi,,,,,,,
applyFileOverlay for layout
applyFileOverlay for anim
applyFileOverlay for animator
applyFileOverlay for interpolator
applyFileOverlay for xml
applyFileOverlay for raw
applyFileOverlay for color
applyFileOverlay for menu
applyFileOverlay for mipmap
      (new resource id ic_launcher from \
      .\bin\res\drawable-hdpi\ic_launcher.png)
      (new resource id ic_launcher from \
      .\bin\res\drawable-ldpi\ic_launcher.png)
      (new resource id ic_launcher from \
      .\bin\res\drawable-mdpi\ic_launcher.png)
      (new resource id main from .\res\layout\main.xml)
    Writing symbols for class R.
```

I think my "aapt" package command is working. The main output is the .\gen\com \herongyang\R.java file. What do you think?

"javac" - Java Compilation Command

This section describes 'javac', the Java compilation command, provided from the JDK (Java Development Kit) package.

The next tool used in the "ant -verbose debug" command is the "javac" tool, which comes from JDK (Java Development Kit).

If you are new to the "javac" tool, you can run it with "-help" option to get some usage information:

```
C:\herong\HelloAndroid>\Progra~1\Java\jdk1.8.0_45\bin\javac -help


Usage: javac <options> <source files>
where possible options include:
-g                      Generate all debugging info
-g:none                 Generate no debugging info
-g:{lines,vars,source} Generate only some debugging info
-nowarn                 Generate no warnings
-verbose                Output messages about what the compiler is \
                        doing
-deprecation            Output source locations where deprecated APIs \
                        are used
-classpath <path>       Specify where to find user class files and \
                        annotation processors
-cp <path>              Same as -classpath
-sourcepath <path>      Specify where to find input source files
-bootclasspath <path>   Override location of bootstrap class files
-extdirs <dirs>         Override location of installed extensions
-endorseddirs <dirs>    Override location of endorsed standards path
-proc:{none,only}       Control whether annotation processing and/or \
                        compilation is done.
-processor <class1>[,<class2>,<class3>...] Names of the annotation \
                        processors to run; bypasses default discovery \
                        process
-processorpath <path>   Specify where to find annotation processors
-d <directory>          Specify where to place generated class files
```

```
-s <directory>          Specify where to place generated source files
-implicit:{none,class}  Specify whether or not to generate class files \
                        forimplicitly referenced files
-encoding <encoding>    Specify character encoding used by source files
-source <release>       Provide source compatibility with specified \
                        release
-target <release>       Generate class files for specific VM version
-version                Version information
-help                   Print a synopsis of standard options
-Akey[=value]           Options to pass to annotation processors
-X                      Print a synopsis of nonstandard options
-J<flag>                Pass <flag> directly to the runtime system
-Werror                 Terminate compilation if warnings occur
@<filename>             Read options and filenames from file
```

The "javac" command line used by the "ant -verbose debug" command should be like this:

```
C:\herong\HelloAndroid>\Progra~1\Java\jdk1.8.0_45\bin\javac
-sourcepath .\src;.\gen -d .\bin\classes -classpath .\bin\classes;.\;
\local\android-sdk-windows\tools\support\annotations.jar
-target 1.5 -source 1.5
-bootclasspath \local\android-sdk...\platforms\android-15\android.jar;
\local\android-sdk...\add-ons\addon-goo...-google-22\libs\effects.jar;
\local\android-sdk...\add-ons\addon-goo...-google-22\libs\usb.jar;
\local\android-sdk...\add-ons\addon-goo...google-22\libs\maps.jar
-encoding UTF-8 -g
```

You can test it yourself.

"dx.bat --dex" Command - Converting .class Files into .dex File

This section describes the 'dx.bat --dex' command that can be used to convert Java byte code (.class) files into a Dalvik executable (.dex) file.

The next tool used in the "ant -verbose debug" command is the "dex" tool, which converts Java byte code into a .dex (Dalvik Executable) file.

Looking at the output of "ant -verbose debug", I have created this "dx.bat --dex" command to perform the byte code conversion step of the build process. The dx.bat calls a Java application to do the actual conversion work. This is how the command works on the HelloAndroid project:

```
C:\herong\HelloAndroid>
    \local\android-sdk-windows\build-tools\22.0.1\dx.bat --dex
    --verbose --output .\bin\classes.dex    .\bin\classes

processing ...\bin\classes\com\herongyang\BuildConfig.class...
processing ...\bin\classes\com\herongyang\HelloAndroid.class...
processing ...\bin\classes\com\herongyang\R$attr.class...
processing ...\bin\classes\com\herongyang\R$drawable.class...
processing ...\bin\classes\com\herongyang\R$layout.class...
processing ...\bin\classes\com\herongyang\R$string.class...
processing ...\bin\classes\com\herongyang\R.class...

C:\herong>dir \herong\HelloAndroid\bin\classes.dex

    2,328 classes.dex
```

I think the command worked correctly. All *.class files are converted into a single .dex file: classes.dex.

"apkbuilder" Command - Packaging and Signing .apk File

This section describes that the 'apkbuilder' tool is used to package the .dex file with resource files into a .apk file and sign the .apk file. But no details on how the 'apkbuilder' tool is invoked.

When builder the debug version of an Android application, the "ant -verbose debug" command used the "apkbuilder" tool. It only the following 2 lines in the output:

```
-package:
[apkbuilder] Current build type is different than previous build:
             forced apkbuilder run.
[apkbuilder] Creating HelloAndroid-debug-unaligned.apk and signing
             it with a debug key...
```

So I have no clue on how the "apkbuilder" tool is invoked to package the .dex file with resource files into a single .apk file and how the .apk file is signed.

"zipalign" Command - Aligning File Locations in .apk Package

This section describes the 'zipalign' tool for aligning file locations in an .apk package (really a .zip file) to decreases memory usage when running the application.

The last tool used in the "ant -verbose debug" command is the "zipalign" tool, which optimize the .apk package file by aligning file locations in the .apk package to decreases memory usage when running the application.

Looking at the output of "ant -verbose debug", I have created this "zipalign" command to perform the package optimization step of the build process. This is how the command works on the HelloAndroid project:

```
C:\herong\\HelloAndroid>
    \local\android-sdk-windows\build-tools\22.0.1\zipalign
    -f -v 4 .\bin\HelloAndroid-debug-unaligned.apk
    .\bin\HelloAndroid-debug.apk

Verifying alignment of .\bin\HelloAndroid-debug.apk (4)...
      53 res/layout/main.xml (OK - compressed)
     766 AndroidManifest.xml (OK - compressed)
    1352 resources.arsc (OK)
    2824 res/drawable-hdpi/ic_launcher.png (OK)
    6856 res/drawable-ldpi/ic_launcher.png (OK)
    8456 res/drawable-mdpi/ic_launcher.png (OK)
   10697 classes.dex (OK - compressed)
```

```
   12241 META-INF/MANIFEST.MF (OK - compressed)
   12671 META-INF/CERT.SF (OK - compressed)
   13136 META-INF/CERT.RSA (OK - compressed)
 Verification successful
```

Okay. The "zipalign" command worked. There are 10 files in the .apk package file: .\bin
\HelloAndroid-debug.apk.

"aapt dump" Command - Printing Contents of .apk Package

This section describes the 'aapt dump' command for providing the list of all files, the resource table and the manifest of an .apk package file.

After figuring out roughly how the "ant debug" build process works. Now I am interested to review the content of the final .apk package file: .\bin\HelloAndroid-debug.apk using the "aapt list" command:

```
C:\herong\HelloAndroid>
   \local\android-sdk-windows\build-tools\\22.0.1\aapt
   list -a bin\HelloAndroid-debug.apk

AndroidManifest.xml
res/drawable-hdpi-v4/ic_launcher.png
res/drawable-ldpi-v4/ic_launcher.png
res/drawable-mdpi-v4/ic_launcher.png
res/drawable-xhdpi-v4/ic_launcher.png
res/layout/main.xml
resources.arsc
classes.dex
META-INF/MANIFEST.MF
META-INF/CERT.SF
META-INF/CERT.RSA

Resource table:
Package Groups (1)
```

```
Package Group 0 id=0x7f packageCount=1 name=com.herongyang
   Package 0 id=0x7f name=com.herongyang
      type 1 configCount=4 entryCount=1
         spec resource 0x7f020000 com.herongyang:drawable/ic_launcher:...
         config ldpi-v4:
            resource 0x7f020000 com.herongyang:drawable/ic_launcher: t=...
         config mdpi-v4:
            resource 0x7f020000 com.herongyang:drawable/ic_launcher: t=...
         config hdpi-v4:
            resource 0x7f020000 com.herongyang:drawable/ic_launcher: t=...
         config xhdpi-v4:
            resource 0x7f020000 com.herongyang:drawable/ic_launcher: t=...
      type 2 configCount=1 entryCount=1
         spec resource 0x7f030000 com.herongyang:layout/main: flags=0x...
         config (default):
            resource 0x7f030000 com.herongyang:layout/main: t=0x03 d=0x...
      type 3 configCount=1 entryCount=1
         spec resource 0x7f040000 com.herongyang:string/app_name: flag...
         config (default):
            resource 0x7f040000 com.herongyang:string/app_name: t=0x03 ...
(s=0x0008 r=0x00)


Android manifest:
N: android=http://schemas.android.com/apk/res/android
  E: manifest (line=2)
    A: android:versionCode(0x0101021b)=(type 0x10)0x1
    A: android:versionName(0x0101021c)="1.0" (Raw: "1.0")
    A: package="com.herongyang" (Raw: "com.herongyang")
    A: platformBuildVersionCode=(type 0x10)0x16 (Raw: "22")
    A: platformBuildVersionName="5.1.1-1819727" (Raw: "5.1.1-1819727")
    E: application (line=6)
      A: android:label(0x01010001)=@0x7f040000
      A: android:icon(0x01010002)=@0x7f020000
      A: android:debuggable(0x0101000f)=(type 0x12)0xffffffff
      E: activity (line=7)
        A: android:label(0x01010001)=@0x7f040000
        A: android:name(0x01010003)="HelloAndroid" (Raw: "HelloAndroid")
```

```
      E: intent-filter (line=9)
        E: action (line=10)
          A: android:name(0x01010003)="android.intent.action.MAIN"...
        E: category (line=11)
          A: android:name(0x01010003)="android.intent.category.LAU...
```

Pretty good. "aapt dump" command provides me the list of all files in the package. It also provides me the resource table and the manifest of the package.

META-INF Files - Digests, Signature and Certificate

This section describes META-INF files in an .apk package file: MANIFEST.MF - manifest file, CERT.SF - signature file and CERT.RSA - the real signature file with certificate.

In the previous tutorial, we learned that the debug package of an Android application is automatically signed by a debug key in the "ant debug" build process. Now I am interested to how signatures are stored in package file.

1. Copy the .apk file to a .zip file:

```
C:\herong\HelloAndroid>copy bin\HelloAndroid-debug.apk package.zip
        1 file(s) copied.
```

2. Unzip "package.zip" to \herong\package folder.

3. Open the manifest file, META-INF\MANIFEST.MF, in the package folder in a text editor. You will see a list of all files in the package with their SHA1 digests (Base64 encoded strings):

```
Manifest-Version: 1.0
Created-By: 1.0 (Android)

Name: res/layout/main.xml
SHA1-Digest: NXEzfMpms988J98yXEUXqh9u9ug=

Name: AndroidManifest.xml
SHA1-Digest: 0f22NLU8Ebm1krUUO0GjGIIl4zU=
```

```
Name: res/drawable-mdpi/ic_launcher.png
SHA1-Digest: 7Ft/Rirt+l/JRX2KjDREScdbCZk=


Name: res/drawable-hdpi/ic_launcher.png
SHA1-Digest: Vj/qhxk8ic8FE0/kT6E3vgRJ4mE=


Name: resources.arsc
SHA1-Digest: 5kllfCdPWbdy9w3CYz9lXYfN1Do=


Name: classes.dex
SHA1-Digest: ostS2N/xSK7OaaQ4m2rCAq8iD0k=


Name: res/drawable-ldpi/ic_launcher.png
SHA1-Digest: i7vxaosoiS+9HzKB7ZgIsXMYRLY=
```

4. Open the signature file, META-INF\CERT.SF, in the package folder in a text editor. You will see a list of all files in the package again with their SHA1 digests again. But this time, each digest is the digest of the 3-line entry of that file in the Manifest file.

```
Signature-Version: 1.0
Created-By: 1.0 (Android)
SHA1-Digest-Manifest: UOE6fu4Pq1ddGXiJC5iAOkOtDVI=


Name: res/layout/main.xml
SHA1-Digest: +IKkn6R+Vr90Oy+4cVnVwXvkqXw=


Name: AndroidManifest.xml
SHA1-Digest: 8GD9vp78dBfzFq7uRbunWZs2XjU=


Name: res/drawable-mdpi/ic_launcher.png
SHA1-Digest: zSBo0hBNc4K46aIFvlD4ZmQBHcg=


Name: res/drawable-hdpi/ic_launcher.png
SHA1-Digest: YuN8HjuH/csIGA1V8jxQw62DV0A=


Name: resources.arsc
SHA1-Digest: lU1eIHhOCyd3E+nBCgPiv27Vb+M=
```

```
Name: classes.dex
SHA1-Digest: k/Tdh4GY0wZKoL/g28iE7z3uGLI=


Name: res/layout/main_original.xml
SHA1-Digest: dD4LMOZORFmtPpAZwc0R48/FAik=


Name: res/drawable-ldpi/ic_launcher.png
SHA1-Digest: edY5GhthxxpZN3rJpWsoorrticI=
```

5. The real signature of the package is actually stored in the META-INF\CERT.RSA file in the package folder. The CERT.RSA also contains the certificate of the public key for you to verify the signature.

6. You can use the "keytool" command to view the certificate:

```
C:\herong\HelloAndroid>\Progra~1\Java\jdk1.7.0_03\bin\keytool \
    -printcert -file package\META-INF\CERT.RSA


Owner: CN=Android Debug, O=Android, C=US
Issuer: CN=Android Debug, O=Android, C=US
Serial number: 4427b9db
Valid from: Sun Mar 01 14:43:33 EDT 2012 until: \
    Tue Mar 25 14:43:33 EDT 2042
Certificate fingerprints:
        MD5:   47:F7:5B:83:5E:F0:19:08:15:7D:1B:80:67:96:9A:03
        SHA1: CA:59:3A:44:F5:08:D7:43:96:E2:EE:2C:10:91:0F:86:3C:...
        SHA256: BE:29:82:5E:4A:F6:81:D4:AA:E7:2E:D8:AB:66:B4:E2:7...
94:81:08:62:D9:AE:38:66:F9:66:1F
        Signature algorithm name: SHA256withRSA
        Version: 3


Extensions:

#1: ObjectId: 2.5.29.14 Criticality=false
SubjectKeyIdentifier [
KeyIdentifier [
0000: B4 41 2F 4A 00 AF 4B E1   2A A8 C6 E8 DA 55 13 FB  .A/J..K.*...
```

```
0010: 02 64 48 87                                          .dH.
    ]
    ]
```

As I expected, this certificate is a self-signed certificate, which can not be verified by any root certificate authorities. I guess for debugging purpose, this is good enough.

Building Your Own Web Browser

This chapter provides tutorial notes on the android.webkit.WebView class. Topics include building your own Web browser with the WebView class; setting INTERNET permission for the application; using WebViewClient subclass to interface with Web page rendering; saving Web pages as Web archive files.

Takeaways:

- android.webkit.WebView is a complex view class that allows you to build your own Web browser.

- INTERNET permission is needed if the application needs to access Internet.

- Callback methods can be implemented in a WebViewClient subclass to interface with the Web page rendering process.

- saveWebArchive() method can be used to same the Web content into a Web archive file.

- A Web archive file is an XML of Base64 encoded Web page resources.

android.webkit.WebView - Web Browser Base Class

This section provides a tutorial example on how to create an Android project to build your own Web browser using the android.webkit.WebView class. The first version failed with 'Webpage not available' error.

Android SDK offers a nice view class, android.webkit.WebView, that helps you to build your version of a Web browser. Here is my first version of AndroidWeb application:

Create AndroidWeb project with the "android create project" command:

```
C:\herong>\local\android-sdk-windows\tools\android create project \
   -k com.herongyang.web -a AndroidWeb -t 2 -p .\AndroidWeb
```

Edit the activity class Java code stored at \herong\AndroidWeb\src\com\herongyang \web\AndroidWeb.java:

```
/* AndroidWeb.java
 * Version 1.0 - Show Google home page
 * Copyright (c) 2015, HerongYang.com, All Rights Reserved.
 */
package com.herongyang.web;

import android.app.Activity;
import android.os.Bundle;
import android.webkit.WebView;
public class AndroidWeb extends Activity {
   @Override
   public void onCreate(Bundle savedInstanceState) {
      super.onCreate(savedInstanceState);

      WebView view = new WebView(this);
      view.loadUrl("http://www.google.com/");
      setContentView(view);
   }
}
```

Build the debug package and install it to the emulator using the "ant" command:

```
C:\herong\AndroidWeb>\local\apache-ant-1.8.3\bin\ant debug
```

```
C:\herong\AndroidWeb>\local\apache-ant-1.8.3\bin\ant installd
```

Run AndroidWeb on the emulator. Too bad. AndroidWeb 1.0 is not working. The following message is showing on the screen:

```
Webpage not available


The webpage at http://www.google.com/ could not be loaded because:


net:ERR_CACHE_MISS
```

AndroidWeb Webpage not available Error

The error is not very helpful. I will try to find the root cause in the next tutorial.

By the way, the same program running in Android SDK R17 gave the following error message:

```
Webpage not available


The webpage at http://www.google.com/ might be temporarily down or
it may have moved permanently to a new web address.


Suggestions:
   Make sure you have a data connection
   Reload this webpage later
```

```
Check the address you entered
```

AndroidWeb - My Own Web Browser

This section provides a tutorial example on how to make my own Web browser, AndroidWeb, to work. The INTERNET permission needs to added to the Android project manifest file.

To figure out what's wrong with my AndroidView 1.0, I looked at the log entries with the "adb logcat" command. Nothing is related to this error.

I went back to the Android SDK document, and found this information: *Because this application needs access to the Internet, you need to add the appropriate permissions to the Android manifest file. Open the AndroidManifest.xml file and add the following as a child of the <manifest> element: <uses-permission android:name="android.permission.INTERNET" />*

Okay. I modified the \herong\AndroidWeb\AndroidManifest.xml file to include the INTERNET permission line:

```
<?xml version="1.0" encoding="utf-8"?>
<!-- AndroidWeb_AndroidManifest.xml
  - Version 2.0 - Adding INTERNET permission
  - Copyright (c) 2015, HerongYang.com, All Rights Reserved.
-->
<manifest xmlns:android="http://schemas.android.com/apk/res/android"
    package="com.herongyang.web"
    android:versionCode="1"
    android:versionName="1.0">
    <application android:label="@string/app_name"
        android:icon="@drawable/ic_launcher">
        <activity android:name="AndroidWeb"
            android:label="@string/app_name">
            <intent-filter>
                <action android:name="android.intent.action.MAIN" />
                <category
                    android:name="android.intent.category.LAUNCHER" />
```

```
        </intent-filter>
     </activity>
   </application>
   <uses-permission android:name="android.permission.INTERNET" />
</manifest>
```

Rebuild the debug package, reinstall it to the emulator and run it. Google search home page is displayed!

AndroidWeb - My Own Web Browser

WebViewClient Subclass - Content Rendering Callbacks

This section provides a tutorial example on how to implement a subclass of android.webkit.WebViewClient with callback methods to interface with the rendering process of the WebView content.

In the next release of my AndroidWeb, I want to play with the android.webkit.WebViewClient class, which allows you to implement some callback methods to interface with the rendering process of the WebView content.

Key callback methods in android.webkit.WebViewClient class are:

- onFormResubmission(WebView view, Message dontResend, Message resend) - As the host application if the browser should resend data as the requested page was a result of a POST.

- onLoadResource(WebView view, String url) - Notify the host application that the WebView will load the resource specified by the given url.

- onPageFinished(WebView view, String url) - Notify the host application that a page has finished loading.

- onPageStarted(WebView view, String url, Bitmap favicon) - Notify the host application that a page has started loading.

- onReceivedError(WebView view, int errorCode, String description, String failingUrl) - Report an error to the host application.

To use WebViewClient, you need to:

- Implement a subclass of WebViewClient with your own version of callback methods.

- Create an object of your subclass.

- Assign the object to the WebView using the setWebViewClient() method before calling loadUrl().

Here is how I implemented my subclass of WebViewClient to write log entries to see how Web pages are loaded to WebView:

```
/* AndroidWeb.java
 * Version 3.0 - Adding a WebViewClient
 * Copyright (c) 2012, HerongYang.com, All Rights Reserved.
 */
package com.herongyang.web;

import android.app.Activity;
import android.os.Bundle;
import android.webkit.WebView;
import android.webkit.WebViewClient;
```

```
import android.content.Context;
import java.io.*;
import java.util.*;
public class AndroidWeb extends Activity {
    @Override
    public void onCreate(Bundle savedInstanceState) {
        super.onCreate(savedInstanceState);

        WebView view = new WebView(this);
        AndroidWebClient client = new AndroidWebClient();
        view.setWebViewClient(client);
        view.loadUrl("http://www.google.com/");
        setContentView(view);
    }
    private class AndroidWebClient extends WebViewClient {
        @Override
        public void onPageStarted(WebView view, String url,
            android.graphics.Bitmap favicon) {
            logLine(view, "onPageStarted() called: url = "+url);
        }
        public void onPageFinished(WebView view, String url) {
            logLine(view, "onPageFinished() called: url = "+url);
        }
        public void onLoadResource(WebView view, String url) {
            logLine(view, "onLoadResource() called: url = "+url);
        }
        public void logLine(WebView view, String msg) {
            try {
                FileOutputStream fos =
                    view.getContext()
                    .openFileOutput("Activity.log", Context.MODE_APPEND);
                OutputStreamWriter out = new OutputStreamWriter(fos);
                out.write((new Date()).toString()+": "+msg+"\n");
                out.close();
                fos.close();
            } catch (Exception e) {
                e.printStackTrace(System.err);
```

```
        }
      }
    }
  }
```

I also increased version values in AndroidManifest.xml.
android:versionCode="20150301" must be an integer acting like a build number.
android:versionName="3.0" is the string representing version of the application.

```xml
<?xml version="1.0" encoding="utf-8"?>
<!-- AndroidWeb_AndroidManifest.xml
  - Version 3.0 - Adding INTERNET permission
  - Copyright (c) 2015, HerongYang.com, All Rights Reserved.
-->
<manifest xmlns:android="http://schemas.android.com/apk/res/android"
    package="com.herongyang.web"
    android:versionCode="20150301"
    android:versionName="3.0">
    <application android:label="@string/app_name"
        android:icon="@drawable/ic_launcher">
        <activity android:name="AndroidWeb"
            android:label="@string/app_name">
            <intent-filter>
                <action android:name="android.intent.action.MAIN" />
                <category
                    android:name="android.intent.category.LAUNCHER" />
            </intent-filter>
        </activity>
    </application>
    <uses-permission android:name="android.permission.INTERNET" />
</manifest>
```

Rebuild the debug package, reinstall it to the emulator and run it. Google search home page is displayed again.

Copy the log file out of the emulator and view it:

```
C:\herong>\local\android-sdk-windows\platform-tools\adb \
    pull /data/data/com.herongyang.web/files/Activity.log Activity.log
```

```
C:\herong\AndroidWeb>type Activity.log
20:17:24 onPageStarted() called: url = http://www.google.com/
20:17:24 onLoadResource() called: url = http://www.google.com/
20:17:25 onPageStarted() called: url = https://www.google.com/?gws_...
20:17:27 onLoadResource() called: url = https://ssl.gstatic.com/gb/...
20:17:28 onLoadResource() called: url = https://ssl.gstatic.com/gb/...
20:17:29 onLoadResource() called: url = https://www.google.com/imag...
20:17:30 onPageFinished() called: url = https://www.google.com/?gws...
```

My WebViewClient subclass works! The log file tells me that:

- Callback methods are called in this order: onPageStarted(), onLoadResource(), ..., onPageFinished().

- Those resource URLs are strange to me. They look like Base64 encoded image files but have no remote server names.

saveWebArchive() Method - Saving Web Archive Files

This section provides a tutorial example on how to use the saveWebArchive() method to save Web page content in WebView to Web archive files in the application's files folder.

Now let me make the WebViewClient subclass more useful. In the onPageFinished() callback method, I want to save the Web page as a Web archive file using the saveWebArchive() method. Here is my AndroidWeb version 3.1:

```
/* AndroidWeb.java
 * Version 3.1 - Saving content as Web archive file
 * Copyright (c) 2015, HerongYang.com, All Rights Reserved.
 */
package com.herongyang.web;

import android.app.Activity;
import android.os.Bundle;
import android.webkit.WebView;
import android.webkit.WebViewClient;
```

```
import android.content.Context;
import java.io.*;
import java.util.*;
public class AndroidWeb extends Activity {
    @Override
    public void onCreate(Bundle savedInstanceState) {
        super.onCreate(savedInstanceState);

        WebView view = new WebView(this);
        AndroidWebClient client = new AndroidWebClient();
        view.setWebViewClient(client);
        view.loadUrl("http://www.google.com/");
        setContentView(view);
    }
    private class AndroidWebClient extends WebViewClient {
        @Override
        public void onPageStarted(WebView view, String url,
            android.graphics.Bitmap favicon) {
            logLine(view, "onPageStarted() called: url = "+url);
        }
        public void onPageFinished(WebView view, String url) {
            logLine(view, "onPageFinished() called: url = "+url);
            // view.saveWebArchive("Google.xml"); // Incorrect use
            view.saveWebArchive(getFilesDir().getAbsolutePath()
                + File.separator + System.currentTimeMillis()+".xml");
        }
        public void onLoadResource(WebView view, String url) {
            logLine(view, "onLoadResource() called: url = "+url);
        }
        public void logLine(WebView view, String msg) {
            try {
                FileOutputStream fos =
                    view.getContext()
                    .openFileOutput("Activity.log", Context.MODE_APPEND);
                OutputStreamWriter out = new OutputStreamWriter(fos);
                out.write((new Date()).toString()+": "+msg+"\n");
                out.close();
```

```
        fos.close();
     } catch (Exception e) {
        e.printStackTrace(System.err);
     }
  }
 }
}
```

Do you see the commented out line of view.saveWebArchive("Google.xml")? This will produce the following error in the main log buffer, because saveWebArchive() is expecting a full path name for the output file:

```
D/webcoreglue( 1301): saveWebArchive: Failed to initialize xml writer.
```

Rebuild the debug package, reinstall it to the emulator and run it. Google search home page is displayed again.

Enter "herongyang", search and select my Web site. Some Web archive files should be saved in the application "files" folder now.

```
C:\herong>\local\android-sdk-windows\platform-tools\adb shell
# ls -l /data/data/com.herongyang.web/files
ls -l /data/data/com.herongyang.web/files
-rw------- u0_a73   u0_a73   95072 20:26 1435501582525.xml
-rw------- u0_a73   u0_a73   62359 20:26 1435501590670.xml
-rw------- u0_a73   u0_a73   59273 20:26 1435501592254.xml
-rw------- u0_a73   u0_a73   14874 20:26 1435501596675.xml
-rw-rw---- u0_a73   u0_a73    2658 20:26 Activity.log
```

AndroidWeb version 3.1 is working! See next tutorial on how to open the Web archive .xml files.

Web Archive File - XML File of Base64 Encoded Data

This section provides a tutorial example on how to view contents of a Web archive file, which is really an XML file with Base64 encoded data.

In previous tutorials I use able to build my own Web browser, AndroidWeb, to visit Web sites and save page contents into Web archive files. In this tutorial, I want to spend some time to explore those Web archive files.

First copy AndroidWeb "files" folder from the emulator to my Windows file system:

```
C:\herong>\local\android-sdk-windows\platform-tools\adb
    pull /data/data/com.herongyang.web/files .\files

pull: building file list...
pull: /data/data/com.herongyang.web/files/Activity.log
    -> .\files/Activity.log
pull: /data/data/com.herongyang.web/files/1323772666133.xml
    -> .\files/1335017266133.xml
pull: /data/data/com.herongyang.web/files/1323772679558.xml
    -> .\files/1335017279558.xml
pull: /data/data/com.herongyang.web/files/1323772686866.xml
    -> .\files/1335017286866.xml
4 files pulled. 0 files skipped.
```

I have 3 Web archive .xml files, because I visited 3 Web pages in the previous tutorial:

- 1323772666133.xml - Web archive file for the Google search home page.

- 1323772679558.xml - Web archive file for the Google search result page.

- 1323772686866.xml - Web archive file for my home page.

Open 1323772666133.xml in a Web browser, I see this XML file structure:

```
<?xml version="1.0" ?>
<Archive>
 <mainResource>
  <ArchiveResource>
   <url>aHR0cDovL3d3dy5nb29nbGUuY29tLw==</url>
   <mimeType>dGV4dC9odG1s</mimeType>
   <textEncoding>dXRmLTg=</textEncoding>
   <frameName />
   <data>PCFkb2N0eXBlIGh0bWw+PGh0bWwgbWFuaWZlc3Q9Imh0dHA6Ly...</data>
  </ArchiveResource>
 </mainResource>
```

```
<subresources>
 <ArchiveResource>
  <url>ZGF0YTppbWFnZS9wbmc7YmFzZTY0LGlWQk9SdzBLR2dvQUFBQU5T...</url>
  <mimeType>aW1hZ2UvcG5n</mimeType>
  <textEncoding>VVMtQVNDSUk=</textEncoding>
  <frameName />
  <data>iVBORw0KGgoAAAANSUhEUgAAAFQAAABUCAYAAAAcaxDBAAAABH...</data>
 </ArchiveResource>
 <ArchiveResource>
  <url>ZGF0YTppbWFnZS9wbmc7YmFzZTY0LGlWQk9SdzBLR2dvQUFBQU5T...</url>
  <mimeType>aW1hZ2UvcG5n</mimeType>
  <textEncoding>VVMtQVNDSUk=</textEncoding>
  <frameName />
  <data>iVBORw0KGgoAAAANSUhEUgAAAFQAAABUCAYAAAAcaxDBAAAABH...</data>
 </ArchiveResource>
 <ArchiveResource>
  <url>ZGF0YTppbWFnZS9naWY7YmFzZTY0LFIwbEdPRPRGBZUFLSUhB...</url>
  <mimeType>aW1hZ2UvZ2lm</mimeType>
  <textEncoding>VVMtQVNDSUk=</textEncoding>
  <frameName />
  <data>R0lGODlhGAAeAKIHAOvr69DQ0N3d3b+/v8DAwP////Pz8////y...</data>
 </ArchiveResource>
 <ArchiveResource>
  <url>ZGF0YTppbWFnZS9wbmc7YmFzZTY0LGlWQk9SdzBLR2dvQUFBQU5T...</url>
  <mimeType>aW1hZ2UvcG5n</mimeType>
  <textEncoding>VVMtQVNDSUk=</textEncoding>
  <frameName />
  <data>iVBORw0KGgoAAAANSUhEUgAAAFQAAABUCAYAAAAcaxDBAAAABH...</data>
 </ArchiveResource>
 <ArchiveResource>
  <url>ZGF0YTppbWFnZS9wbmc7YmFzZTY0LGlWQk9SdzBLR2dvQUFBQU5T...</url>
  <mimeType>aW1hZ2UvcG5n</mimeType>
  <textEncoding>VVMtQVNDSUk=</textEncoding>
  <frameName />
  <data>iVBORw0KGgoAAAANSUhEUgAAACYAAAAmCAYAAACoPemuAAAAX...</data>
 </ArchiveResource>
 <ArchiveResource>
```

```
 <url>ZGF0YTppbWFnZS9wbmc7YmFzZTY0LGlWQk9SdzBLR2dvQUFBQU5T...</url>
 <mimeType>aW1hZ2UvcG5n</mimeType>
 <textEncoding>VVMtQVNDSUk=</textEncoding>
 <data>iVBORw0KGgoAAAANSUhEUgAAAFQAAABUCAYAAAAcaxDBAAAABH...</data>
</ArchiveResource>
<ArchiveResource>
 <url>ZGF0YTppbWFnZS9wbmc7YmFzZTY0LGlWQk9SdzBLR2dvQUFBQU5T...</url>
 <mimeType>aW1hZ2UvcG5n</mimeType>
 <textEncoding>VVMtQVNDSUk=</textEncoding>
 <data>iVBORw0KGgoAAAANSUhEUgAAAFQAAABUCAYAAAAcaxDBAAAABH...</data>
</ArchiveResource>
<ArchiveResource>
 <url>ZGF0YTppbWFnZS9wbmc7YmFzZTY0LGlWQk9SdzBLR2dvQUFBQU5T...</url>
 <mimeType>aW1hZ2UvcG5n</mimeType>
 <textEncoding>VVMtQVNDSUk=</textEncoding>
 <data>iVBORw0KGgoAAAANSUhEUgAAAFQAAABUCAYAAAAcaxDBAAAABH...</data>
</ArchiveResource>
<ArchiveResource>
 <url>ZGF0YTppbWFnZS9wbmc7YmFzZTY0LGlWQk9SdzBLR2dvQUFBQU5T...</url>
 <mimeType>aW1hZ2UvcG5n</mimeType>
 <textEncoding>VVMtQVNDSUk=</textEncoding>
 <data>iVBORw0KGgoAAAANSUhEUgAAAFQAAABUCAYAAAAcaxDBAAAABH...</data>
</ArchiveResource>
<ArchiveResource>
 <url>ZGF0YTppbWFnZS9wbmc7YmFzZTY0LGlWQk9SdzBLR2dvQUFBQU5T...</url>
 <mimeType>aW1hZ2UvcG5n</mimeType>
 <textEncoding>VVMtQVNDSUk=</textEncoding>
 <data>iVBORw0KGgoAAAANSUhEUgAAAFQAAABUCAYAAAAcaxDBAAAABH...</data>
</ArchiveResource>
<ArchiveResource>
 <url>ZGF0YTppbWFnZS9wbmc7YmFzZTY0LG...</url>
 <mimeType>aW1hZ2UvcG5n</mimeType>
```

```
    <textEncoding>VVMtQVNDSUk=</textEncoding>
    <frameName />
    <data>iVBORw0KGgoAAAANSUhEUgAAACAAAAAgCAYAAABzenr0AAADIm...</data>
   </ArchiveResource>
   <ArchiveResource>
    <url>aHR0cDovL3d3dy5nb29nbGUuY29tL2ltYWdlcy9zcnByL2xvZ28z...</url>
    <mimeType>aW1hZ2UvcG5n</mimeType>
    <textEncoding />
    <frameName />
    <data>iVBORw0KGgoAAAANSUhEUgAAARMAAABfCAMAAAD8mtMpAAAC/V...</data>
   </ArchiveResource>
  </subresources>
  <subframes>
   <Archive>
    <mainResource>
     <ArchiveResource>
      <url>YWJvdXQ6Ymxhbms=</url>
      <mimeType>dGV4dC9odG1s</mimeType>
      <textEncoding />
      <frameName>d2dqZg==</frameName>
      <data />
     </ArchiveResource>
    </mainResource>
    <subresources />
    <subframes />
   </Archive>
  </subframes>
 </Archive>
```

This tells me that:

- A Web archive file is an XML file.

- All data contents in a Web archive file are Base64 encoded.

- Each <ArchiveResource> element represents a resource that is used to build the Web page.

- I need to find a tool to read a Web archive file and convert the content back to a Web page.

Android Command Line Shell

This chapter provides tutorial notes on Android command line shell. Topics include introduction of Bourne Shell; Unix/Linux command line programs; Android command line tools; running Java application on Dalvik VM.

Takeaways:

- Bourne Shell is the default command line shell on Android systems.

- Many Unix/Linux command line programs are supported on Android systems.

- "am" allows you to manage application activities.

- "dalvikvm" allows you to run Java applications.

- "dumpsys" allows you to dump information of a given system service.

- "monkey" allows you to perform monkey testing.

- "screenrecord" allows you to record screen activities in MP4 format.

- "pm" allows you to manage application packages.

What Is the Bourne Shell?

This section provides a quick introduction of the Bourne shell which is the default shell on the Android system, which is based on the Linux system, which is based on Unix system.

The Bourne shell is a Unix shell introduced by Stephen Bourne in 1977. The Bourne shell replaced the Thompson shell and became the default shell of Unix systems. Bourne shell is also the default shell for the Android system, which is based on the Linux system, which is based on the Unix system.

The Bourne shell is a command-line interpreter that provides a traditional user interface for the Unix-based operating systems. Users direct the operation of the computer by entering commands as text for a command line interpreter to execute or by creating text scripts of one or more such commands.

The Bourne shell has the following main features:

- Built-in Commands - The ability to use a few useful commands built into the shell.

- Command Path Variable - The ability to define a list of paths where the shell can search for external program to execute.

- Command Substitution - The ability to execute extra commands in sub shells and uses their output in the command line.

- Filename Substitution - The ability to expand filename wildcard characters with real file names.

- Input and Output Redirection - The ability to change standard input and/or output from terminal console to files.

- Job Control - The ability to suspend an interactive job and resume it at a later time, or send it into the "background".

- Execution Control Commands - The ability to execute commands conditionally and repeatedly.

- Execution Pipes - The ability to pipe output of one command into another command as input.

- Quotation and Escape Sequences - The ability to protect special characters with single quotes and backslashes.

- Shell Scripts - The ability to write shell scripts with execution flow control and variables.

- Signal Handling - The ability to trap interruption signals (errors).

- Variable Substitution - The ability to reference values of built-in and user defined shell variables.

The Bourne shell is the default shell supported on Android systems. You can invoke it remotely using the Android Debugging Bridge (abd) tool your connected desktop computer as described in "Android Debug Bridge (adb) Tool" chapter.

If you have "adb" installed as part of the Android SDK Platform Tools of Android Studio package, the "adb" program file is located in the "platform-tools" sub-directory. You can include "platform-tools" in the PATH environment variable, so you can run the "adb" command without specifying the path name. For example, this is what I did on macOS computer:

```
herong$ export PATH=$PATH:~/Applications/platform-tools/


herong$ adb devices
List of devices attached
10.0.0.150:5555 device


herong$ adb shell

milan:/ $ uname -a
Linux 4.19.191+ #1 SMP PREEMPT Tue Apr 25 04:32:44 CDT 2023 aarch64


milan:/ $ exit
```

If you are using a Windows computer, setting up the PATH environment variable is slightly different:

```
herong> set PATH=%PATH%;\local\platform-tools


herong> adb devices
List of devices attached
emulator-5554    offline


herong> adb shell df

Filesystem        Size     Used     Free    Blksize
/dev             242.9M    24.0K   242.8M      4096
/sys/fs/cgroup   242.9M    12.0K   242.9M      4096
/mnt/asec        242.9M     0.0K   242.9M      4096
/mnt/obb         242.9M     0.0K   242.9M      4096
```

See next tutorials on using the "adb shell" interface to run Bourne shell built-in commands and some commonly used Android system commands.

Bourne Shell Command Line Examples

This section provides a quick introduction of the Bourne shell which is the default shell on the Android system, which is based on the Linux system, which is based on Unix system.

Below is an example of Bourne shell session on my Android emulator. Explanations are provided in "()" below the output of the command.

```
herong> adb shell
#

        (Starting a Bourne shell session on the Android emulator)


# set
set
ANDROID_ASSETS=/system/app
ANDROID_BOOTLOGO=1
ANDROID_DATA=/data
ANDROID_PROPERTY_WORKSPACE=8,0
ANDROID_ROOT=/system
ASEC_MOUNTPOINT=/mnt/asec
BOOTCLASSPATH=/system/framework/core.jar:/system/framework/core-ju...
ANDROID_STORAGE=/storage
IFS='
'
LD_LIBRARY_PATH=/vendor/lib:/system/lib
LOOP_MOUNTPOINT=/mnt/obb
OPTIND=1
PATH=/sbin:/vendor/bin:/system/sbin:/system/bin:/system/xbin
PS1='# '
PS2='> '
PS4='+ '
        (Displays the values of all shell variables)
```

```
# PS1=\$
PS1=\$
$
      (Sets the shell prompt to the dollar sign $)

$ cd /sdcard/Download
cd /sdcard/Download
      (Changes directory to /sdcard/Download)

$ D=`pwd`
D=`pwd`
      (Sets the current working directory to variable D)

$ echo $D
echo $D
/sdcard/Download
      (Displays the value in variable D)

$ date
date
Sub Mar  1 22:20:19 GMT 2015
      (Displays the date)

$ cat > myself
cat > myself
I am trying to learn Android systems
I am trying to learn Android systems
^D
      (Creates a file and lets you to enter some text)

$ ls -l
ls -l
----rwxr-x system   sdcard_rw       36 2015-03-01 22:24 myself
      (Lists the contents of the current directory in long format)

$ cat myself
cat myself
```

```
I am trying to learn Android systems
        (Displays the contents of "myself" on the screen)


$ mkdir test
mkdir test
        (Makes a new directory)


$ touch test/myfile
touch test/myfile
        (Touches a file - Creates a new empty file)


$ rm test/myfile
rm test/myfile
        (Removes a file)


$ rmdir test
rmdir test
        (Removes a directory)
```

Unix/Linux Command Line Programs

This section provides a list of commonly used Unix/Linux command line programs that can be executed on the Bourne shell on Android systems.

Here is a list of commonly used Unix/Linux/Android command line programs that can be executed on in the Bourne shell on a connected device through the "adb shell" interface:

- cat - Program cat (short for "concatenate") concatenates files into a single file.

- chmod - Program chmod (short for "change mode") changes access modes of files and directories to control what permissions a user can have.

- cmp - Program cmp (short for "compare") compares two files of any type and writes the results to the standard output.

- dalvikvm - Program dalvikvm (short for "Dalvik VM") launches a JVM to run a Java program.

- dd - Program dd copies and converts raw data.

- df - Program df (short for "disk free") displays free spaces of mounted file systems.

- dumpsys - Program dumpsys dumps information about system services.

- env - Program env (short for "environment") prints all environmental veriables.

- id - Program id (short for "identifier") prints the uid (user id) and gid (group id) of the current user.

- getprop - Program getprop (short for "get property") gets a system property, or lists them all.

- gzip - Program df (short for "GNU ZIP") compresses files in ZIP format.

- kill - Program kill send signals to running processes to exit.

- ln - Program ln (short for "link") creates a link to a file or directory.

- ls - Program ls (short for "list) lists files and sub-directories of a given directory.

- mkdir - Program mkdir (short for "make directory") makes a new directory.

- mount - Program mount mounts a file system to the system's file system hierarchy. It also displays currently-mounted files systems.

- mv - Program mv (short for "move") moves files or directories to other places in file system hierarchy.

- netcfg - Program netcfg (short for "netword configuration") creates and modifies network configuration profiles.

- netstat - Program netstat (short for "network statistics") displays network connections (both incoming and outgoing), routing tables, and a number of network interface statistics.

- rm - Program rm (short for "remove") removes files and directories from the file system hierarchy.

- rmdir - Program rmdir (short for "remove directory") removes an existing directory.

- ping - Program ps pings a remote host to measure the round-trip time.

- printenv - Program printenv (short for "print environment") prints current environment variables.

- ps - Program ping displays statuses of currently-running processes on the system.

- top - Program top displays and updates sorted information about processes continuously.

- umount - Program umount (short for "un-mount") removes a file system from the system's file system hierarchy.

- vmstat - Program vmstat (short for "virtual memory statistics") displays summary information about operating system memory.

Android Command Line Tools

This section provides a list of commonly used Android command line tools that can be executed on the Bourne shell.

The Android system also provided its own programs that you can run on the Bourne shell command line. Here are some examples:

adb (Android Debug Bridge) - "adb" is a command line tool that normally provided on an external system to perform remote access to Android systems. But it is also provided on Android systems that you ran it locally. Here is an example session of running "adb shell" on my Android emulator:

```
herong> adb shell
   (Running "adb shell" on my Windows system)


# adb shell
   (Running "adb shell" on my Android emulator)


adb shell
* daemon not running. starting it now on port 5038 *
* daemon started successfully *
# exit
exit
#
```

am (Activity Manager) - "am" is a command line tool that allows you to manage activities like: starting an application activity, stop activities, monitor activities, etc. Here is an example session of running "am start" to start my "AndroidWeb" application:

```
herong> adb shell am start com.herongyang.web/.AndroidWeb
am start com.herongyang.web/.AndroidWeb
Starting: Intent { act=android.intent.action.MAIN cat=
   [android.intent.category.LAUNCHER]
   cmp=com.herongyang.web/.AndroidWeb }
```

dumpsys - "dumpsys" is a command line tool that dumps information about system services. Here is an example session:

```
herong> adb shell dumpsys procstats
CURRENT STATS:
* system / 1000 / v31:
   TOTAL: 100% (251MB-252MB-253MB/139MB-147MB-156MB/537MB-532MB-...)
   Persistent: 100% (251MB-252MB-253MB/139MB-147MB-156MB/537MB-...)
* com.motorola.actions / u0a204 / v301071708:
   TOTAL: 99% (16MB-17MB-18MB/13MB-13MB-14MB/115MB-116MB-117MB over 2)
* com.android.bluetooth / 1002 / v31:
   TOTAL: 99% (25MB-26MB-27MB/15MB-16MB-17MB/92MB-96MB-99MB over 2)
   Persistent: 99% (25MB-26MB-27MB/15MB-16MB-17MB/92MB-96MB-...)
* com.android.systemui / u0a297 / v31:

...
```

dalvikvm (Dalvik VM) - "dalvikvm" is a command line tool that allows you to launch the Dalvik VM to run a Java class in DEX format. Here is an example session of running "dalvikvm -version":

```
herong> adb shell dalvikvm -showversion
dalvikvm -showversion
ART version 2.1.0
```

logcat - "logcat" is a command line tool that allows you to dump log entries from 3 log buffers: main, events and radio. Here is an example session of running "logcat" on my Android emulator:

```
herong> adb shell
```

```
# logcat *:E
logcat *:E
--------- beginning of system
--------- beginning of crash
E/AndroidRuntime( 1819): FATAL EXCEPTION: main
E/AndroidRuntime( 1819): Process: com.herongyang.debug, PID: 1819
E/AndroidRuntime( 1819): java.lang.RuntimeException: Unable to start
activity ComponentInfo{com.herongyang.debug/com.herongyang.debug.
AndroidDebug}: java.lang.IllegalStateException: The specified child
already has a parent. You must call removeView() on the child's parent
first.
'''
^C
```

monkey - "monkey" is a command line tool that allows you to perform a monkey testing on an application. Here is an example session of running "monkey" to perform a monkey test on my "AndroidWeb" application:

```
herong> adb shell

# monkey -p com.herongyang.web 500
monkey -p com.herongyang.web 500
    // Injection Failed
    // activityResuming(com.android.documentsui)
    // Injection Failed
    // activityResuming(com.android.documentsui)
    // Injection Failed
Events injected: 500
## Network stats: elapsed time=31980ms (0ms mobile, 0ms wifi, 31980ms
not connected)
```

pm (package manager) - "pm" is a command line tool that allows you to manage application packages. Here is an example session of running "pm" to list features and packages:

```
herong> adb shell

# pm list features
pm list features
```

```
feature:reqGlEsVersion=0x0

feature:android.hardware.audio.output

feature:android.hardware.bluetooth

feature:android.hardware.camera

feature:android.hardware.camera.any

feature:android.hardware.camera.autofocus

...


# pm list packages

pm list packages

package:com.android.smoketest

package:com.example.android.livecubes

package:com.android.providers.telephony

package:com.herongyang.web

package:com.android.providers.calendar

package:com.android.providers.media

package:com.android.protips

package:com.android.launcher

package:com.android.documentsui

package:com.android.gallery

package:com.android.externalstorage

package:com.android.htmlviewer

package:com.android.quicksearchbox

package:com.android.mms.service

package:com.android.providers.downloads

package:net.sf.andpdf.pdfviewer

package:com.android.browser

...
```

screenrecord - "screenrecord" is a command line tool that allows you to record the display of device in a MPEG-4 file. Here is an example session:

```
herong> adb shell


# screenrecord /sdcard/Movies/demo.mp4


(go to the device and play with some apps)
(press Control + C to stop)
```

```
# ls -l /sdcard/Movies/
-rw-rw---- 1 root everybody 166173285 2023-06-01 22:15 demo.mp4
```

More tutorial examples on using these command line tools are provided in other sections.

"dalvikvm" Command to Run Java Application

This section provides a tutorial example on how to use 'dalvikvm' command line tool to run a Java application on the Dalvik VM (Virtual Machine).

Since "dalvikvm" is a Java virtual machine, you can use it to run regular Java applications as shown in this tutorial:

1. Write a simple Java application called Hello.java:

```
class Hello {
   public static void main(String[] a) {
      System.out.println("Hello world!");
   }
}
```

2. Compile the application with Java SE 6:

```
herong> "%java_home%/bin/java" -version
java version "1.8.0_45"
...

herong> "%java_home%/bin/javac" Hello.java
```

3. Convert .class file to .dex file:

```
herong> copy Hello.class \local\platform-tools
   (dx.bat requires class files in the same folder as the command)

herong> dx.bat
   --dex --output=Hello.dex Hello.class
```

```
UNEXPECTED TOP-LEVEL EXCEPTION:
com.android.dx.cf.iface.ParseException: bad class file magic (cafebabe)
    or version (0034.0000)
    at com.android.dx.cf.direct.DirectClassFile.parse0
        (DirectClassFile.java:472)
...
```

4. Recompile with lower JDK version:

```
herong> "%java_home%/bin/javac" -target 1.7 -source 1.7 Hello.java
warning: [options] bootstrap class path not set in conjunction with
-source 1.7
1 warning
```

5. Convert .class file to .dex file:

```
herong> copy Hello.class \local\platform-tools


herong> \local\platform-tools\dx.bat
    --dex --output=Hello.dex Hello.class
```

6. Copy .dex file to the Android system:

```
herong> adb push Hello.dex /sdcard/Download
4 KB/s (736 bytes in 0.167s)
```

7. Run the application with "dalvikvm":

```
herong> adb shell

# cd /sdcard/Download
cd /sdcard/Download

# dalvikvm -cp Hello.dex Hello
dalvikvm -cp Hello.dex Hello

Hello world!
```

Very nice! This confirms that dalvikvm is just another JVM that can run Java applications.

Samsung Galaxy Tab 3 Mini Tablet

This chapter provides tutorial notes on the Android mini tablet - Samsung Galaxy Tab 3. Topics include Android tablet system basic information; running background processes and foreground applications; connecting tablet to computer as USB storage drive, transferring files using Bluetooth radio; using Wi-Fi network to access Internet; setting up Gmail access; downloading applications from Google Play Store.

Takeaways:

- Android tablet system supports multi-tasking and allows you to run multiple background processes and foreground applications.

- The USB cable allows you to use your Android tablet as USB storage drive. This gives you a way to exchange files on tablet's SD Card with your computer.

- Bluetooth connection also gives you a way to transfer files between your tablet and your computer.

- The Wi-Fi function allows your tablet to access the Internet using your home Wi-Fi network.

- Setting up Gmail mail box access on an Android tablet is easy.

- Downloading applications from Google Play Store to Android tablet is also easy.

About My Samsung Galaxy Tab 3 Mini Tablet

This section provides a tutorial example on how to view basic information on a Samsung Galaxy mini tablet, running Android 4.4.2.

Here is how my Android mini tablet, Samsung Galaxy Tab 3, looks like:

Samsung Galaxy Tab 3

The technical specifications say:

```
Dimensions   188 x 111.1 x 9.9 mm
Display      7" TFT (1024 x 600)
CPU          Dual Core Application Processor, 1.2GHz
Memory       8GB / 16GB ROM + 1GB RAM
Video        30fps and HD (720p)
Camera       3MP
Storage      8GB
Weight       300g
```

```
Operating System     Android 4.4.2
I/O Port     MicroSD, Micro USB, 3.5mm Audio Port;
Battery      Capacity: 4000 mAh, Audio Playback: 109 hours,
             Video Playback: 7 hours
```

To review basic information on the mini tablet, tap on "Settings", then "About device". I see the following information:

```
Device name - SM-T210R
Model number - SM-T210R
Android version - 4.4.2
Kernel version - 3.4.5-2364900
Build number - KOT49H.T210RUEU0CNI1
```

Ok. My Android version 4.4.2 is not that old. It was released on December 9, 2013.

Samsung Galaxy Storage Usage

This section provides a tutorial example on how to view tablet storage size and usage. Samsung Galaxy Tab 3 comes with 8GB total storage.

After checking the Android OS version on my mini tablet, I want to know how much storage I have.

Tap on "Settings", then "Storage". I see the following information:

```
Total space - Total device capacity: 8.00GB


System memory - The minimum amount of storage space required to run
    the system: 2.72GB


Used space - The amount of storage space current being used: 1.53GB


Cached data: 330MB


Miscellaneous files - The amount of memory used to store miscellaneous
    files: 254MB
```

Not too bad. The mini tablet came with 8GB. I have used about 4.8GB. About 3.2GB free space is available on the mini tablet.

Running Services - Background Processes

This section provides a tutorial example on how to review running services, or background processes, on my Android mini tablet. Those background processes are started automatically and running all the time.

Since Android is a multi-tasking system, let's see what are currently running on my tablet.

Tap on "Settings", "Application Manager", then "Running". I see a long list of items displayed:

```
Settings                          37.0MB
Factory Test                       1.1MB
Software update                    4.9MB
MTP application                    1.4MB
com.marvell.powergadget            1.9MB
SmartcardService                   0.9MB
Weather Daemon                     3.1MB
Google Play service               20.0MB
Media                              3.3MB
Group Play                         0.8MB
S Voice                            3.5MB
PageBuddyNoticSvc                  0.7MB
com.sec.android.app.keyguard       1.2MB
com.sec.android.app.FlashBarService 8.8MB
Samsung keyboard                   8.1MB


RAM 425MB used, 408MB free
```

It seems to me that only background apps are listed here. The running Android system and running foreground apps are not listed and they are using about 328MB, The total RAM used by background apps is about 97MB, and the total RAM used is 425MB. The difference is 328MB.

Connect tablet to Computer using Bluetooth

This section provides a tutorial example on how to connect an Android tablet to a Windows computer using Bluetooth radio. Once connected, you can transfer files between the tablet and computer.

1. Turn on Bluetooth function on the laptop computer.

2. On the Android mini tablet, tap on "Settings", then turn on Bluetooth by sliding the Bluetooth switch. The tablet automatically searches the nearby Bluetooth devices. I see my laptop Bluetooth device displayed with other Bluetooth devices nearby.

3. Tap on my laptop Bluetooth device name to make a pairing request to the computer.

4. On the computer, accept the paring request, which should contain a pairing code for identification purpose.

5. On the tablet, tap on "OK" to finish up the pairing process.

To send a music file from computer to tablet, right-click on the music file to select "Send to\Bluetooth" in the context menu to start the sending process. Go to your tablet to receive the music file.

To send a music file from tablet to computer, tap on "Applications", then "Music". Tap and hold on the music to select the "Bluetooth" in the pop up menu to start the sending process. Go to your computer to receive the music file.

Connect tablet Storage to Computer via USB

This section provides a tutorial example on how to use the USB cable to connect the storage in the tablet to a computer as a removable drive on the computer.

My Android tablet also came with a USB cable that can be used to connect the storage on my tablet as an external storage to my laptop for exchange files. Here is how it works:

1. Turn on my tablet and my laptop. Then connect them with the USB cable.

2. On the laptop, the AutoPlay screen shows up asking you how to open the storage on the connected tablet.

3. Click on "Open device to view files". Windows Explorer shows up with the tablet storage listed as "SM-T210R" next to "Local Disk (C:)"

4. Click on "Tablet" under "SM-T210R. Directories and files stored in the tablet storage show up. See the picture below:

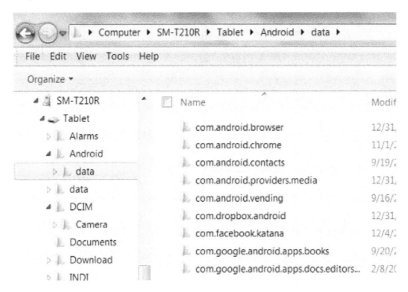

Samsung Galaxy Tab 3 USB Storage

Using Wi-Fi to Connect to Internet

This section provides a tutorial example on how to turn on the 'Wi-Fi' function to connect the tablet to the Internet through home Wi-Fi network.

To connect my Samsung Galaxy Tab 3 mini tablet to the Internet, I need to use my home Wi-Fi network:

1. Tap on "Settings", and go to the "Wireless & networks" section.

2. Turn on "Wi-Fi" by sliding the "Wi-Fi" switch. I see my Wi-Fi SID displayed with other Wi-Fi SIDs in the neighborhood. My SID should have the strongest signal icon.

3. Tap on my Wi-Fi SID and enter my Wi-Fi password to finish up the connection.

Now I can browse the Internet, download files, or play on-line games through my Wi-Fi home network.

Setting up Gmail Access on Android tablet

This section provides a tutorial example on how to set up Gmail access on Android tablets: 'Settings' > 'Account and sync' > 'Add account'.

If you want to read emails from your Gmail mailbox or download more applications, you need to do account setup on your Android tablet.

1. Tap on "Settings" and go to the "Accounts" section. You will see a list of Internet access accounts that you have already set up.

2. Tap on the "Add account" link at the top right cornet, then "Next".

3. Select "Google". Then follow instructions on the screen to finish the set up process.

4. Tap on "Applications", then "Gmail". You will see incoming emails listed on the screen now.

If you have more than one Gmail mailbox, you can set up them on your tablet by repeating the "Add account" process.

If you want to remove any mailbox, tap on the Gmail address, then "Remove account".

Of course, you can add other types of accounts too, like Skype, Twitter, Facebook, etc.

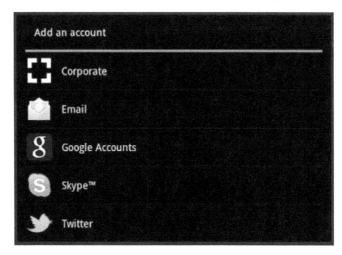

Android Tablet Add an Account

Downloading and Installing from "Play Store"

This section provides a tutorial example on how to download and install applications from Google's 'Play Store'. Read permissions requested by the application carefully before using the application.

Downloading and installing Android application is easy. Here is what you need to do to install the Tetris game as an example.

1. Make sure you have done the Gmail account set up as presented in the previous tutorial.

2. Tap on "Applications", then "Play Store". Go to the "Apps" section.

3. Tap the Search icon to search for "Tetris". Then tap on "Tetris Classis" in the search result. You will see "Tetris Classis" download screen.

4. Tap on the "Download" button. The system will install automatically after download is completed.

Now "Tetris Classic" will be available in the application list for to play. Enjoy it!

USB Debugging Applications on Samsung Tablet

This chapter provides tutorial notes on debugging application on Samsung mini tablet. Topics include installing Samsung USB device driver on Windows; Turning on USB debugging interface on Samsung tablet; running 'adb -d' commands on USB connected device; installing application through USB connection; Android API levels and platform versions.

Takeaways:

* USB cable connection can charge the tablet from the computer.

* USB cable connection can also turn your Samsung tablet into USB storage drive for the computer.

* USB cable connection can also provide debugging interface for the Android SDK package on the computer to install and debug applications on the tablet. But you need to install the USB driver on the computer first.

* The ADB tool has a switch to select the emulator or connected device: "adb -e" for emulator and "adb -d" for device.

* "ant installd" can install an application to the emulator or the connected device, but only if one of them exists.

- "adb install" can install an application to the emulator or the connected device, even both of them exist. "adb -e install" works for the emulator. "adb -d install" works for the connected device.

Samsung USB Driver for Mobile Phones

This section provides a tutorial example on how to download and install Samsung USB Driver for Mobile Phones, which is needed to run Samsung Galaxy Tab 3 mini tablet in debug mode.

By default, when you connect your Samsung Galaxy Tab 3 mini tablet to a Windows computer with a USB cable, the Windows computer will charge the battery on the mini tablet and access its storage as an external drive.

But the USB cable also allows you to run the mini tablet in debugging mode for you to perform development tasks on the mini tablet. This requires Samsung Mobile Device drivers to be installed on your Windows system. Some Windows systems may install required drivers for you automatically. But you should follow this tutorial to ensure all drivers are installed correctly:

1. On your Windows system, visit the "Samsung Android USB Driver for Windows" page at http://developer.samsung.com/technical-doc/view.do?v=T000000117.

2. Click "SAMSUNG_USB_Driver_for_Mobile_Phones.zip (15.3MB)" to download "SAMSUNG_USB_Driver_for_Mobile_Phones.zip".

3. Unzip "SAMSUNG_USB_Driver_for_Mobile_Phones.zip" and run "SAMSUNG_USB_Driver_for_Mobile_Phones.exe". It will install SAMSUNG USB Driver for Mobile Phones V1.5.51.0.

4. Wait until the installation is done. Windows will display a software driver installation icon in the task bar area.

5. Click on the software driver installation icon. You will see a list of drivers and their installation statuses.

```
Bluetooth Peripheral Device          No Driver fund
Bluetooth Peripheral Device          No Driver fund
Bluetooth Peripheral Device          No Driver fund
Bluetooth Peripheral Device          No Driver fund
```

```
SAMSUNG Mobile USB Composite Device    Ready to use
MTP USB Device                         Failed
SAMSUNG Mobile USB Modem               Ready to use
SAMSUNG Mobile USB ADB Interface       Ready to use
```

Ok. Some drivers failed to install. But the important one "SAMSUNG Mobile USB ADB Interface" seems to be installed properly.

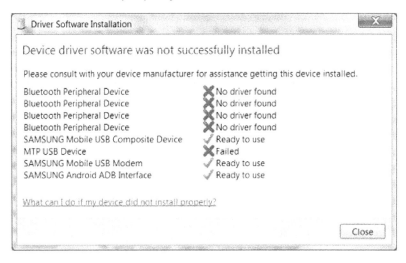

SAMSUNG USB Driver for Mobile Phones

Turning on USB Debugging on Samsung Galaxy Tab 3

This section provides a tutorial example on how to turn on 'USB Debugging' on Samsung Galaxy Tab 3 mini tablet by tapping 'Build Number' 7 times.

With Samsung USB Driver for Mobile Phones installed on my Windows system, I am ready to run my Samsung Galaxy Tab 3 in debug mode.

1. Connect Samsung Galaxy Tab 3 mini tablet to a Windows computer with a USB cable. Windows will install proper device drivers to support the mini tablet.

2. On the mini tablet, tap on "Home", "Settings", "About Device" and find the build number at the bottom. Then tap "Build number" 7 times. Yes, 7 times! The "Developer options" shows in the menu.

3. Tap on "Developer options". You will see some development settings:

```
    Desktop backup password

    Stay awake

    Bluetooth HCI snoop log

    Process stats
Debugging

    USB debugging - Debug mode when USB is connected

    Revoke USB debugging authorizations

    Include bug reports in power menu

    Allow mock locations

    Select debug app

    Wait for debugger

    Verify apps via USB
Input

    Show touches

    Show pointer location
Drawing

    Show screen updates

    show layout boundaries

    Force RTL layout

    Window animation scale

    Transition animation scale

    Animator duration scale

    Simulate secondary displays

...
```

4. Tap on the "USB debugging" checkbox to turn on the setting. You will get the confirmation message:

```
Allow USB debugging?


USB debugging is intended for development purposes only. It can be
used to copy data between your computer and your device, install
applications on your device without notification, and read log data.
[OK] [Cancel]
```

5. Tap on "OK" to confirm.

Running "adb" on USB Debugging Interface

This section provides a tutorial example on how to run 'adb' commands on Samsung Android mini tablet through the USB debugging interface. 'adb -d' is to run commands on the USB connected Android device. But if there is only 1 device, '-d' option is not needed.

With my Samsung Galaxy Tab 3 mini tablet connected in USB debugging mode, I can try some Android SDK debugging tools on my Windows computer now.

1. Try the ADB (Android Debugging Bridge) tool to list the device:

```
C:\herong>\local\android-sdk-windows\platform-tools\adb devices
List of devices attached
5200e5505ae3a000   unauthorized
```

Cool. My tablet is showing up as "5200e5505ae3a000". But it is flagged as "unauthorized" for some reason.

2. Go back to the tablet, go to "Settings > Developer options", uncheck "USB debugging" and check it again.

3. Tap OK on the warning message. You will see an authorization request message:

```
Allow USB debugging?
The computer's RSA key fingerprint is "....".
[x] Always allow from this computer.
```

4. Check "Always allow..." and tap OK.

5. Go back to Windows computer, and run the "adb devices" command again:

```
C:\herong>\local\android-sdk-windows\platform-tools\adb devices
List of devices attached
5200e5505ae3a000   device
```

6. Run some other "adb" commands:

```
C:\herong>\local\android-sdk-windows\platform-tools\adb -d shell \
    uptime
up time: 1 days, 02:25:28, idle time: 1 days, 10:38:29, sleep time: 08:35:28
```

```
C:\herong>\local\android-sdk-windows\platform-tools\adb shell \
   ping localhost
PING localhost (127.0.0.1) 56(84) bytes of data.
64 bytes from localhost (127.0.0.1): icmp_seq=1 ttl=64 time=0.291 ms
64 bytes from localhost (127.0.0.1): icmp_seq=2 ttl=64 time=0.173 ms
64 bytes from localhost (127.0.0.1): icmp_seq=3 ttl=64 time=0.166 ms
...
   Ctrl-C


C:\herong>\local\android-sdk-windows\platform-tools\adb -d shell


shell@lt02wifi:/ $ df
/mnt/secure/asec: Permission denied
Filesystem             Size      Used      Free    Blksize
/dev                  416.2M    164.0K    416.0M     4.0K
/mnt/secure           416.2M      0.0K    416.2M     4.0K
/mnt/asec             416.2M      0.0K    416.2M     4.0K
/mnt/obb              416.2M      0.0K    416.2M     4.0K
/preload              196.7M    182.6M     14.1M     4.0K
/system                 1.4G      1.2G    218.1M     4.0K
/efs                   11.8M      4.1M      7.7M     4.0K
/cache                196.7M     51.4M    145.3M     4.0K
/data                   5.3G      2.1G      3.2G     4.0K
/NVM                   15.7M      4.2M     11.5M     4.0K
/tmp                  416.2M      0.0K    416.2M     4.0K
/mnt/shell/emulated     5.3G      2.1G      3.2G     4.0K


shell@lt02wifi:/ $ exit
exit


C:\herong>\local\android-sdk-windows\platform-tools\adb -d logcat
...
...
I/ServiceManager(  119): Waiting for service com.marvell.FileMonito...
I/ServiceManager(  119): Waiting for service com.marvell.FileMonito...
I/ServiceManager(  119): Waiting for service com.marvell.FileMonito...
```

```
V/AlarmManager(  548): waitForAlarm result :8
D/KeyguardClockWidgetService(  930): onReceive action=android.inten...
V/AlarmManager(  548): ClockReceiver onReceive() ACTION_TIME_TICK
D/KeyguardUpdateMonitor(  645): received broadcast android.intent.a...
D/KeyguardUpdateMonitor(  645): handleTimeUpdate
D/STATUSBAR-IconMerger(  645): checkOverflow(420), More:false, Req:...
I/ServiceManager(  119): Waiting for service com.marvell.FileMonito...
I/ServiceManager(  119): Waiting for service com.marvell.FileMonito...
W/        (  119): FileMonitorService not published, waiting...
...
   Ctrl-C
```

What I learned here are:

- I have one Android device connected to my Windows system to play: "5200e5505ae3a000" representing the mini tablet connected on USB.

- Authorization on the mini tablet is required to allow USB debugging

- If there is only 1 Android device connected, I can run "adb" command without the "-d" option.

- You need to press "<Ctrl>-C" to stop some "adb" commands.

Installing Application to Tablet using "ant installd"

This section provides a tutorial example on how to install the debug package of my 'HelloAndroid' application to my Samsung mini tablet using the 'ant installd' command through the USB debugging interface.

I think I am ready try to install my own applications on my Samsung mini tablet and debug/test them.

Let's try to install the "HelloAndroid" debug package to my tablet first using the "ant installd" command. See previous tutorials on how to build the debug package.

You may need to shutdown the Android emulator to run "ant installd", because it can not support 2 connected Android devices.

```
C:\herong\HelloAndroid>\local\apache-ant-1.8.3\bin\ant installd
```

```
Buildfile: C:\herong\HelloAndroid\build.xml

-set-mode-check:

-set-debug-files:

install:
    [echo] Installing C:\herong\HelloAndroid\bin\HelloAndr
oid-debug.apk onto default emulator or device...
    [exec]      pkg: /data/local/tmp/HelloAndroid-debug.apk
    [exec] Success
    [exec] 812 KB/s (14980 bytes in 0.018s)

installd:

BUILD SUCCESSFUL
Total time: 6 seconds
```

It works! "ant installd" installed my debug package of "HelloAndroid" to my mini tablet through the USB debugging interface.

To verify, go to the tablet and tap on "Applications". You will see "HelloAndroid" listed and ready to run.

Installing Application to Tablet using "adb -d install"

This section provides a tutorial example on how to install the debug package of my 'HelloAndroid' application to my Samsung tablet using the 'adb -d install' command through the USB debugging interface.

The Android SDK document also mentions another way to install application packages to the USB connected tablet device using the "adb -d install path/to/your/app.apk" command.

1. Go to Samsung tablet. Tap on "Applications", then "HelloAndroid". You will see "Hello, Android" displayed on the screen.

2. Tap on "Settings", then "Application manager". You will see "HelloAndroid" listed under "Downloaded" tab.

3. Tap on "HelloAndroid" and "Uninstall" to uninstall "HelloAndroid".

4. Go to Windows computer, try to install the "HelloAndroid" debug package to my tablet again using the "adb -d install" command.

```
C:\herong\HelloAndroid>\local\android-sdk-windows\platform-tools\adb
    -d install bin\HelloAndroid-debug.apk


2089 KB/s (14980 bytes in 0.007s)
        pkg: /data/local/tmp/HelloAndroid-debug.apk
Success
```

5. Go to the tablet again. You will see "HelloAndroid" is ready to run again.

6. You can uninstall "HelloAndroid" using the "adb -d uninstall" command:

```
C:\herong\HelloAndroid>\local\android-sdk-windows\platform-tools\adb
    -d uninstall com.herongyang
Success
```

Note that the "adb -d uninstall" command takes the Java class package name as the argument. "com.herongyang" is the package name for my "HelloAndroid" application.

Installing "AboutAndroid" to Samsung Tablet

This section provides a tutorial example on how to install my 'AboutAndroid' application to my Samsung tablet. 'HelloAndroid' needs to be uninstalled first, because both applications share the same Java package name 'com.herongyang'.

My first application "HelloAndroid" works on my Samsung tablet, now let's see what will happen to my second application "AboutAndroid".

1. Uninstall "HelloAndroid", then install "AboutAndroid". Keeping "HelloAndroid" on the tablet will cause installation problem with "AboudAndroid", because both "HelloAndroid" and "AboutAndroid" use the same Java class package name.

```
C:\herong\AboutAndroid>\local\android-sdk-windows\platform-tools\adb
```

```
      -d uninstall com.herongyang
Success


C:\herong\cod\AboutAndroid>\local\android-sdk-windows\platform-tools\adb
   -d install -s bin\AboutAndroid-debug.apk
868 KB/s (23132 bytes in 0.026s)
        pkg: /sdcard/tmp/AboutAndroid-debug.apk
Success
```

2. Go to the tablet. Tap on "Applications", then "AboutAndroid" to run the application. You will see the output:

```
System properties
-----------
java.vm.specification.vendor: The Android Project
java.vm.name: Dalvik
java.vm.specification.version: 0.9
java.vendor.url: http://www.android.com/
user.home: /
java.ext.dirs:
java.specification.name: Dalvik Core Library
file.encoding: UTF-8
java.runtime.version: 0.9
user.name: root
java.library.path: /vendor/lib;/system/lib
os.version: 3.4.5-2364900
android.icu.unicode.version: 6.2
java.boot.class.path: /system/frameword/core.jar;...
os.arch: armv7I
java.io.tmpdir: /data/data/com.herongyang/cache
java.vm.version: 1.6.0
http.agent: Dalvik/1.6.0 (Linux; U; Android 4.4.2; SM-T210R...
android.openssl.version: OpenSSL 1.0.1e 11 Feb 2013
java.home: /system
java.class.version: 46.0
...

Environment variables
```

```
------------
ANDROID_SOCKET_zygot: 9

EMULATED_STORAGE_SOURCE: /mnt/shell/emulated

SECONDARY_STORAGE: /storage/extSdCard

ANDROID_STORAGE: /storage

EXTERNAL_STORAGE: /storage/emulated/legacy

ANDROID_ASSETS: /system/app

ASEC_MOUNTPOINT: /mnt/asec

PATH: /sbin;/vendor/bin;/system/sbin;/system/bin;/system/xbin

ANDROID_DATA: /data

ANDROID_ROOT: /system

LD_LIBRARY_PATH: /vendor/lib;/system/lib;/lib

...


Environment folders
------------
Data folder: /data

Download cache folder: /cache

External storage folder: /storage/emulated/0

Root folder: /system


Application context info
------------
Cache folder: /data/data/com.herongyang/cache

External cache folder: /storage/emulated/0/Android/data/com.herong...

File folder: /data/data/herongyang/files

OBB folder: /storage/emulated/0/Android/obb/com.herongyang

Package name: com.herongyang

Package code path: /data/app/com.herongyang-1.apk

Package resource path: /data/app/com.herongyang-1.apk
```

Note that you may get execution errors, if the device Android version is not compatible with AboutAndroid build version.

Android Tablet - LG-V905R

This chapter provides tutorial notes on the Android tablet - LG-V905R. Topics include Android tablet system basic information; running background processes and foreground applications; connecting tablet to computer as USB storage drive, transferring files using Bluetooth radio; using Wi-Fi network to access Internet; setting up Gmail access; downloading applications from Google Play Store.

Takeaways:

- Android tablet system supports multi-tasking and allows you to run multiple background processes and foreground applications.

- The USB cable allows you to use your Android tablet as USB storage drive. This gives you a way to exchange files on tablet's SD Card with your computer.

- Bluetooth connection also gives you a way to transfer files between your tablet and your computer.

- The Wi-Fi function allows your tablet to access the Internet using your home Wi-Fi network.

- Setting up Gmail mail box access on an Android tablet is easy.

- Downloading applications from Google Play Store to Android tablet is also easy.

About My LG-V905R Android Tablet

This section provides a tutorial example on how to view basic information a LG-V905R Android tablet, running Android 3.0.1.

Here is how my Android tablet, LG-V905R, looks like:

LG-V905R Android Tablet

The technical specifications say:

```
Dimensions    243 x 149.4 x 12.8mm
Display       8.9" Capacitive Touch Screen (1280 x 768)
CPU           NVIDIA Tegra 2 (T20) Cortex-A9 Dual Core 1GHz
Video         Playing: 720p (1080p HDMI out) - H.263 D1, H.264, MPEG4;
              Recording: 720p - H.264, MPEG4; 3D Recording: 720p - H.264
Camera        5MP x 2 (Stereoscopic), 2MP (Video Conferencing)
Storage       32GB
Weight        625g
Operating System    Android 3.0 Honeycomb
I/O Port      3.5mm Audio Port; Power Port; Micro USB, Mini HDMI,
              Stereo Speakers
Memory        LP-DDR2
Battery       Capacity: 6400 mAh, Standby: 15 days,
              Video Playback: 10 hours
```

To review basic information on the tablet, tap on "Settings", then "About tablet". I see the following information:

```
System updates
Status - Status of the battery, network, and...
Battery use - What has been using the battery
Legal information
Model number - LG-V925R
Android version - 3.0.1
Baseband version - V905R-V10c
Kernel version - 2.6.36.3+ OptimusPad@wuthGoogle #1
Build number - HRI66
```

Ok. My Android version 3.0.1 is not that old. Android 3.0.1 was released on October 19, 2011.

Tablet Memory Usage

This section provides a tutorial example on how to view tablet memory size and usage.

After checking the Android OS version on my tablet, I want to know how much storage I have on my tablet.

Tap on "Settings", then "Storage". I see the following information:

```
Internal storage
   Total 28.35GB


Media 573MB


Application 481MB


Available 27.32GB
```

Not too bad. The tablet came with 28GB. I have only used about 1GB. Lot of free space available on the tablet.

Running Services - Background Processes

This section provides a tutorial example on how to review running services, or background processes, on my Android tablet. Those background processes are started automatically and running all the time.

Since Android is a multi-tasking system, let's see what are currently running on my tablet.

Tap on "Settings", "Applications", then "Running services". I see a long list of items displayed:

```
LGESystemService          4.3MB
SpeakerSwitch             4.9MB
Google Service             10MB
Maps                      7.3MB
Android keyboard          8.4MB


RAM 108MB used, 364MB free
```

It seems to me that those are background processes that are started automatically and running all the time. I should leave them alone.

Connect tablet to Computer using Bluetooth

This section provides a tutorial example on how to connect an Android tablet to a Windows computer using Bluetooth radio. Once connected, you can transfer files between the tablet and computer.

1. Turn on Bluetooth function on the laptop computer.

2. On the Android tablet, tap on "Settings", then "Bluetooth settings".

3. Tap on the checkbox next to "Bluetooth" to turn on the "Bluetooth" function on the tablet.

4. Tap on the "Find nearby devices". You will your laptop Bluetooth device displayed with other Bluetooth devices nearby.

5. Tap on my laptop Bluetooth device name to make a pairing request to the computer.

6. On the computer, accept the paring request, which should contain a pairing code for identification purpose.

7. On the tablet, tap on "Pair" to finish up the pairing process. The status message should say "Paired but not connected" now.

To send a music file from computer to tablet, right-click on the music file to select "Send to\Bluetooth" in the context menu to start the sending process. Go to your tablet to receive the music file.

To send a music file from tablet to computer, tap on "Applications", then "Music". Tap and hold on the music to select the "Bluetooth" in the pop up menu to start the sending process. Go to your computer to receive the music file.

Connect tablet Storage to Computer via USB

This section provides a tutorial example on how to use the USB cable to connect the storage in the tablet to a computer as a removable drive on the computer.

My Android tablet also came with a USB cable that can be used to connect the storage on my tablet as an external storage to my laptop for exchange files. Here is how it works:

1. Turn on my tablet and my laptop. Then connect them with the USB cable.

2. On the laptop, the AutoPlay screen shows up asking you how to open the storage on the connected tablet.

3. Click on "Open device to view files". Windows Explorer shows up with the tablet storage listed as "LG-V905R" next to "Local Disk (C:)"

4. Click on "Device Storage". Directories and files stored in the tablet storage show up. See the picture below:

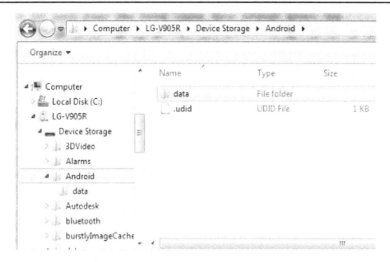

LG-V905R Android Tablet USB Storage

Using Wi-Fi to Connect to Internet

This section provides a tutorial example on how to turn on the 'Wi-Fi' function to connect the tablet to the Internet through home Wi-Fi network.

To connect my tablet to the Internet, I need to use my home Wi-Fi network:

1. Tap on "Settings", "Wireless & networks", then "Wi-Fi settings".

2. Tap on the checkbox next to "Wi-Fi" to turn on the "Wi-Fi" function. I see my Wi-Fi SID displayed with other Wi-Fi SIDs in the neighborhood. My SID should have the strongest signal icon.

3. Tap on my Wi-Fi SID and enter my Wi-Fi password to finish up the connection.

Now I can browse the Internet, download files, or play on-line games through my Wi-Fi home network.

Setting up Gmail Access on Android tablet

This section provides a tutorial example on how to set up Gmail access on Android tablets: 'Settings' > 'Account and sync' > 'Add account'.

If you want to read emails from your Gmail mailbox or download more applications, you need to do account setup on your Android tablet.

1. Tap on "Settings", then "Account & sync". You will see a list of Internet access accounts that you have already set up.

2. Tap on the "Add account" link at the top right cornet, then "Next".

3. Select "Google". Then follow instructions on the screen to finish the set up process.

4. Tap on "Applications", then "Gmail". You will see incoming emails listed on the screen now.

If you have more than one Gmail mailbox, you can set up them on your tablet by repeating the "Add account" process.

If you want to remove any mailbox, tap on the Gmail address, then "Remove account".

Of course, you can add other types of accounts too, like Skype, Twitter, Facebook, etc.

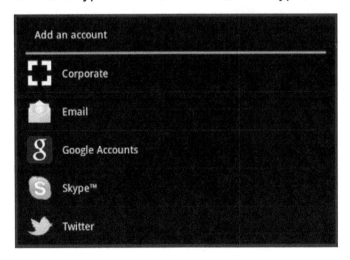

Android Tablet Add an Account

Downloading and Installing from "Play Store"

This section provides a tutorial example on how to download and install applications from Google's 'Play Store'. Read permissions requested by the application carefully before using the application.

Downloading and installing Android application is easy. Here is what you need to do to install the Tetris game.

1. Make sure you have done the Gmail account set up as presented in the previous tutorial.

2. Tap on "Applications", then "Play Store". Go to the "Apps" section.

3. Tap the Search icon to search for "Tetris". Then tap on "Tetris Classis" in the search result. You will see "Tetris Classis" download screen.

4. Tap on the "Download" button. The system will install automatically after download is completed.

Now "Tetris Classic" will be available in the application list for to play. Enjoy it!

USB Debugging Applications on LG-V905R Tablet

This chapter provides tutorial notes on debugging application on LG-V905R tablet. Topics include installing LG USB device driver on Windows; Turning on USB debugging interface on LG-V905R tablet; running 'adb -d' commands on USB connected device; installing application through USB connection; Android API levels and platform versions.

Takeaways:

- USB cable connection can charge the tablet from the computer.

- USB cable connection can also turn your LG-V905R tablet into USB storage drive to the computer.

- USB cable connection can also provide debugging interface for the Android SDK package on the computer to install and debug applications on the tablet. But you need to install the USB driver on the computer first.

- The ADB tool has a switch to select the emulator or connected device: "adb -e" for emulator and "adb -d" for device.

- "ant installd" can install an application to the emulator or the connected device, but only if one of them exists.

- "adb install" can install an application to the emulator or the connected device, even both of them exist. "adb -e install" works for the emulator. "adb -d install" works for the connected device.

Turning on USB Debugging on LG-V905R

This section provides a tutorial example on how to turn on 'USB Debugging' on LG-V905R Android tablets in the 'Settings > Applications > Development' area.

Of course, you can connect an Android table to a Windows system in USB debugging mode in the same way as connecting an Android phone. This requires you to install the LG USB Device Driver on the Windows system as described earlier in the book first.

Then you need to turn on the USB Debugging function on the tablet to allow me to do testing and debugging applications on the tablet through the USB connection.

1. Turn on the LG-V905R tablet and connect it to the Windows computer with the USB cable.

2. Tap on "Home", "Settings", "Applications", then "Development". You will see 3 development settings:

```
USB debugging - Debug mode when USB is connected       [ ]
Stay awake - Screen will never sleep while charging    [ ]
Allow mock locations - Allow mock locations            [ ]
```

3. Tap on the checkbox to turn on the "USB debugging" setting. You will get the confirmation message:

```
Allow USB debugging?


USB debugging is intended for development purposes only. It can be
used to copy data between your computer and your device, install
applications on your device without notification, and read log data.
[OK] [Cancel]
```

4. Tap on "OK" to confirm.

5. On your computer, Windows will display a "Your device is ready to use" icon in the task bar area. Click on it see details:

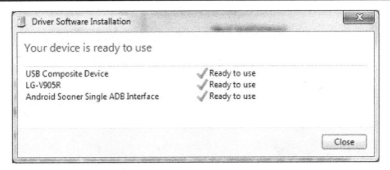

LG-V905R USB Driver for Debugging

The "Android Sooner Single ADB Interface" driver is probably the key driver the USB debugging connection:

- USB Composite Device

- LG-V905R

- Android Sooner Single ADB Interface

Viewing LG-V905R Android USB Device in Control Panel

This section provides a tutorial example on how to view the LG Android USB device in Windows Control Panel and see its detailed properties.

To verify the Android USB debugging connection, you can look at the device properties in the control panel.

1. On the Windows computer, go to "Control Panel\Hardware and Sound\Devices and Printers". You see a "LG AndroidNet Phone" icon listed as a connected device.

LG-V905R Tablet as Device on Windows

2. Right-click on "LG AndroidNet Phone" and select "Properties". You see some general properties.

2. Click on the "Hardware" tab. You see a list of device functions:

```
LG AndroidNet Tablet


Device Functions:
Android Sooner Single ADB Interface ADB Interface
LG-V905R                            Portable Devices
USB Composite Device               Universal Serial Bus Controller


Device Function Summary
Manufacture: Google, Inc.
Location: 0000.001d.0000.001.002.000.000.000.000
Device status: This device is working properly
```

Ok. The LG Android USB Device driver is installed and running properly. However, the word "Phone" is used in its icon and name, even the actual device is a tablet.

Running "adb" on LG-V905R USB Debugging Interface

This section provides a tutorial example on how to run 'adb' commands on LG-V905R Android tablet through the USB debugging interface. 'adb -d' is to run commands on the USB connected Android device. But if there is only 1 device, '-d' option is not needed.

With my LG-V905R Android tablet connected in USB debugging mode, I can try some Android SDK debugging tools on my Windows computer now.

The first I want to try is the ADB (Android Debugging Bridge) tool:

```
C:\herong>\local\android-sdk-windows\platform-tools\adb devices
List of devices attached
028841C6433F5617         device


C:\herong>\local\android-sdk-windows\platform-tools\adb -d shell \
   uptime
up time: 03:53:55, idle time: 06:46:15, sleep time: 00:29:12


C:\herong>\local\android-sdk-windows\platform-tools\adb shell \
   ping localhost
PING localhost (127.0.0.1) 56(84) bytes of data.
64 bytes from localhost (127.0.0.1): icmp_seq=1 ttl=64 time=0.291 ms
64 bytes from localhost (127.0.0.1): icmp_seq=2 ttl=64 time=0.173 ms
64 bytes from localhost (127.0.0.1): icmp_seq=3 ttl=64 time=0.166 ms


C:\herong>\local\android-sdk-windows\platform-tools\adb -d shell
shell@android:/ $ df
df
Filesystem          Size    Used    Free    Blksize
/dev                331M    36K     331M    4096
/mnt/asec           331M    0K      331M    4096
/mnt/obb            331M    0K      331M    4096
/system             393M    202M    191M    4096
/data               28G     1G      27G     4096
/cache              393M    6M      387M    4096
/mnt/sdcard         28G     1G      27G     4096
```

```
shell@android:/ $ exit
exit

C:\herong>\local\android-sdk-windows\platform-tools\adb -d logcat
...
ommand(): intent = Intent { act=tango.service.KEEP_ALIVE flg=0x4 cm...
V/Tango.Utils(  455): 2012 06 29 14:16:55.579 [455.455] Read Tango....
D/Tango.MessageService(  455): 2012 06 29 14:16:55.584 [455.455]   ...
D/BatteryService(  123): level:99 scale:100 status:4 health:2 prese...
D/Tango.MessageService(  455): 2012 06 29 14:19:55.583 [455.455]   ...
V/Tango.Utils(  455): 2012 06 29 14:19:55.585 [455.455] Read Tango....
D/Tango.MessageService(  455): 2012 06 29 14:19:55.588 [455.455]   ...
D/BatteryService(  123): level:99 scale:100 status:4 health:2 prese...
D/SntpClient(  123): request time failed: java.net.UnknownHostExcep...
D/SntpClient(  123): request time failed: java.net.UnknownHostExcep...
D/SntpClient(  123): request time failed: java.net.UnknownHostExcep...
...
^C
```

What I learned here are:

* I have one Android device connected to my Windows system to play: "028841C6433F5617" representing the LG-V905R tablet connected on USB. The Android emulator is turned off at this moment.

* If there is only 1 Android device connected, I can run "adb" command without the "-d" option.

* You need to press "<Ctrl>-C" to stop "adb logcat" command. Otherwise it will continuously print new log data on the screen.

Installing Application to Tablet using "ant installd" Command

This section provides a tutorial example on how to install the debug package of my 'HelloAndroid' application to my LG-V905R tablet using the 'ant installd' command through the USB debugging interface.

I think I am ready try to install my own applications on my LG-V905R tablet and debug/test them.

Let's try to install the "HelloAndroid" debug package to my tablet first using the "ant installd" command. See previous tutorials on how to build the debug package.

You may need to shutdown the Android emulator to run "ant installd", because it can not support 2 connected Android devices.

```
C:\herong\HelloAndroid>\local\apache-ant-1.8.3\bin\ant installd

Unable to locate tools.jar.
Expected to find it in C:\Program Files\Java\jre7\lib\tools.jar
Buildfile: C:\herong\HelloAndroid\build.xml

-set-mode-check:

-set-debug-files:

install:
     [echo] Installing C:\herong\HelloAndroid\bin\HelloAndr
oid-debug.apk onto default emulator or device...
     [exec]     pkg: /data/local/tmp/HelloAndroid-debug.apk
     [exec] Success
     [exec] 1125 KB/s (14980 bytes in 0.013s)

installd:

BUILD SUCCESSFUL
Total time: 3 seconds
```

Ok. We have an error here. The default Java environment on my Windows system is JRE 1.6, which does not have the tools.jar, which required by "ant"

I need to set the JAVA_HOME variable to point to the JDK environment, which contains the tools.jar file.

Go to the emulator Windows and close it. Then rerun the "ant installd" command:

```
C:\herong\HelloAndroid>set "JAVA_HOME=\Program Files\java\jdk1.7.0_03"
```

```
C:\herong\HelloAndroid>\local\apache-ant-1.8.3\bin\ant installd
Buildfile: C:\herong\HelloAndroid\build.xml

-set-mode-check:

-set-debug-files:

install:
     [echo] Installing C:\herong\HelloAndroid\bin\HelloAndr
oid-debug.apk onto default emulator or device...
     [exec]     pkg: /data/local/tmp/HelloAndroid-debug.apk
     [exec] 1218 KB/s (14980 bytes in 0.012s)
     [exec] Success

installd:

BUILD SUCCESSFUL
Total time: 2 seconds
```

It works this time! "ant installd" installed my debug package of "HelloAndroid" to my LG-V905R tablet through the USB debugging interface.

To verify, go to the tablet and tap on "Applications". You will see "HelloAndroid" listed and ready to run.

Installing Application to Tablet using "adb -d install" Command

This section provides a tutorial example on how to install the debug package of my 'HelloAndroid' application to my LG-V905R tablet using the 'adb -d install' command through the USB debugging interface.

The Android SDK document also mentions another way to install application packages to the USB connected tablet device using the "adb -d install path/to/your/app.apk" command.

1. Go to LG-V905R tablet. Tap on "Home", "Applications", then "HelloAndroid". You will see "Hello, Android" displayed on the screen.

2. Tap on "Home", "Settings", "Applications", then "Managing applications". You will see "HelloAndroid" displayed in the application list.

3. Tap on "HelloAndroid" and "Uninstall" to uninstall "HelloAndroid".

4. Go to Windows computer, try to install the "HelloAndroid" debug package to my tablet again using the "adb -d install" command.

```
C:\herong\HelloAndroid>\local\android-sdk-windows\platform-tools\adb
   -d install bin\HelloAndroid-debug.apk


914 KB/s (14980 bytes in 0.016s)
        pkg: /data/local/tmp/HelloAndroid-debug.apk
Success
```

5. Go to the tablet again. You will see "HelloAndroid" is ready to run again.

6. You can uninstall "HelloAndroid" using the "adb -d uninstall" command:

```
C:\herong\HelloAndroid>\local\android-sdk-windows\platform-tools\adb
   -d uninstall com.herongyang
Success
^C
```

Note that the "adb -d uninstall" command takes the Java class package name as the argument. "com.herongyang" is the package name for my "HelloAndroid" application.

Installing "AboutAndroid" to LG-V905R Tablet

This section provides a tutorial example on how to install my 'AboutAndroid' application to my LG-V905R tablet. 'HelloAndroid' needs to be uninstalled first, because both applications share the same Java package name 'com.herongyang'.

My first application "HelloAndroid" works on my LG-V905R tablet, now let's see what will happen to my second application "AboutAndroid".

1. Uninstall "HelloAndroid", then install "AboutAndroid". Keeping "HelloAndroid" on the tablet will cause installation problem with "AboudAndroid", because both "HelloAndroid" and "AboutAndroid" use the same Java class package name.

```
C:\herong\AboutAndroid>\local\android-sdk-windows\platform-tools\adb
   -d uninstall com.herongyang
Success


C:\herong\cod\AboutAndroid>\local\android-sdk-windows\platform-tools\adb
   -d install -s bin\AboutAndroid-debug.apk
778 KB/s (23132 bytes in 0.029s)
      pkg: /sdcard/tmp/AboutAndroid-debug.apk
Success
```

2. Go to the tablet. Tap on "Home", "Applications", then "AboutAndroid" to run the application. You will see the output:

```
System properties
------------
java.vm.version: 1.5.0
java.vm.name: Dalvik
user.dir: /
javax.net.ssl.trustedStore: /system/etc/security/cacerts.bks
java.io.tmpdir: /sdcard
java.runtime.name: Android Runtime
http.agent: Dalvik/1.5.0 (Linux; U; Android 3.0.1; LG-V905R Build/H...
java.net.preferIPv6Addresses: true
java.boot.class.path: /system/frameword/core.jar;...
java.library.path: /vendor/lib;/system/lib
file.encoding: UTF-8
java.vm.specification.version: 0.9
java.vm.specification.vendor: The Android Project
o.name: Linux
android.vm.dexfile.true
java.specification.name: Dalvik Core Library
os.version: 2.6.36.3+
os.arch: armv7I
java.runtime.version: 0.9
java.class.version: 46.0
```

```
Environment variables
------------
ANDROID_SOCKET_zygot: 9
EXTERNAL_STORAGE: /mnt/sdcard
ANDROID_ASSETS: /system/app
ASEC_MOUNTPOINT: /mnt/asec
PATH: /sbin;/vendor/bin;/system/sbin;/system/bin;/system/xbin
ANDROID_DATA: /data
ANDROID_ROOT: /system

Environment folder
------------
Data folder: /data/data/com.herongyang/cache
External cache folder: /mnt/sdcard/Android/data/com.herongyang/cache
File folder: /data/data/com.herongyang/files
Package name: com.herongyang
Package code path: /data/app/com.herongyang-1.apk
Package resource path: /data/app/com.herongyang-1.apk
```

Note that you may get execution errors, if tablet Android version is not compatible with AboutAndroid build version.

Android Phone - LG-P925g

This chapter provides tutorial notes on the Android phone - LG-P925g. Topics include Android phone system basic information; running background processes and foreground applications; connecting phone to computer as USB storage drive, transferring files using Bluetooth radio; using Wi-Fi network to access Internet; setting up Gmail access; downloading applications from Google Play Store.

Takeaways:

- Android phone system supports multi-tasking and allows you to run multiple background processes and foreground applications.

- The USB cable allows you to use your Android phone as USB storage drive. This gives you a way to exchange files on phone's SD Card with your computer.

- Bluetooth connection also gives you a way to transfer files between your phone and your computer.

- The Wi-Fi function allows your phone to access the Internet using your home Wi-Fi network. This will save cost on the data transfer charge on your cell phone bill.

- Setting up Gmail mail box access on an Android phone is easy.

• Downloading applications from Google Play Store to Android phone is also easy.

About My LG-P925g Android Phone

This section provides a tutorial example on how to view basic information a LG-P925g Android phone.

I got my first Android phone, LG-P925g, not long ago. Here is how it looks like:

LG-P925g Android Phone

The technical specifications say:

```
Technology         GSM

Form Factor        Bar

Camera             Dual 5MP stereoscopic 3D camera with auto-focus

Smartphone         Android 2.2 OS, upgradable to 2.3

Touch Screen       Large 4.3" Capacitive Touch Screen

Frequency          Quad-band GSM/GPRS/EDGE; 850/900/1800/1900 MHz...

DataTransmission   HSDPA 14.4 Mbps, HSUPA 5.7 Mbps

Dimensions         5.07" (H) x 2.67" (W) x 0.47" (D)

Weight             5.93 oz.

Display            16M Color 3D TFT, 800 x 480 Pixels, 4.3"

USB                2.0 High Speed
```

```
Standard Battery      1,500 mAh

Talk Time             Up to 6 Hours*

Standby Time          Up to 13 Days*

Internal Memory       512 MB RAM, 8GB (eMMC) ROM;

                      preinstalled 6GB microSD card

microSD Memory Slot Supports up to a 32GB memory card
```

To review basic information on the phone, tap on "Settings", then "About Phone". I see the following information:

```
Status - Phone number, signal, etc.

Battery use - What has been using the battery

Legal information

Model number - LG-P925g

Android version - 2.2.2

Baseband version - L6260_MODEM_SIC_01...

Kernel version - 2.6.35.7

Build number - FRG83G

Software version - LGP925g-V10c...
```

Ok. My Android version 2.2.2 is not that old. Android 2.2.2 was released on 22 January 2011. But Google released 2.3.3, 2.3.4, 2.3.5, and 2.3.6 very quickly after 2.2.2. I may need to do a upgrade on phone soon.

Phone Memory and SD (Secure Digital) Card

This section provides a tutorial example on how to view phone memory size and SD (Secure Digital) card size. LG-P925g came with a preinstalled internal SD card.

After checking the Android OS version on my phone, I want to know how much storage I have on my phone.

Tap on "Settings", then "SD card & phone storage settings". I see the following information:

```
USB connection mode

   Mass storage only [ ]
```

```
SD card
   Total space - Unavailable
   Available space - Unavailable

Internal SD card
   Total space - 5.57 GB
   Available space - 5.32 GB
   Format internal SD card

Internal phone storage
   Available space - 859 MB
```

Not too bad. The phone came with preinstall internal SD (Secure Digital) card. And I can add another SD card, if I want to.

Running Services - Background Processes

This section provides a tutorial example on how to review running services, or background processes, on my Android phone. Those background processes are started automatically and running all the time.

Since Android is a multi-tasking system, let's see what are currently running on my phone.

Tap on "Settings", "Applications", then "Running services". I see a long list of items displayed:

```
de.emsys.usbmode.control              1.6MB
   Process: de.emsys.usbmode.control
   Usb Mode Control                   21:50:09
de.emsys.usbmode.service              1.7MB
   Process: de.emsys.usbmode.service
   UsbModeService                     21:50:09
Message Widget                        2.0MB
   Process: com.lge.sizechangable.message
   messageViewManage                  21:50:09
```

```
What's New                          2.7MB
   Process: com.android.whatsnew
   SyncService                        12:30
Google Play Store                   6.5MB
   Process: com.android.vending
   ContentSyncService              4:16:10
On-Screen Phone                     2.0MB
   Process: com.lge.osp
   On-Screen Phone                21:50:08
Calendar Storage                    2.3MB
   Process com.android.provider.calendar
Google Service Framework           11MB
   Process: com.google.process.gapps
   Google Messaging Service       21:50:09
LG PC Suite                         1.9MB
   Process: com.mobileleader.sync
   ObexService                        17:40
DRM Service                         1.7MB
   Process: com.lge.drmservice
   DrmService                     21:50:08
Weather                             3.5MB
   Process: com.lge.sizechangable.weather
   WeatherTimerService               21:23
Video Player                        1.5MB
   Process: com.lifevibes.lgevideoplayer
   AppHelperService                12:51:30
Android keyboard
   Process: com.android.inputmethod.latin
   Android keyboard               21:50:09

Other: 94MB in 9   Avail: 88MB+129MB in 16
```

It seems to me that those are background processes that are started automatically and running all the time. I should leave them alone.

Running Applications - Background and Foreground Processes

This section provides a tutorial example on how to review running applications, including both background processes and foreground processes, on my Android phone.

In the previous tutorial, I reviewed what are running as background processes on my phone. In this tutorial, I want to review all processes, including background and foreground, that are currently running.

Tap on "Settings", "Applications", than "Manage applications". I see 4 tabs showing up: "Downloaded", "Running", "All" and "On SD card".

Tap on "Running" tab. I see a long list of items displayed:

```
Alarm/Clock
Android keyboard
Android System
Bluetooth Share
Browser
Calendar Storage
com.android.provider.appl
com.android.provider.user
contact Storage
de.emsys.usbmode.control
Dialer
Dialer Storage
Download Manager
DRM Protected Content Storage
DRM Service
E-mail
Fonts
Gallery
Gmail
Google Play Books
Google Play Store
Google Search
```

```
Google Service Framework

Home

LG PC Suite

LGMITS Service

Media Storage

Message Widget

Messaging

Music

My Updates

On-Screen Phone

Settings

Settings Storage

Social+

Video Player

Voice Control

Weather

What's New
```

If you want stop any running application, you tap on its name. Then tap on the "Force stop" button.

Connect Phone to Computer using Bluetooth

This section provides a tutorial example on how to connect an Android phone to a Windows computer using Bluetooth radio. Once connected, you can transfer files between the phone and computer.

1. Turn on Bluetooth function on the laptop computer.

2. On the Android phone, tap on "Settings", then "Bluetooth settings".

2. Tap on the checkbox next to "Bluetooth" to turn on the "Bluetooth" function on the phone. You will your laptop Bluetooth device displayed with other Bluetooth devices nearby.

3. Tap on your laptop Bluetooth device name to make a pairing request to the computer.

4. On the computer, accept the paring request, which should contain a pairing code for identification purpose.

5. On the phone, tap on "Pair" to finish up the pairing process. The status message should say "Paired but not connected" now.

To send a music file from computer to phone, right-click on the music file to select "Send to\Bluetooth" in the context menu to start the sending process. Go to your phone to receive the music file.

To send a music file from phone to computer, tap on "Applications", then "Music". Tap and hold on the music to select the "Bluetooth" in the pop up menu to start the sending process. Go to your computer to receive the music file.

Connect Phone SD Card to Computer via USB

This section provides a tutorial example on how to use the USB cable to connect SD card in the phone to the computer as a removable drive on the computer.

My Android phone also came with a USB cable that can be used to connect the SD card on my phone as a storage to my laptop for exchange files. Here is how it works:

1. Turn on my phone and my laptop. Then connect them with the USB cable.

2. On the phone, you will see the USB connection message:

```
USB connected


You have connected your phone to your computer via USB.
Select the button below if you want to copy files between
your computer and your Android's SD card.


[Turn on USB storage]
```

3. Tap on "Turn on USB storage". you will see a warning message saying that when the SD card is connected to the laptop as a USB storage to the laptop. Applications that are using the SD card will be stopped to avoid data corruption.

```
Turn on USB storage
```

```
If you turn USB storage, some applications you are using will
stop and may unavailable until you turn off USB storage.
```

```
[OK] [Cancel]
```

4. Tap on "OK". You will see another message:

```
USB storage in use
```

```
Before turn off USB storage, make sure you have unmounted ("ejected")
your Android's SD card from your computer.
```

```
[Turn off USB storage]
```

5. Look at the laptop now. You will see a removable drive E: is listed in the Windows Explorer.

6. Check the property of that removable drive E. You will see the total capacity is 5.57 GB. This matches the size of the internal SD card on my phone.

7. Copy some music .mp3 files from the laptop to the E:\Music folder

8. Eject the removable drive E: on the laptop.

10. Go back to the phone and tap "Turn off USB storage". You will see a quick message in the status bar saying "scanning media files". This tells me that Android is checking files that have been copied to the SD card.

11. Tap "Application" and "Music". Then select the music files copied from the laptop to enjoy the music on the phone.

Using Wi-Fi Function to Reduce Data Cost

This section provides a tutorial example on how to turn on the 'Wi-Fi' function to reduce data transfer cost when you are at home next to your home Wi-Fi network.

To save "Data Service" cost on you cell phone bill, you should turn the Wi-Fi function on your Android phone to use your home Wi-Fi network.

1. Tap on "Settings", "Wireless & networks", then "Wi-Fi settings".

2. Tap on the checkbox next to "Wi-Fi" to turn on the "Wi-Fi" function. You will your Wi-Fi SID displayed with other Wi-Fi SIDs in the neighborhood. You SID should have the strongest signal icon.

3. Tap on your Wi-Fi SID and enter your Wi-Fi password to finish up the connection.

Now you can browse the Internet, download files, or play on-line games through your Wi-Fi home network.

Without using the "Wi-Fi" function, the cell phone service provider will charge you for the amount of data transferred whenever you use the Internet.

Setting up Gmail Access on Android Phone

This section provides a tutorial example on how to set up Gmail access on Android phones: 'Settings' > 'Account and sync' > 'Add account'.

If you want to read emails from your Gmail mailbox or download more applications, you need to do account setup on your Android phone.

1. Tap on "Settings", then "Account & sync". You will see a list of Internet access accounts that you have already set up.

2. Tap on the "Add account" button, then "Next".

3. Tap on "Create", if you don't have a Google Account. Tap on "Sign in", if you already have a Google Account.

4. Follow instructions on the screen to finish the set up process.

5. Tap on "Applications", then "Gmail". You will see incoming emails listed on the screen now.

If you have more than one Gmail mailbox, you can set up them on your phone by repeating the "Add account" process.

If you want to remove any mailbox, tap on the Gmail address, then "Remove account".

Downloading and Installing from "Play Store"

This section provides a tutorial example on how to download and install applications from Google's 'Play Store'. Read permissions requested by the application carefully before using the application.

Downloading and installing Android application is easy. Here is what you need to do to install the Tetris game.

1. Make sure you have done the Gmail account set up as presented in the previous tutorial.

2. Tap on "Applications", then "Play Store". Go to the "Apps" section.

3. Tap the Search icon to search for "Tetris". Then tap on "TETRIS free" in the search result. You will see "TETRIS free" installation screen.

4. Tap on the "Install" button. You will see the list permissions requested by this application:

```
PERMISSIONS

Storage - Modify/delete SD card content
Phone calls - Read phone state and identity
Network communication - Allows the application to accept cloud
    to device messages from application's service, full Internet
    access
System tools - Change network connectivity, prevent phone from
    sleeping
Network communication - View Wi-Fi state, view network state
Hardware controls - Control vibrator
```

5. Tap on "Accept & download". You will see the download progress bar displayed.

6. The system will install automatically after download is completed.

Before playing the game, you should look at those permissions again. I don't understand why a "Tetris" game needs to have this permission: "Phone calls - Read phone state and identity"

USB Debugging Applications on LG-P925g Phone

This chapter provides tutorial notes on debugging application on LG-P925g phone. Topics include installing LG USB device driver on Windows; Turning on USB debugging interface on LG-P925g phone; running 'adb -d' commands on USB connected device; installing application through USB connection; Android API levels and platform versions.

Takeaways:

- USB cable connection can charge the phone from the computer.

- USB cable connection can also turn your phone into USB storage drive to the computer.

- USB cable connection can also provide debugging interface for the Android SDK package on the computer to install and debug applications on the phone. But you need to install the USB driver on the computer first.

- The ADB tool has switch to select the emulator or connected device: "adb -e" for emulator and "adb -d" for device.

- "ant installd" can install an application to the emulator or the connected device, but only if one of them exists.

- "adb install" can install an application to the emulator or the connected device, even both of them exist. "adb -e install" works for the emulator. "adb -d install" works for the connected device.

- You need to stay with API Level 7 when developing a new Android application, if you want the application to run on 99% of existing Android devices.

Installing LG USB Device Driver on Windows

This section provides a tutorial example on how to install the LG USB device driver for LG-P925g Android phone on Windows system. This is needed to test your Android application developed on Windows on LG phones via a USB connection.

If you are developing applications on Windows and would like to connect an Android-powered device to test them, then you need to install the appropriate USB driver.

Here is what I did to install the USB driver on my Windows system for my LG-P925g Android phone.

1. On my Windows computer, go to LG Mobile Support Web site at: http://www.lg.com/us/support/mobile-devices/phone-support.

2. Follow the link "Click here to download your mobile driver" in the "Download Drivers / Phone Updates" section.

3. Save the download file to: "\temp\LGUnitedMobileDriver S4981MAN36AP22 ML WHQL Ver 3.6.exe", and wait for the download to finish.

4. Double-click on that downloaded file to start installing the driver.

5. Follow the instructions to finish the installation.

6. Turn on the LG-P925g phone and connect it to the Windows computer with the USB cable. Windows will display a "Your device is ready to use" icon in the task bar area. Click on it see details:

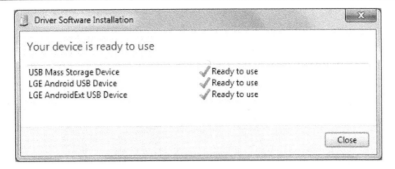

LG-P925g USB Driver for Windows

This is good. Now I can use my phone from my Windows system as:

- USB Mass Storage Device

- LGE Android USB Device

- LGE AndroidExt USB Device

Viewing LG Android USB Device in Control Panel

This section provides a tutorial example on how to view the LG Android USB device in Windows Control Panel and see its detailed properties.

To verify the LG USB device driver installation, you can look at the device properties in the control panel.

1. On the Windows computer, go to "Control Panel\Hardware and Sound\Devices and Printers". You see a "LG AndroidNet Phone" icon listed as a connected device.

LG-P925g Phone as Device on Windows

2. Right-click on "LG AndroidNet Phone" and select "Properties". You see some general properties.

2. Click on the "Hardware" tab. You see a list of device functions:

```
LG AndroidNet Phone

Device Functions:
E:\                          Portable Devices
F:\                          Portable Devices
LGE Android USB Device       Disk drives
LGE AndroidExt USB Device    Disk drives
USB Mass Storage Device      Universal Serial Bus controllers

Device Function Summary
Manufacture: LGE
Location: on UMBus Enumerator
Device status: This device is working properly
```

Ok. The LG Android USB Device driver is installed and running properly.

Turning on USB Debugging on LG-P925g

This section provides a tutorial example on how to turn on 'USB Debugging' on LG-P925g
Android phones in the 'Settings > Applications > Development' area.

After installing the LG USB driver on my Windows system for my LG Android phone, I am ready to turn on the USB Debugging function on my phone to allow me to do testing and debugging my application on my phone through the USB connection.

1. Turn on the LG-P925g phone and connect it to the Windows computer with the USB cable. You will get the USB connected message, which asks you to "Turn on USB storage". Ignore that message, because we don't want use the phone just as a USB storage.

2. Tap on "Home", "Settings", "Applications", then "Development". You will see 3 development settings:

```
USB debugging - Debug mode when USB is connected        [ ]
Stay awake - Screen will never sleep while charging     [ ]
Allow mock locations - Allow mock locations             [ ]
```

3. Tap on the checkbox to turn on the "USB debugging" setting. You will get the confirmation message:

```
Allow USB debugging?


USB debugging is intended for development purposes only. It can be
used to copy data between your computer and your device, install
applications on your device without notification, and read log data.
[OK] [Cancel]
```

4. Tap on "OK" to confirm.

5. On your computer, Windows will display a "Your device is ready to use" icon in the task bar area. Click on it see details:

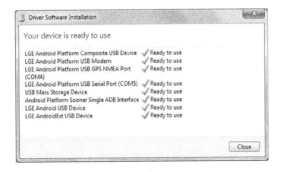

LG-P925g USB Driver for Debugging

This is getting better. There are more functions that are available on the USB connection now:

- LGE Android Platform Composite USB Device

- LGE Android Platform USB Modem

- LGE Android Platform USB GPS NMEA Port (COM4)

- LGE Android Platform USB Serial Port (COM5)

- USB Mass Storage Device

- Android Platform Sooner Single ADB Interface

- LGE Android USB Device

- LGE AndroidExt USB Device

Viewing USB Debugging Devices in Control Panel

This section provides a tutorial example on how to view the LG Android USB Debugging devices in Windows Control Panel. Each device represents a different interface that Windows can use through the USB connection.

Since more devices are added to my Windows system when I turned on "USB Debugging" on my phone, I want to check their properties in the Control Panel.

1. On the Windows computer, go to "Control Panel\Hardware and Sound\Devices and Printers". You do see more icons listed as connected devices representing different interfaces Windows can through the USB connection.

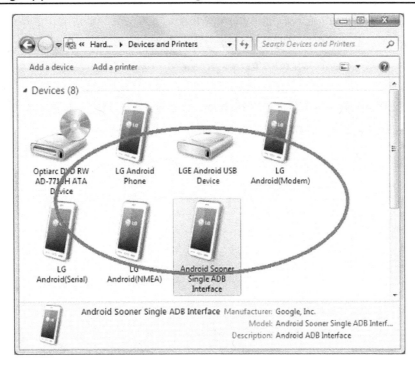

LG-P925g Phone as USB Debugging Device

2. Right-click on "Android Sooner Single ADB Interface" and select "Properties". You
see some general properties:

```
Device Information


Manufacture: Google Inc.

Model: Android Sooner Single ADB Interface

Model number: Unavailable

Categories: Phone

Description: Android ADB Interface
```

Interesting, the actual ADB (Android Debugging Bridge) interface driver is produced by
Google and included in the LG USB driver package that I installed earlier.

You continue to check other detailed properties to know more about this driver.

Running "adb" on LG-P925g USB Debugging Interface

*This section provides a tutorial example on how to run 'adb' commands on LG-P925g
Android phone through the USB debugging interface. 'adb -d' is to run commands on the
USB device. 'adb -e' is to run commands on the emulator.*

With my LG-P925g Android phone connected in USB debugging mode, I can try some
Android SDK debugging tools on my Windows computer now.

The first I want to try is the ADB (Android Debugging Bridge) tool:

```
C:\herong>\local\android-sdk-windows\platform-tools\adb devices
List of devices attached
emulator-5554    device
6B30002400000001        device


C:\herong>\local\android-sdk-windows\platform-tools\adb shell date
error: more than one device and emulator


C:\herong>\local\android-sdk-windows\platform-tools\adb -e shell date
Sun Apr 1 23:29:21 GMT 2012


C:\herong>\local\android-sdk-windows\platform-tools\adb -d shell date
Sun Apr 1 19:29:33 GMT 2012


C:\herong>\local\android-sdk-windows\platform-tools\adb -e shell \
    ping localhost
PING localhost (127.0.0.1) 56(84) bytes of data.
64 bytes from localhost (127.0.0.1): icmp_seq=1 ttl=64 time=2.52 ms
64 bytes from localhost (127.0.0.1): icmp_seq=2 ttl=64 time=3.69 ms


C:\herong>\local\android-sdk-windows\platform-tools\adb -d shell \
    ping localhost
ping: icmp open socket: Operation not permitted


C:\herong>\local\android-sdk-windows\platform-tools\adb -d shell
$ df
df
/dev: 226052K total, 12K used, 226040K available (block size 4096)
/lgdrm: 2011K total, 1059K used, 952K available (block size 1024)
/mnt/asec: 226052K total, 0K used, 226052K available (block size 4096)
```

```
/mnt/tmp: 4096K total, 0K used, 4096K available (block size 4096)

/system: 613840K total, 530296K used, 83544K available (block size 4096)

/data: 1032088K total, 153872K used, 878216K available (block size 4096)

/misc: 3963K total, 1058K used, 2905K available (block size 1024)

/cache: 63472K total, 4144K used, 59328K available (block size 4096)

/mnt/sdcard: 5844864K total, 2368480K used, 3476384K available (bl...

/mnt/secure/asec: Permission denied

$exit

exit


C:\herong>\local\android-sdk-windows\platform-tools\adb -d logcat
--------- beginning of /dev/log/system
I/ActivityManager(  194): Starting activity: Intent { act=android....

I/ActivityManager(  194): process name to start: com.android.setti...

I/ActivityManager(  194): Start proc com.android.settings for acti...

W/Watchdog(  194): handleMessage monitor is completed.

W/Watchdog(  194): handleMessage mCompleted is true...

I/ActivityManager(  194): process name to start: com.lge.hiddenmen...

I/ActivityManager(  194): Start proc com.lge.hiddenmenu for conten...

D/PowerManagerService(  194): setTimeoutLocked mPolicy.isKeyguardS...

D/PowerManagerService(  194): setTimeoutLocked mPolicy.isKeyguardS...

D/PowerManagerService(  194): setTimeoutLocked mPolicy.isKeyguardS...

D/PowerManagerService(  194): setTimeoutLocked mPolicy.isKeyguardS...

I/ActivityManager(  194): Starting activity: Intent { act=android....

...

^C
```

What I learned here are:

- I have two Android devices on my Windows system to play with now: "emulator-5554" is the Android emulator, and "6B30002400000001" is the LG-P925g phone connected on USB.

- If there are more than 1 device connected, the "adb" command requires an option to specify which device to use: "-e" is for the emulator, and "-d" is for the real device.

- The "shell date" command returns 2 different time stamps from my emulator and my device, because the clock on the emulator is wrong and needs to be configured.

- It looks like the USB Debugging interface on my real LG Android device does not have the root permission. The "shell ping localhost" command returns a permission error on the device.

- You need to press "<Ctrl>-C" to stop "adb logcat" command. Otherwise it will continuously print new log data on the screen.

Installing Application to Phone using "ant installd" Command

This section provides a tutorial example on how to install the debug package of my 'HelloAndroid' application to my LG-P925g phone using the 'ant installd' command through the USB debugging interface.

I think I am ready try to install my own applications on my LG-P925g phone and debug/ test them.

Let's try to install the "HelloAndroid" debug package to my phone first using the "ant installd" command. See previous tutorials on how to build the debug package.

```
C:\herong\HelloAndroid>\local\apache-ant-1.8.3\bin\ant installd
Buildfile: C:\herong\HelloAndroid\build.xml

-set-mode-check:

-set-debug-files:

install:
     [echo] Installing
           C:\herong\HelloAndroid\bin\HelloAndroid-debug.apk
           onto default emulator or device...
     [exec] error: more than one device and emulator

BUILD FAILED
C:\local\android-sdk-windows\tools\ant\build.xml:1194:
The following error occurred while executing this line:
C:\local\android-sdk-windows\tools\ant\build.xml:1208:
```

USB Debugging Applications on LG-P925g Phone

```
exec returned: 1


Total time: 0 seconds
```

Ok. We have an error here. I have both the emulator and the USB device running. The "ant" command does not know which one to use.

I don't see how to provide a command option to help the "ant" command. I am going to shut down my Android emulator to resolve the problem.

Go to the emulator Windows and close it. Then rerun the "ant installd" command:

```
C:\herong\HelloAndroid>\local\apache-ant-1.8.3\bin\ant installd
Buildfile: C:\herong\HelloAndroid\build.xml


-set-mode-check:


-set-debug-files:


install:
     [echo] Installing
           C:\herong\HelloAndroid\bin\HelloAndroid-debug.apk
           onto default emulator or device...
     [exec]     pkg: /data/local/tmp/HelloAndroid-debug.apk
     [exec] Success
     [exec] 228 KB/s (14980 bytes in 0.064s)


installd:


BUILD SUCCESSFUL
Total time: 2 seconds
```

It works this time! "ant installd" installed my debug package of "HelloAndroid" to my LG-P925g phone through the USB debugging interface.

To verify, go to the phone and tap on "Applications". You will see "HelloAndroid" listed in the "Downloads" section.

Android Tutorials - Herong's Tutorial Examples (v3.05, 2023)   HerongYang.com

Installing Application to Phone using "adb -d install" Command

This section provides a tutorial example on how to install the debug package of my 'HelloAndroid' application to my LG-P925g phone using the 'adb -d install' command through the USB debugging interface.

The Android SDK document also mentions another way to install application packages to the USB connected phone device using the "adb -d install path/to/your/app.apk" command.

1. Go to LG-P925g phone. Tap on "Home", "Applications", then "HelloAndroid". You will see "Hello, Android" displayed on the screen.

2. Tap on "Home", "Settings", "Applications", then "Managing applications". You will see "HelloAndroid" displayed in the application list.

3. Tap on "HelloAndroid" and "Uninstall" to uninstall "HelloAndroid".

4. Go to Windows computer, try to install the "HelloAndroid" debug package to my phone again using the "adb -d install" command.

```
C:\herong\HelloAndroid>\local\android-sdk-windows\platform-tools\adb
   -d install bin\HelloAndroid-debug.apk

731 KB/s (14980 bytes in 0.020s)
      pkg: /data/local/tmp/HelloAndroid-debug.apk
Success
^C
```

Note that for some reason the "adb -d install" command does exit by itself. I need to press "<Ctrl>-C" to break it.

5. Go to the phone again. You will see "HelloAndroid" is ready to run again.

6. You can uninstall "HelloAndroid" using the "adb -d uninstall" command:

```
C:\herong\HelloAndroid>\local\android-sdk-windows\platform-tools\adb
   -d uninstall com.herongyang
```

```
Success
^C
```

Note that the "adb -d uninstall" command takes the Java class package name as the argument. "com.herongyang" is the package name for my "HelloAndroid" application.

"adb -d install" Command Options

This section provides a tutorial example on how to use 'adb -d install' command options. '-r' is to reinstall an application without uninstall it. '-s' is to install an application on the SD Card instead of the internal memory.

To have a better control of the application installation process, I looked at the "adb" command document again. It gives the following command options:

```
adb install [-l] [-r] [-s] <file> - push this package file to the
   device and install it
   ('-l' means forward-lock the app)
   ('-r' means reinstall the app, keeping its data)
   ('-s' means install on SD card instead of internal storage)

adb uninstall [-k] <package> - remove this app package from the device
   ('-k' means keep the data and cache directories)
```

Now try some of those options:

1. Testing the reinstall option "-r":

```
C:\herong\HelloAndroid>\local\android-sdk-windows\platform-tools\adb
   -d install bin\HelloAndroid-debug.apk
812 KB/s (14980 bytes in 0.018s)
      pkg: /data/local/tmp/HelloAndroid-debug.apk
Success
^C

C:\herong\HelloAndroid>\local\android-sdk-windows\platform-tools\adb
   -d install bin\HelloAndroid-debug.apk
812 KB/s (14980 bytes in 0.018s)
```

```
        pkg: /data/local/tmp/HelloAndroid-debug.apk
Failure [INSTALL_FAILED_ALREADY_EXISTS]
^C


C:\herong\HelloAndroid>\local\android-sdk-windows\platform-tools\adb
    -d install -r bin\HelloAndroid-debug.apk
975 KB/s (14980 bytes in 0.015s)
        pkg: /data/local/tmp/HelloAndroid-debug.apk
Success
^C
```

2. Testing the SD Card installation option "-s":

```
C:\herong\HelloAndroid>\local\android-sdk-windows\platform-tools\adb
    -d install -r -s bin\HelloAndroid-debug.apk
504 KB/s (14980 bytes in 0.029s)
        pkg: /sdcard/tmp/HelloAndroid-debug.apk
Success
^C
```

Go to the phone. Tap on "Home", "Settings", "Applications", "Managing applications", then "On SD Card". You will "HelloAndroid" displayed in the application list.

You can try other command options yourself.

Installing "AboutAndroid" to LG-P925g Phone

This section provides a tutorial example on how to install my 'AboutAndroid' application to my LG-P925g phone. 'HelloAndroid' needs to be uninstalled first, because both applications share the same Java package name 'com.herongyang'.

My first application "HelloAndroid" works on my LG-P925g phone, now let's see what will happen to my second application "AboutAndroid".

1. First, install the "AboutAndroid" debug package to my phone using the "adb -d install" command. See previous tutorials on how to build the debug package.

```
C:\herong\AboutAndroid>\local\android-sdk-windows\platform-tools\adb
```

```
    -d -s install bin\AboutAndroid-debug.apk
806 KB/s (23132 bytes in 0.028s)
        pkg: /data/local/tmp/AboutAndroid-debug.apk
Failure [INSTALL_FAILED_ALREADY_EXISTS]
^C
```

What's wrong with the installation? This is the first time installing the "AboutAndroid" package on my phone. Why I am getting the "INSTALL_FAILED_ALREADY_EXISTS" error?

After checking "AndroidManifest.xml" files from both "HelloAndroid" and "AboutAndroid" applications, I notice that both applications are sharing the same Java class package name - package="com.herongyang". This means that I can not install both "HelloAndroid" and "AboutAndroid" applications on to the same Android phone.

When building any future applications, remember to give different Java package name for each application.

2. Uninstall "HelloAndroid", then install "AboutAndroid".

```
C:\herong\AboutAndroid>\local\android-sdk-windows\platform-tools\adb
    -d uninstall com.herongyang
Success
^C

C:\herong\cod\AboutAndroid>\local\android-sdk-windows\platform-tools\adb
    -d install -s bin\AboutAndroid-debug.apk
778 KB/s (23132 bytes in 0.029s)
        pkg: /sdcard/tmp/AboutAndroid-debug.apk
Success
^C
```

3. Go to the phone. Tap on "Home", "Applications", then "AboutAndroid" to run the application. You will see an error message on the screen:

```
Sorry!


The application AboutAndroid (process com.herongyang)
has stopped unexpectedly. Please try again.
```

```
[Force close]
```

What's wrong with my "AboutAndroid" application? It's a very simple application trying to display system information in a text view object.

See the next tutorial on how to resolve this error.

Developing Applications with Android API Level 7

This section describes why 'AboutAndroid' fails to run on Android 2.2.2 phone. The getObbDir() method is supported only on Android 2.3.4 (API Level 10) and higher. To run on 99% of existing Android devices, you need to develop the application with API Level 7.

In this tutorial, I want to try to figure out why "AboutAndroid" crashes on my LG-P925g phone.

1. Go to the LG-P925g phone and run "AboutAndroid" again. You will get the application crash error message again.

2. Go to the Windows computer and check the log buffer using the "adb -d logcat" command:

```
C:\herong\AboutAndroid>\local\android-sdk-windows\platform-tools\adb
   -d logcat AndroidRuntime:E *:S

--------- beginning of /dev/log/main
--------- beginning of /dev/log/system
E/AndroidRuntime( 8681): FATAL EXCEPTION: main
E/AndroidRuntime( 8681): java.lang.NoSuchMethodError:
                    com.herongyang.AboutAndroid.getObbDir
E/AndroidRuntime( 8681):   at com.herongyang.AboutAndroid.onCreate
                    (AboutAndroid.java:61)
E/AndroidRuntime( 8681):   at android.app.Instrumentation.callActiv...
E/AndroidRuntime( 8681):   at android.app.ActivityThread.performLau...
E/AndroidRuntime( 8681):   at android.app.ActivityThread.handleLaun...
E/AndroidRuntime( 8681):   at android.app.ActivityThread.access$230...
E/AndroidRuntime( 8681):   at android.app.ActivityThread$H.handleMe...
E/AndroidRuntime( 8681):   at android.os.Handler.dispatchMessage(Ha...
```

```
E/AndroidRuntime( 8681):    at android.os.Looper.loop(Looper.java:12...
E/AndroidRuntime( 8681):    at android.app.ActivityThread.main(Activ...
E/AndroidRuntime( 8681):    at java.lang.reflect.Method.invokeNative...
E/AndroidRuntime( 8681):    at java.lang.reflect.Method.invoke(Metho...
E/AndroidRuntime( 8681):    at com.android.internal.os.ZygoteInit$Me...
E/AndroidRuntime( 8681):    at com.android.internal.os.ZygoteInit.ma...
E/AndroidRuntime( 8681):    at dalvik.system.NativeStart.main(Native...
```

The log buffer does have some details about the crash: getObbDir() method is not supported by my LG-P925g phone.

This is because my LG-P925g phone is running Android 2.2.2, which has the API level of 8, while the getObbDir() method was introduced since API Level 11.

Now we learned that when develop a new Android application, we can not go with the classes and methods offered in the latest version of the API, if you want your application to run on existing Android devices currently used by millions of users.

Here is diagram of usage share of the different Android versions as of 2 April 2012 from wikipedia.com:

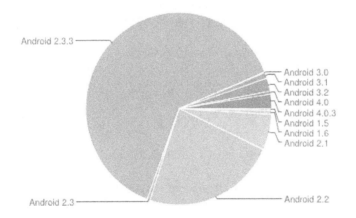

Usage Share of Android Versions as of 2012

So if you want your new application to cover 99% of existing Android devices, you need to develop it with Android API level 7, which should run on Android 2.1 and higher devices. Do not use anything higher than Android API level 7.

I think you know how to modify "AboutAndroid" Java code to make it work on LG-P925g. Try it yourself.

Archived Tutorials

This chapter contains some outdated tutorial notes and example codes from previous versions of this book.

Archived: Downloading and Installing JDK 1.7

This section describes how to download and install Java SE Development Kit 7u3 on a Windows system.

To develop Android applications in Java language, you need to have a copy of JDK (Java Development Kit) installed on your machine. The latest version of JDK is Java SE Development Kit 7u3. Here is what I did to download and install Java SE Development Kit 7u3 on my Windows system.

1. Open the Java SE Download page with this URL: http://www.oracle.com/technetwork/java/javase/downloads/.

2. Click the download button below "JDK" in the "Java SE 7u3" section. You will see a new page with a list of different download files of "Java SE Development Kit 7u3".

3. Click the "Accept License Agreement" option.

4. Locate the line "Windows x86 (32-bit) 84.12 MB" and click on "jdk-7u3-windows-i586.exe" to start download.

5. Save the download file to C:\download\jdk-7u3-windows-i586.exe and wait for the download to finish.

6. Double-click on C:\download\jdk-7u3-windows-i586.exe to start the installation wizard. The installation wizard will guide you to finish the installation.

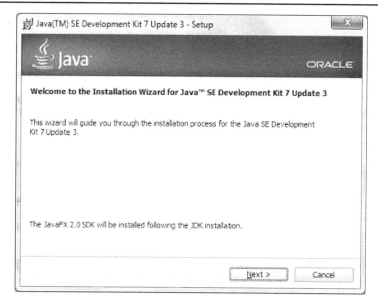

Java SE Development Kit 7 Setup

To verify the installation, open a command window to try the java command. If you are getting the following output, your installation was ok:

```
C:\herong>"\Program Files\Java\jdk1.7.0_03\bin\java.exe" -version

java version "1.7.0_03"
Java(TM) SE Runtime Environment (build 1.7.0_03-b05)
Java HotSpot(TM) Client VM (build 22.1-b02, mixed mode, sharing)
```

Archived: Downloading and Installing Android SDK R17

This section provides a tutorial example on how to download and install Android SDK (Software Development Kit) Revision 17 on Windows systems.

This tutorial was based on Android SDK R17 with Android 4.0.3 and left here as a reference.

If you want to develop applications for Android systems, you need to start with the following two steps to create an Android development environment on your Windows system:

- Download and install Android SDK starter package.

- Download and install libraries and tools to help you build applications for specific Android platforms.

Here is what I did to download and install the Android SDK Revision 17 starter package:

1. Go to the Android SDK download page at http://developer.android.com/sdk/.

2. Click "android-sdk_r17-windows.zip" in the Windows section. The browser will start the download process.

3. Save the downloaded file to C:\download\android-sdk_r17-windows.zip. The file size should be 37,417,953 bytes.

4. Unzip the downloaded file to C:\local\android-sdk-windows.

5. Double-click on "C:\local\android-sdk-windows\SDK Manager.exe". The "Android SDK Manager" windows will show up:

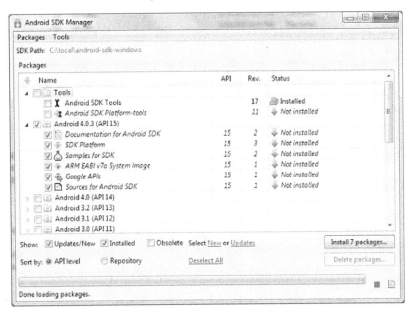

Android SDK Manager R17

Cool. Android SDK Revision 17 starter package is installed now. Read next tutorials to learn how to install Android platform emulator.

Archived: Running Android SDK Manager

This section provides a tutorial example on how to run Android SDK Manager to see what additional tools and libraries that are available from the Android developer center.

This tutorial was based on Android SDK R17 with Android 4.0.3 and left here as a reference.

After installing the Android SDK starter package, you can use the Android SDK Manager to see what additional tools and libraries that are available from the Android developer center.

Double-click on "C:\local\android-sdk-windows\SDK Manager.exe". The "Android SDK Manager" windows will show up with a list of libraries and tools for different versions of Android platforms that are currently available for download:

- Tools/Android SDK Tools - Basic tools installed already as part of the starter package.

- Tools/Android SDK Platform-tools - Common tools to build applications.

- Android 4.0.3 (API15) (Released on Dec. 16, 2011) - Libraries and tools for Android 4.03 platforms.

- Android 4.0 (API14) (Released on Oct. 19, 2011) - Libraries and tools for Android 4.0 platforms.

- Android 3.2 (API13) (Released on Jul. 15, 2011) - Libraries and tools for Android 3.2 platforms.

- Android 3.1 (API12) (Released on May 10, 2011) - Libraries and tools for Android 3.1 platforms.

- Android 3.0 (API11) (Released on Feb. 22, 2011) - Libraries and tools for Android 3.0 platforms.

- Android 2.3.3 (API10) (Released on Feb. 9, 2011) - Libraries and tools for Android 2.3.3 platforms.

- Android 2.2 (API8) (Released on May 20, 2010) - Libraries and tools for Android 2.2 platforms.

- Android 2.1 (API7) (Released on Jan. 12, 2010) - Libraries and tools for Android 2.1 platforms.

- Android 1.6 (API4) (Released on Sep. 15, 2009) - Libraries and tools for Android 1.6 platform.

- Android 1.5 (API3) (Released on Apr. 30, 2009) - Libraries and tools for Android 1.5 platform.

- Extra - Additional libraries for USB driver and other interfaces.

Read the next tutorial on how to download and install libraries and tools for Android 4.0 platforms.

Archived: Installing Android Platform 4.0.3 and Libraries

This section provides a tutorial example on how to install Android platform libraries and tools using Android SDK Manager.

This tutorial was based on Android SDK R17 with Android 4.0.3 and left here as a reference.

If you want to develop applications for mobile devices that are running the Android systems, you need to download and install libraries and tools for the latest Android platform using the Android SDK Manager:

1. Double-click on "C:\local\android-sdk-windows\SDK Manager.exe" to run the Android SDK Manager.

2. Review those libraries and tools that are preselected for you:

```
...
[x] Android 4.0.3 (API15)
    [x] Documentation for Android SDK
    [x] SDK Platform
    [x] Sample for SDK
    [x] ARM EABI v7a System Image
    [x] Sources for Android SDK
...
[ ] Extras
    ...
```

```
    [x] Google USB Driver

    ...
```

4. Click the "Install 7 packages..." button. The "Choose Packages to Install" window will show up:

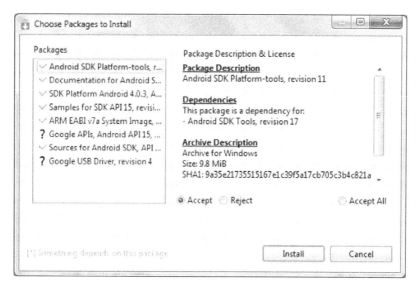

Android SDK Manager R17 - Installing Platform

5. Click the "Accept All" option and click the "Install" button. Android SDK Manager will start to download those selected packages.

6. Wait for the download process to finish and Double-click C:\local\android-sdk-windows\docs\index.html to view the documentation.

Archived: Verifying Android Platform Installation

This section provides a tutorial example on how to verify Android platform installation using the 'android' tool provided in the Android SDK starter package.

This tutorial was based on Android SDK R17 with Android 4.0.3 and left here as a reference.

After installing the latest Android platform packages using the Android SDK Manager, you need to run the "android" tool provided in the Android SDK starter package to verify the installation.

Go to a Windows command line window and run this command:

```
C:\herong\>\local\android-sdk-windows\tools\android list target
Available Android targets:
----------
id: 1 or "android-15"
     Name: Android 4.0.3
     Type: Platform
     API level: 15
     Revision: 3
     Skins: HVGA, QVGA, WQVGA400, WQVGA432, WSVGA, WVGA800 (default),
        WVGA854, WXGA720, WXGA800
     ABIs : armeabi-v7a
----------
id: 2 or "Google Inc.:Google APIs:15"
     Name: Google APIs
     Type: Add-On
     Vendor: Google Inc.
     Revision: 1
     Description: Android + Google APIs
     Based on Android 4.0.3 (API level 15)
     Libraries:
      * com.google.android.media.effects (effects.jar)
          Collection of video effects
      * com.android.future.usb.accessory (usb.jar)
          API for USB Accessories
      * com.google.android.maps (maps.jar)
          API for Google Maps
     Skins: WVGA854, WQVGA400, WSVGA, WXGA720, HVGA, WQVGA432, WVGA800
        (default), QVGA, WXGA800
     ABIs : armeabi-v7a
```

The output confirms that:

- 1 Android platform is installed. The version number is 4.0.3, which was released on Dec. 16, 2011. The API (Application Programming Interface) level is 15.3. This platform should allow me to build test my applications for any mobile devices that running Android 4.0.3 system.

- 1 Add-on is also installed. This add-on represents the Google API for Android 4.0.3.

Read the next tutorials on how to create and run an Android emulator on your Windows system.

Archived: Creating Android Virtual Device (AVD)

This section provides a tutorial example on how to create an Android Virtual Device (AVD), which is an emulator configuration that lets you to model an actual Android device.

This tutorial was based on Android SDK R17 with Android 4.0.3 and left here as a reference.

In order to run the Android emulator on your Windows system, you need to create an Android Virtual Device (AVD), which is an emulator configuration that lets you to model an actual device by defining hardware and software options to be emulated by the Android Emulator.

Here is what I did to create an AVD:

1. Double-click on "C:\local\android-sdk-windows\AVD Manager.exe". The "Android Virtual Device Manager" window shows up.

2. Click "New" button. The "Create new Android Virtual Device (AVD)" window shows up:

Create Android Virtual Device (AVD) - R17

3. Keep all default values and enter these new values:

```
Name: MyAVD
Target: Android 4.0.3 - API Level 15
SD Card/Size: 32 MiB
```

4. Click "Create AVD" button. The "Result of creating AVD 'MyAVD'" message box shows up.

5. Click "OK" to close the message box. A new AVD "MyAVD" is listed in the "Android Virtual Device Manager" window now.

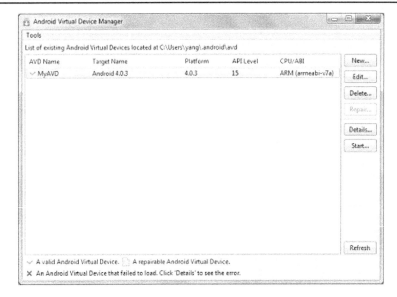

Android Virtual Device (AVD) Manager - R17

Read the next tutorials on how to run an Android emulator with the AVD you created on your Windows system.

Archived: Launching Android Emulator in AVD Manager

This section provides a tutorial example on how to launch an Android emulator with the Android Virtual Device (AVD) created in the AVD Manager.

This tutorial was based on Android SDK R17 with Android 4.0.3 and left here as a reference.

With the Android Virtual Device (AVD) created as shown in the previous tutorial, you can run a Android emulator on your Windows system now.

1. Double-click on "C:\local\android-sdk-windows\AVD Manager.exe". "MyAVD", the AVD created earlier will show up in the AVD list.

2. Select "MyAVD" and click the "Start..." button. The "Launch Options" box will show up.

3. Keep all default values and click "Launch". The Android emulator window will show up:

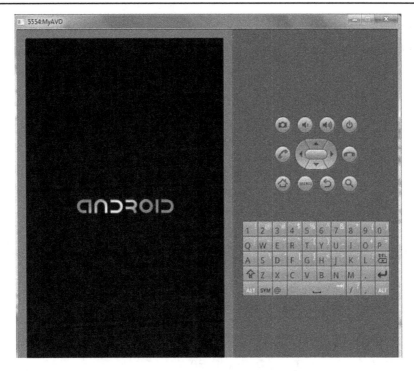

Android Emulator R17 - Start Screen

Congratulations! You have successfully created an Android emulator on Windows system.

Archived: Android Emulator Built-in Applications

This section describes the Android emulator home screen and built-in applications.

This tutorial was based on Android SDK R17 with Android 4.0.3 and left here as a reference.

1. Double-click on "C:\local\android-sdk-windows\AVD Manager.exe" to start the AVD Manager.

2. Select "MyAVD" and click the "Start..." button to start the Android emulator.

3. Wait for the emulator to finish boot the system. The emulator will display a blank screen with a locker icon.

4. Drag the locker icon to the unlock position at right to unlock the system. The emulator will display the home screen with icons to access built-in applications:

- Google icon - The Google client for you to search Web pages.

- Camera icon - The camera tool for you to take pictures with you computers built-in camera.

- Phone icon - The phone client for you to make phone calls.

- Contact icon - The contact manager for you to record contact names and phone numbers.

- Application icon - The application container for you to view all applications that are currently installed in the emulator.

- Message icon - The text message client for you to exchange text messages with your friends.

- Browser icon - The Web browser for you to browse Web pages on the Internet.

You can also flick the emulator screen with your mouse to see more icons like a real mobile device. The picture below shows the emulator's home screen:

Android Emulator R17 - Home Screen

Archived: Android Emulator Built-in Web Browser

This section provides a tutorial example on how to use the Android emulator's built-in Web browser to visit a home page.

This tutorial was based on Android SDK R17 with Android 4.0.3 and left here as a reference.

To the test emulator, let's use its browser to visit my home page.

1. Launch the Android emulator and unlock the screen.

2. Click the "Google" icon and enter "herongyang" by click the key pad on the screen.

3. Click the enter key. Google will display the search result which includes my web site www.herongyang.com.

4. Click on my web site. My home page will show up in the Android emulator.

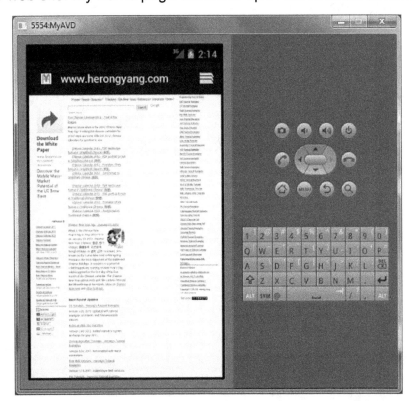

Android Emulator R17 - herongyang.com Page

As you can see, my home page is mobile device friendly at this moment. I need to spend some time to work on it.

Archived: Downloading and Installing Apache Ant 1.8

This section describes how to download and install Apache Ant 1.8.3 on a Windows system. Apache Ant is a popular Java application build tool that allows you to automate the Java application build process.

To develop Android applications in Java language, you also need to install Apache Ant, which is a popular Java application build tool that allows you to automate the Java application build process.

Here is what I did to download and install Apache Ant 1.8.3 on my Windows system.

1. Go to Apache Ant home page: http://ant.apache.org/ and click "Download / Binary Distributions" in the menu.

2. Click the link "apache-ant-1.8.3-bin.zip" next to ".zip archive:" in the "Current Release of Ant" section to start download.

3. Save the download file to C:\download\apache-ant-1.8.3-bin.zip and wait for the download to finish.

4. Unzip C:\download\apache-ant-1.8.3-bin.zip to folder C:\local\apache-ant-1.8.3.

5. Set JAVA_HOME as a system environment variable to point to the JDK 1.7 home folder:

```
set JAVA_HOME=C:\Progra~1\Java\jdk1.7.0_03
```

To verify the installation, open a command window to try the "ant" command. If you are getting the following output, your installation is done correctly:

```
C:\herong>\local\apache-ant-1.8.3\bin\ant -version
Apache Ant(TM) version 1.8.3 compiled on February 26 2012
```

Archived: "HelloAndroid" - First Android Project

This section provides a tutorial example on how to create the first Android project, HelloAndroid, using the 'android' command. Java source file and resource files are automatically created.

This tutorial was based on Android SDK R17 with Android 4.0.3 and left here as a reference.

Now let's try to create a new Android application project called: HelloAndroid. I want the project home folder to be \herong\HelloAndroid and source code package to be com.herongyang.

Go to a command window and run the following commands to create the project, HelloAndroid:

```
C:\>cd \herong
C:\herong>\local\android-sdk-windows\tools\android create project \
   --package com.herongyang --activity HelloAndroid --target 2 \
   --path .\HelloAndroid

Created project directory: C:\herong\HelloAndroid
Created directory C:\herong\HelloAndroid\src\com\herongyang

Added file C:\herong\HelloAndroid\src\com\herongyang\HelloAndroid.java
Created directory C:\herong\HelloAndroid\res
Created directory C:\herong\HelloAndroid\bin
Created directory C:\herong\HelloAndroid\libs
Created directory C:\herong\HelloAndroid\res\values
Added file C:\herong\HelloAndroid\res\values\strings.xml
Created directory C:\herong\HelloAndroid\res\layout
Added file C:\herong\HelloAndroid\res\layout\main.xml
Created directory C:\herong\HelloAndroid\res\drawable-hdpi
Created directory C:\herong\HelloAndroid\res\drawable-mdpi
Created directory C:\herong\HelloAndroid\res\drawable-ldpi
Added file C:\herong\HelloAndroid\AndroidManifest.xml
Added file C:\herong\HelloAndroid\build.xml
```

```
Added file C:\herong\HelloAndroid\proguard-project.txt
```

The output from the command tells me that:

- A Java source code file, com\herongyang\HelloAndroid.java, is created in the .\src folder.

- 2 resource files, values\strings.xml and layout\main.xml, are created in the .\res folder.

- 3 project-level files, AndroidMainifest.xml, build.xml, and proguard-project.txt, are created in the .\ folder.

See next tutorial on how to modify the Java source code generated by the "android" tool.

Archived: Building the Debug Binary Package

This section provides a tutorial example on how to build the debug binary package of the HelloAndroid application using the Apache Ant tool and the build file.

This tutorial was based on Android SDK R17 with Android 4.0.3 and left here as a reference.

Let me try to build the "debug" binary output first.

```
C:\>cd \herong\HelloAndroid
C:\herong\HelloAndroid>\local\apache-ant-1.8.3\bin\ant debug
Buildfile: C:\herong\HelloAndroid\build.xml

-set-mode-check:

-set-debug-files:

-set-debug-mode:

-debug-obfuscation-check:

-setup:
```

```
      [echo] Creating output directories if needed...
     [mkdir] Created dir: C:\herong\HelloAndroid\bin\res
      [echo] Gathering info for HelloAndroid...
     [setup] Android SDK Tools Revision 17
     [setup] Project Target: Google APIs
     [setup] Vendor: Google Inc.
     [setup] Platform Version: 4.0.3
     [setup] API level: 15
     [setup]
     [setup] ------------------
     [setup] Resolving library dependencies:
     [setup] No library dependencies.
     [setup]
     [setup] ------------------
     [setup] API<=15: Adding annotations.jar to the classpath.
     [setup]
     [setup] ------------------
     [setup] WARNING: No minSdkVersion value set. Application will
             install on all Android versions.

-build-setup:
     [mkdir] Created dir: C:\herong\HelloAndroid\gen
     [mkdir] Created dir: C:\herong\HelloAndroid\bin\classes


-pre-build:

-code-gen:
      [echo] ----------
      [echo] Handling aidl files...
      [aidl] No AIDL files to compile.
      [echo] ----------
      [echo] Handling RenderScript files...
[renderscript] No RenderScript files to compile.
      [echo] ----------
      [echo] Handling Resources...
      [aapt] Generating resource IDs...
      [echo] ----------
```

```
    [echo] Handling BuildConfig class...
[buildconfig] Generating BuildConfig class.


-pre-compile:


-compile:
    [javac] Compiling 3 source files to
            C:\herong\HelloAndroid\bin\classes


-post-compile:


-obfuscate:


-dex:
      [dex] Converting compiled files and external libraries into
            C:\herong\HelloAndroid\bin\classes.dex...


-crunch:
   [crunch] Crunching PNG Files in source dir:
            C:\herong\HelloAndroid\res
   [crunch] To destination dir: C:\herong\HelloAndroid\bin\res
   [crunch] Processing image to cache: C:\herong\HelloAndroid\res...
   [crunch]   (processed image to cache entry C:\herong\HelloAndr...
   [crunch] Processing image to cache: C:\herong\HelloAndroid\res...
   [crunch]   (processed image to cache entry C:\herong\HelloAndr...
   [crunch] Processing image to cache: C:\herong\HelloAndroid\res...
   [crunch]   (processed image to cache entry C:\herong\HelloAndr...
   [crunch] Crunched 3 PNG files to update cache


-package-resources:
     [aapt] Creating full resource package...


-package:
[apkbuilder] Current build type is different than previous build:
             forced apkbuilder run.
[apkbuilder] Creating HelloAndroid-debug-unaligned.apk and signing it
             with a debug key...
```

```
-post-package:


-do-debug:
 [zipalign] Running zip align on final apk...
     [echo] Debug Package: C:\herong\HelloAndroid\bin\Hello
Android-debug.apk
[propertyfile] Creating new property file:
  C:\herong\HelloAndroid\bin\build.prop
[propertyfile] Updating property file:
  C:\herong\HelloAndroid\bin\build.prop


-post-build:


debug:


BUILD SUCCESSFUL
Total time: 7 seconds
```

By looking at the output, I think my HelloAndroid binary package, HelloAndroid-debug-unaligned.apk, is ready to be tested on the Android emulator.

Archived: Installing the Debug Binary Package

This section provides a tutorial example on how to install the debug binary package to the Android emulator using the Apache Ant tool and the build file.

This tutorial was based on Android SDK R17 with Android 4.0.3 and left here as a reference.

Now I need to install the debug build, HelloAndroid-debug-unaligned.apk, on the Android emulator. The Android documentation does not have detailed instructions on this step. But I did the following steps to make it happen:

1. Run the Android emulator through the AVD Manager and wait for the emulator to be fully booted.

2. Install HelloAndroid-debug-unaligned.apk to the Android emulator using the Ant tool:

```
C:\>cd \herong\HelloAndroid

C:\herong\HelloAndroid>\local\apache-ant-1.8.3\bin\ant installd

Buildfile: C:\herong\HelloAndroid\build.xml


-set-mode-check:


-set-debug-files:


install:
     [echo] Installing C:\herong\HelloAndroid\bin\HelloAndroid-debug
              .apk onto default emulator or device...
     [exec]    pkg: /data/local/tmp/HelloAndroid-debug.apk
     [exec] Success
     [exec] 46 KB/s (14237 bytes in 0.298s)


installd:


BUILD SUCCESSFUL
Total time: 6 seconds
```

3. Go to Android emulator and click the "Applications" icon. The "HelloAndroid" application is listed in the application list!

Archived: Running the Debug Binary Package

This section provides a tutorial example on how to run the debug binary package that has been installed on the Android emulator.

This tutorial was based on Android SDK R17 with Android 4.0.3 and left here as a reference.

After installing it on the Android emulator, running the HelloAndroid application is easy:

1. Go to the Android emulator and click the "Application" icon. The list of applications will show up.

2. Click on "HelloAndroid". The "HelloAndroid" application screen will show up!

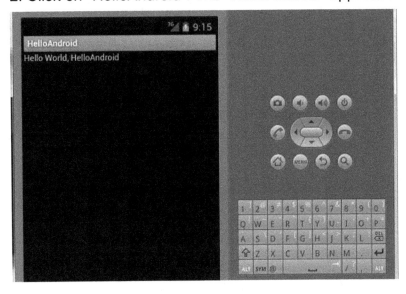

Cool. My first Android application, HelloAndroid, is working nicely!

Archived: Rebuild the Debug Binary Package

This section provides a tutorial example on how to modify the resource file and rebuild the debug binary package of the HelloAndroid application.

This tutorial was based on Android SDK R17 with Android 4.0.3 and left here as a reference.

Whiling running "HelloAndroid" on the emulator, I noticed that the message string does not match what is coded in the Java file!

- "Hello World, HelloAndroid" is the message string displayed on the emulator.

- "Hello, Android" is the message string coded in the Java file.

What happened is that the message string on the TextView defined in the Java file, .\src \com\herongyang\HelloAndroid.java:

```
   ...
   TextView tv = new TextView(this);
   tv.setText("Hello, Android");
   ...
```

is re-defined in the resource file, .\res\layout\main.xml:

```
 ...
 <TextView
    android:layout_width="fill_parent"
    android:layout_height="wrap_content"
    android:text="Hello World, HelloAndroid"
    />
 ...
```

See the next tutorial on how to modify the resource file and re-build the HelloAndroid application.

Archived: Redefine Text in Resource Files

This section describes how the text message string of the TextView gets redefined in the resource file, main.xml.

This tutorial was based on Android SDK R17 with Android 4.0.3 and left here as a reference.

In the previous tutorial, I noticed that the text message string defined the Java source file gets redefined by the resource file. Now I want to modify the resource file and rebuild HelloAnroid to display the original text message.

1. Keep the Android emulator running.

2. Uninstall HelloAndroid from the emulator using the Ant tool:

```
C:\herong\HelloAndroid>\local\apache-ant-1.8.3\bin\ant uninstall
Buildfile: C:\herong\HelloAndroid\build.xml


uninstall:
     [echo] Uninstalling com.herongyang from the default emulator ...
     [exec] Success


BUILD SUCCESSFUL
Total time: 9 seconds
```

3. Modify the resource file, .\res\layout\main.xml, to remove the line android:text="Hello World, HelloAndroid":

```
<?xml version="1.0" encoding="utf-8"?>
<LinearLayout
    xmlns:android="http://schemas.android.com/apk/res/android"
    android:orientation="vertical"
    android:layout_width="fill_parent"
    android:layout_height="fill_parent"
    >
<TextView
    android:layout_width="fill_parent"
    android:layout_height="wrap_content"
    />
</LinearLayout>
```

4. Rebuild HelloAndroid using the Ant tool:

```
C:\herong\HelloAndroid>\local\apache-ant-1.8.3\bin\ant debug
...
```

5. Reinstall HelloAndroid using the Ant tool:

```
C:\herong\HelloAndroid>\local\apache-ant-1.8.3\bin\ant installd
...
```

6. Run HelloAndroid again on the emulator. This time, the test string, "Hello, Android", from the Java source code is displayed:

Now I am happy. I get the exact test message as entered in the Java source code.

Archived: Installing Android PDF Viewer APK File

This section provides a tutorial example on how to install the Android PDF Viewer APK file to the Android emulator using the 'adb' tool provided in the SDK package.

This tutorial was based on Android SDK R17 with Android 4.0.3 and left here as a reference.

If you want to try the Android PDF Viewer on the emulator, you can install the downloaded APK file with the "adb" tool provided in the Android SDK package.

1. Run the Android emulator through the AVD Manager and wait for the emulator to be fully booted.

2. Install AndroidPdfViewer_1_0_1.apk to the Android emulator using the "adb" tool:

```
C:\local\android-sdk-windows\platform-tools>adb install \
   \download\AndroidPdfViewer_1_0_1.apk


1019 KB/s (1433355 bytes in 1.373s)
      pkg: /data/local/tmp/AndroidPdfViewer_1_0_1.apk
Success
```

3. Go to Android emulator and click the "Applications" icon. The "Android PDF Viewer" application is listed in the application list.

4. Click on "Android PDF Viewer" in the application list to run the application:

Android PDF Viewer - Start Screen

Archived: Copy PDF File to Android Emulator's File System

This section provides a tutorial example on how to copy PDF files to the Android emulator's file system using the 'adb' tool provided in the SDK package.

This tutorial was based on Android SDK R17 with Android 4.0.3 and left here as a reference.

To test the Android PDF Viewer, I need to copy PDF files into the emulator's file system. This can also be done with the "adb" command tool.

1. Run the Android emulator through the AVD Manager and wait for the emulator to be fully booted.

2. Copy a PDF file to the Android emulator using the "adb" tool:

```
C:\local\android-sdk-windows\platform-tools>adb push \
    \herong\herong_book_Android.pdf /sdcard/Download


 201 KB/s (641829 bytes in 3.115s)
```

3. Go to Android emulator and run "Android PDF Viewer" again.

4. Click the "Browse" icon next to the "PDF File" field. herong_book_Android.pdf is listed in the /mnt/sdcard/Download folder on the emulator.

5. Click "herong_book_Android.pdf" to select the PDF file and click the "Show" button. My PDF book will be displayed on the Android PDF Viewer:

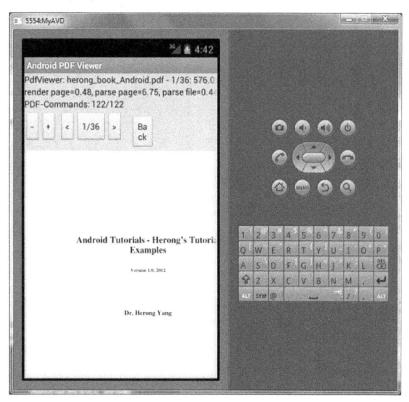

Android PDF Viewer - Herong's Book

Archived: Installing Adobe Reader APK File

This section provides a tutorial example on how to install the Adobe Reader APK file to the Android emulator using the 'adb' tool provided in the SDK package.

This tutorial was based on Android SDK R17 with Android 4.0.3 and left here as a reference.

Let's repeat the process to download and install another APK file of Adobe Reader

1. Run the Android emulator through the AVD Manager and wait for the emulator to be fully booted.

2. Go to http://www.freewarelovers.com/android/app/adobe-reader and click "Download".

3. Click on "Adobe_Reader_9.0.2.apk" in the "Download" section and save the downloaded file to C:\download\Adobe_Reader_9.0.2.apk.

4. Install Adobe_Reader_9.0.2.apk to the Android emulator using the "adb" tool:

```
C:\local\android-sdk-windows\platform-tools>adb install \
   \download\Adobe_Reader_9.0.2.apk

216 KB/s (1839413 bytes in 8.278s)
      pkg: /data/local/tmp/Adobe_Reader_9.0.2.apk
Success
```

5. Go to Android emulator and click the "Applications" icon. The "Adobe Reader" application is listed in the application list.

6. Click on "Adobe Reader" in the application list to run the application, and click "Agree" on the End User License Agreement. "Adobe Reader" will show up with "herong_book_Android.pdf" listed in the /mnt/sdcard/Download folder.

7. Click "herong_book_Android.pdf" to view the content. My PDF book will be displayed on the Android PDF Viewer:

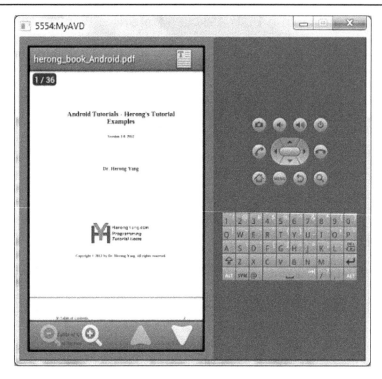

Adobe Reader - Herong's Book

Cool. "Adobe Reader" is official PDF Viewer. It is definitely better than "Android PDF Viewer" install earlier.

Archived: "adb shell" - Remote Shell Interface

This section describes the 'adb shell' command, which gives you a shell interface to the connected Android operating system. The shell interface allows you to manage the Android file system and invoke Android command line programs.

This tutorial was based on Android SDK R17 with Android 4.0.3 and left here as a reference.

Another important command is the "adb shell" command, which gives you a shell interface to the connected Android operating system. The shell interface allows you to manage the Android file system and invoke Android command line programs.

Here is a "adb shell" command session I did on my Android emulator:

```
C:\local\android-sdk-windows\platform-tools>adb shell
```

```
# pwd
pwd
/

# ls -l
ls -l
drwxr-xr-x root    root            2012-04-01 acct
drwxrwx--- system cache            2012-04-01 cache
dr-x------ root    root            2012-04-01 config
lrwxrwxrwx root    root            2012-04-01 d -> /sys/kernel/debug
drwxrwx--x system system           2012-04-01 data
-rw-r--r-- root    root        116 1970-01-01 default.prop
drwxr-xr-x root    root            2012-04-01 dev
lrwxrwxrwx root    root            2012-04-01 etc -> /system/etc
-rwxr-x--- root    root      98676 1970-01-01 init
-rwxr-x--- root    root       2344 1970-01-01 init.goldfish.rc
-rwxr-x--- root    root      17040 1970-01-01 init.rc
drwxrwxr-x root    system           2012-04-01 mnt
dr-xr-xr-x root    root            1970-01-01 proc
drwx------ root    root            2011-11-14 root
drwxr-x--- root    root            1970-01-01 sbin
lrwxrwxrwx root    root            2012-04-01 sdcard -> /mnt/sdcard
drwxr-xr-x root    root            1970-01-01 sys
drwxr-xr-x root    root            2011-12-14 system
-rw-r--r-- root    root        272 1970-01-01 ueventd.goldfish.rc
-rw-r--r-- root    root       3825 1970-01-01 ueventd.rc
lrwxrwxrwx root    root            2012-04-01 vendor -> /system/vendor

# cat default.prop
cat default.prop
#
# ADDITIONAL_DEFAULT_PROPERTIES
#
ro.secure=0
ro.allow.mock.location=1
ro.debuggable=1
persist.sys.usb.config=adb
```

```
# df
df
Filesystem              Size    Used    Free    Blksize
/dev                    252M    32K     252M    4096
/mnt/asec               252M    0K      252M    4096
/mnt/obb                252M    0K      252M    4096
/system                 161M    161M    0K      4096
/data                   124M    13M     110M    4096
/cache                  64M     1M      62M     4096
/mnt/sdcard             126M    907K    125M    512
/mnt/secure/asec        126M    907K    125M    512


# ps
ps
USER      PID PPID VSIZE   RSS     WCHAN       PC            NAME
root      1   0    276     192     c0099f1c 000086e8 S /init
root      2   0    0       0       c004df64 00000000 S kthreadd
root      3   2    0       0       c003fa28 00000000 S ksoftirqd/0
root      4   2    0       0       c004abc0 00000000 S events/0
root      5   2    0       0       c004abc0 00000000 S khelper
root      6   2    0       0       c004abc0 00000000 S suspend
root      7   2    0       0       c004abc0 00000000 S kblockd/0
root      8   2    0       0       c004abc0 00000000 S cqueue
root      9   2    0       0       c0178c7c 00000000 S kseriod
root      10  2    0       0       c004abc0 00000000 S kmmcd
root      11  2    0       0       c006efa8 00000000 S pdflush
root      12  2    0       0       c006efa8 00000000 S pdflush
root      13  2    0       0       c0073480 00000000 S kswapd0
root      14  2    0       0       c004abc0 00000000 S aio/0
root      24  2    0       0       c01764ac 00000000 S mtdblockd
root      25  2    0       0       c004abc0 00000000 S kstriped
root      26  2    0       0       c004abc0 00000000 S hid_compat
root      27  2    0       0       c004abc0 00000000 S rpciod/0
root      28  2    0       0       c0193fd0 00000000 S mmcqd
root      29  1    252     156     c0099f1c 000086e8 S /sbin/ueventd
...
```

```
# exit
exit
```

This is nice. With this shell interface, I have full control of my Android emulator system now.

Archived: "adb push" and "adb pull" Commands

This section describes 'adb push' and 'adb pull' commands, which allows you to copy files to and from the remote Android emulator or device.

This tutorial was based on Android SDK R17 with Android 4.0.3 and left here as a reference.

The "adb" tool also offers you commands to copy files into and from the connected Android emulator or devices.

The "adb push <local> <remote>" copies a file or folder from the local system to the remote emulator or device.

The "adb pull <remote> <local>" copies a file or folder from the remote emulator or device to the local system.

Example 1 - Copying "Silk-Road.jpg" to the /sdcard/Picture folder in the emulator:

```
C:\local\android-sdk-windows\platform-tools>adb push \
   \herong\Pictures\Silk-Road.jpg /sdcard/Picture
258 KB/s (111019 bytes in 0.420s)
```

Example 2 - Copying "init.rc" from the / folder in the emulator:

```
C:\local\android-sdk-windows\platform-tools>adb pull \
   /init.rc \herong
139 KB/s (17040 bytes in 0.119s)
```

Example 3 - Copying all files from the /data/data folder in the emulator:

```
C:\local\android-sdk-windows\platform-tools>adb pull
   /data/app \herong\app
```

```
pull: building file list...
pull: /data/app/GestureBuilder.apk -> \herong\app/GestureBuilder.apk
pull: /data/app/SoftKeyboard.apk -> \herong\app/SoftKeyboard.apk
pull: /data/app/ApiDemos.apk -> \herong\app/ApiDemos.apk
pull: /data/app/SoftKeyboard.odex -> \herong\app/SoftKeyboard.odex
pull: /data/app/CubeLiveWallpapers.apk -> \herong\app/CubeLiveWallp...
pull: /data/app/ApiDemos.odex -> \herong\app/ApiDemos.odex
pull: /data/app/GestureBuilder.odex -> \herong\app/GestureBuilder.odex
pull: /data/app/WidgetPreview.odex -> \herong\app/WidgetPreview.odex
pull: /data/app/CubeLiveWallpapers.odex -> \herong\app/CubeLiveWall...
pull: /data/app/WidgetPreview.apk -> \herong\app/WidgetPreview.apk
pull: /data/app/com.herongyang-1.apk -> \herong\app/com.herongyang-...
pull: /data/app/net.sf.andpdf.pdfviewer-1.apk -> \herong\app/net.sf...
pull: /data/app/com.adobe.reader-1.apk -> \herong\app/com.adobe.rea...
13 files pulled. 0 files skipped.
148 KB/s (7022410 bytes in 46.298s)
```

References

List of reference materials used in this book.

- *What is Android*, https://www.android.com/what-is-android/

- *Android Debug Bridge (adb)*, https://developer.android.com/tools/adb

- *dumpsys (command)*, https://developer.android.com/tools/dumpsys

- *(Android) Architecture overview*, https://source.android.com/docs/core/architecture

- *Android Developers*, http://developer.android.com/

- *Android Developers*, Android marketplace, https://play.google.com/

- *Android & Windows Phone Forums*, http://forum.xda-developers.com/

- *Java SE APIs & Documentation*, http://www.oracle.com/technetwork/java/javase/documentation /api-jsp-136079.html

- *Android Freeware Lovers*, Directory of free Android applications in APK file format, http://www.freewarelovers.com/android/

- *LG Thrill P925 Android Phone*, http://www.lg.com/us/cell-phones/lg-P925-thrill/

Android Tutorials
Herong's Tutorial Examples

v3.05, 2023

Herong Yang
HerongYang.com/Android

This book is a collection of notes and sample codes written
by the author while he was learning Android system. Topics
include Installing of Android SDK on Windows, Creating
and running Android emulators, Developing First Android
Application – HelloAndroid, Creating Android Project with
'android' Command, Building, Installing and Running the
Debug Binary Package, Inspecting Android Application Package
(APK) Files, Using Android Debug Bridge (adb) Tool, Copying
files from and to Android device, Understanding Android File
Systems, Using Android Java class libraries, Using 'adb logcat'
Command for Debugging. Updated in 2023 (Version v3.05)
with ADB tutorials.

*"Thank you so much! I have not known most of listed classes although
I'm not a novice in android developing." -- Buckstabue*

*"Hey man, this is some way cool technical s**t, but another site says the
"adb push" command comes FIRST (not in the middle between the 2
locations like what you've got)." -- RevHectorForbes*

"Thank you so much. It was really helpful for me." -- Pankaj Kumar

HerongYang.com
30+ Tutorial Books
Computers / Programming